MW01613267

Using Narrative Inquiry for Educational Research in the Asia Pacific

Narrative inquiry is being used more widely in the UK, the US, Canada, Australia, New Zealand and Northern European countries to conduct research across a range of disciplines. It is gaining popularity in Hong Kong, Macao and Mainland China, but research in these contexts continues to be dominated by quantitative and more traditional qualitative approaches. Narrative inquirers in these areas can, therefore, find it problematic to have the value of their work acknowledged. This book demonstrates creatively, accessibly and rigorously the ways in which narrative inquiry as a methodological approach, already more firmly established in Australia and New Zealand, is gaining a foothold in other parts of the Asia Pacific region. Contributors to the book write about their use of narrative inquiry in, for example, the Confucian heritage cultures (CHC) of Hong Kong, Singapore and Macao and the Anglo-Celtic cultures of Australia and New Zealand.

Chapters in the book include:

- Creative non-fiction across cultures in Asia Pacific contexts.
- Riding the wave of education reform: Using a reflecting team to explore the professional identities of school counsellors in Hong Kong.
- Is the silent mode on? Researching teachers' voices in Macao through narrative research.
- Narrative inquiry and the exploration of culture for improving teacher education.

This book will appeal to researchers across all sectors of education, in particular those who are exploring the use of qualitative research methods in context. Those interested in comparative education and cross-cultural studies will also find this book valuable.

Sheila Trahar is Reader in International Higher Education at the Graduate School of Education, University of Bristol, UK.

Yu Wai Ming (Flora) is Assistant Professor and Associate Head at the Department of Curriculum and Instruction, Hong Kong Institute of Education.

Routledge Research in Education

For a full list of the titles in this series, please visit www.routledge.com.

Using Narrative Inquiry for Educational Research in the Asia Pacific

Edited by Sheila Trahar and Yu Wai Ming

Routledge
Taylor & Francis Group

LONDON AND NEW YORK

First published 2015
by Routledge
2 Park Square, Milton Park, Abingdon, Oxon OX14 4RN

Simultaneously published in the USA and Canada
by Routledge
711 Third Avenue, New York, NY 10017

Routledge is an imprint of the Taylor & Francis Group, an Informa business

© 2015 Sheila Trahar and Yu Wai Ming

The right of the editors to be identified as the author of the editorial
material, and of the authors for their individual chapters, has been
asserted in accordance with sections 77 and 78 of the Copyright,
Designs and Patents Act 1988.

All rights reserved. No part of this book may be reprinted or
reproduced or utilised in any form or by any electronic, mechanical,
or other means, now known or hereafter invented, including
photocopying and recording, or in any information storage or retrieval
system, without permission in writing from the publishers.

Trademark notice: Product or corporate names may be trademarks
or registered trademarks, and are used only for identification and
explanation without intent to infringe.

British Library Cataloguing in Publication Data
A catalogue record for this book is available from the British Library

Library of Congress Cataloging in Publication Data
Using narrative inquiry for educational research in the Asia
Pacific / edited by Sheila Trahar, Wai Ming Yu.
pages cm
Includes bibliographical references and index.
1. Education—Research—Pacific area. 2. Education—Research—Asia.
3. Narrative inquiry (Research method)—Pacific area. 4. Narrative
inquiry (Research method)—Asia. I. Trahar, Sheila.
LB1028.25.P16U85 2015
370.72—dc23
2014040036

ISBN: 978–1–138–02537–0 (hbk)
ISBN: 978–1–315–77512–8 (ebk)

Typeset in Galliard
by Swales & Willis Ltd, Exeter, Devon, UK

Contents

Notes on contributors

Esther Y. M. Chan is Assistant Professor in the Department of Early Childhood Education in the Hong Kong Institute of Education. Her research interests include teacher knowledge, narrative inquiry, beliefs and practices, culture and children's development.

Crystal Cheung is an EdD candidate at the University of Bristol, UK. She is in the final stages of her doctoral dissertation and works as a clinical psychologist in Hong Kong. She sees the power of stories in her clinical work and this has led her to develop a strong interest in narrative inquiry as a research methodology.

Chan Nai Kwok Francis is the Chief Curriculum Officer of the Catholic Education Office of Hong Kong, leading a team of colleagues to provide professional support to teachers of religious and moral education in over 280 Catholic schools in Hong Kong. He was a teacher and administrator of a secondary school for 15 years before joining the Education Department of Hong Kong as a senior curriculum officer. Then, he served at the Hong Kong Institute of Education for ten years as a senior lecturer. His expertise lies in the preparation of teachers of history, civics, religious and moral education. He received his BA, MA and CEd from the University of Hong Kong, MEd from the University of Bristol and EdD from OISE/University of Toronto.

Wendy Green is a Senior Lecturer in the Tasmanian Institute of Learning and Teaching, University of Tasmania. Her teaching and research concern the internationalisation of higher education; culture, learning and teaching; student and academic mobility; and academic development. She is Convenor of the International Education Association of Australia's Special Interest Group for Internationalisation of the Curriculum (IoC). From 2008 to 2014, she co-convened the Narrative Research Network in Brisbane, Australia. In 2013, she was a Visiting Scholar at the Università Cattolica del Sacro Cuore, Milan.

Jane Horan has her EdD from Bristol University, UK. Her research focuses on cross cultural leadership, unconscious bias and Asian Women Leaders.

Jane is a consultant helping organisations build inclusive and engaged work environments. She has lived in Asia for two decades and previously worked for Kraft, The Walt Disney Company, and CNBC in organisational, leadership and talent management.

Adisorn Juntrasook is Associate Dean at the newly established Faculty of Learning Sciences and Education, Thammasat University, Thailand. Prior to this position, he was a lecturer at the Contemplative Education Center, Mahidol University. His PhD thesis was awarded by the University of Otago in the category of the Divisional List of Exceptional Theses in 2013. Adisorn has professional backgrounds in theatre, expressive arts therapy and education. His research interests include narrative and reflexive methodologies, contemplative and transformative education, academic identities and practices and leadership for social change.

Lau Chun Kwok is a Senior Teaching Fellow in the Department of Curriculum and Instruction of the Hong Kong Institute of Education. He received his education in Hong Kong and Canada. His research interests involve narrative knowledge, cross-cultural experience, service learning and teachers' personal and professional development.

Yu Wai Ming is Associate Head and Assistant Professor of the Department of Curriculum and Instruction at the Hong Kong Institute of Education. She received her university education in the UK and Canada. She uses narrative inquiry in teaching dissertation research and in teaching an undergraduate course in general education. Her research interests are in narrative inquiry, curriculum, assessment and teacher professional development.

Mabel Shek holds a Master's degree in Education and a Master of Social Science degree in Counselling, and is currently a Senior Teaching Fellow in the Department of Special Education and Counselling at the Hong Kong Institute of Education (HKIEd). Mabel was awarded the Excellence in Teaching Award by the Faculty of Education Studies and the President's Award for Outstanding Performance in Teaching by the HKIEd in 2011 and 2012 respectively. She has many years' experience of teaching, training and counselling. Her teaching areas include school counseling, sex education and life skills. She holds an EdD from University of Bristol.

Renée Tan is pursuing her Doctorate in Education in the Narrative Inquiry track at the University of Bristol, UK. She works in the field of workforce development and Continuing Education and Training in Singapore. Her research interests include social and cultural globalism, diversity and inclusivity, narrative inquiry, auto-ethnography and creative ethnographic writing.

Sheila Trahar is Reader in International Higher Education, University of Bristol, UK. Her innovative research in international higher education uses narrative inquiry and autoethnography, reflected in her book *Developing Cultural Capability in International Higher Education: A Narrative Inquiry* (2011). Her edited collections *Learning and Teaching Narrative Inquiry: Travelling in the Borderlands* and *Contextualising Narrative Inquiry: Methodological Approaches for Local Contexts* were published in 2011 and 2013, respectively. Sheila teaches on the Doctor of Education in Bristol and Hong Kong, the Master of Science in Educational Research in Bristol and has led the Master of Education programme in Hong Kong since 2008.

Sou Kuan Vong is currently Associate Professor and Director of the Educational Research Centre in the Faculty of Education, University of Macau. She holds a doctoral degree in Sociology of Education awarded by University of Nottingham, UK. Her research interests are diverse, including educational policy, curriculum issues, citizenship education and teacher education, yet they are held together by a commitment to social justice and an interest in questions of power, knowledge, discourse and practice in educational research.

Matilda Wong holds a doctoral degree in teacher development from the Ontario Institute for Studies in Education, University of Toronto and is currently Assistant Professor in the Faculty of Education, University of Macau. She specialises in English language teaching and teacher education. Her research interests include second language teaching, teacher education and teacher development.

Shijing Xu is Associate Professor at the Faculty of Education, University of Windsor, Canada. She teaches both pre-service and graduate courses at the University of Windsor. Her research interests focus on narrative approaches to intergenerational, bilingual and multicultural educational issues and school–family-community connections in cross-cultural curriculum studies and teacher education. She is directing a seven-year project with Dr. Michael Connelly on reciprocal learning in teacher education and school education between Canada and China, which involves nine partner institutions in Canada and China and is funded by the Social Sciences and Humanities Research Council of Canada (SSHRC) Partnership Grant.

Eunice Pui-yu Yim is a Senior Programme Manager at the Open University of Hong Kong. Her research interests include early childhood education, teacher training, special education, inclusive education, parent education, holistic development in young children and adolescents and cultural identities.

Preface

Sheila Trahar and Yu Wai Ming

Beginnings . . .

Wai Ming: A colleague approached me recently to ask whether I could supervise a doctoral student who was interested in narrative inquiry. I was puzzled about how this student had heard about narrative inquiry, as it isn't included in the research methodology training in our doctoral programme. In response to my query, my colleague told me that this particular student was under pressure to complete his doctorate quickly.

Sheila: I'm really confused! What's the connection between narrative inquiry and completing a doctorate 'quickly'?

Wai Ming: Maybe my colleague thinks narrative inquiry is 'easier' and therefore can be completed in less time than someone using quantitative research . . . .

Sheila: Isn't it funny that people often perceive narrative inquiry as a quick and easy methodology – quite the opposite of our experience?

Wai Ming: True, narrative inquiry gives people the impression of a kind of soft approach. It often uses interviews, which, on the surface, equates to 'go and talk to people, record the conversation, and use it in the research report'. There's no need to design complicated questionnaires or run sophisticated statistical software packages. Some people think that it's a way to avoid learning those strange statistical formulae. Why not use a method they've already mastered – talking and writing?

Sheila: But narrative is so much more than talking and writing. How can we challenge such frustrating misconceptions?

Narrative inquiry, as a methodological approach, has gained much ground in many parts of the world during the past 20 years or so and there are journals and conferences devoted to it. However, it is less well known in contexts such as Hong Kong, China and Singapore, contexts that continue to privilege quantitative research in education and the social sciences. Even in countries with a longer history of narrative inquiry in education such as Canada, the US, the UK,

Australia and New Zealand, its use tends to be constrained to particular areas of research. Our earlier conversation signifies a misconception about narrative inquiry that continues to be widely held in Hong Kong and in other contexts represented in this edited collection – that it is an overly simple way to conduct research. Because it may be perceived as simple, then a further criticism that can be levelled at it is that it demands less of the researcher and is not, therefore, sufficiently rigorous to be credible. Narrative inquiry may be 'popular and engaging' but it is also 'difficult' and the way 'to go about it is much discussed' (Andrews *et al.*, 2013, p. 1). In this edited collection, we set out to challenge what we consider to be misunderstandings about narrative inquiry, held by many people in the Asia Pacific. We demonstrate the ways in which the use of narrative inquiry is being developed creatively, accessibly and rigorously by presenting a rich collection from educational researchers throughout the region.

In assembling the book, we are building on a developing narrative community in Hong Kong and Macao, brought about by a range of factors, two of which are pertinent to us personally. The first is that several people in the region, including some of the contributors, have undertaken doctorates with Michael Connelly, a prominent narrative inquiry scholar, at the Ontario Institute for Studies in Education. The second reason is that there are a growing number of people using narrative inquiry for their doctoral research in completion of the University of Bristol's Doctor of Education (EdD) programme that is taught in Hong Kong. These EdD students are introduced, briefly, to narrative inquiry during their first taught unit, 'Understanding Educational Research' and, following this brief introduction to the approach, several decide to use it in their research, considering it to be the most appropriate methodology for an increasingly broad range of topics. The EdD programme brought us together, as Wai Ming was the external examiner for a doctoral candidate who had been supervised by Sheila. As we got to know one another, we found that we shared a passion for wanting to raise the profile of narrative inquiry in Hong Kong. Recognising that a book on its applicability in the context would be a way to raise local awareness of this methodology, we approached publishers with a proposal. This was accepted by Routledge Singapore who asked us to extend the scope of the book beyond Hong Kong to the Asia Pacific region, which includes Australia and New Zealand. Such a requirement could have been problematic for us. We did not consider that arguments needed to be made for narrative inquiry in those contexts, as it is firmly established and used widely in a range of disciplines. We were fortunate, however, in securing contributions from two people who use narrative inquiry in higher education research, a field that is not yet highly populated, other than perhaps in teacher education, with studies employing this approach. Wendy Green and Adisorn Juntrasook write about their higher education research in Australia and New Zealand respectively, and enable us to sustain and extend our argument, not only for using narrative in those contexts where it is less familiar but also in less traditional fields. Using our various connections throughout other Asian Pacific countries, we assembled a group of narrative inquirers from that region – and the book began to emerge.

Those who use narrative inquiry as a methodological approach, often do so because they want their research to reach a wider public. They risk, therefore, the approbation from the academic community that several contributors to this edited collection have experienced. Because of this, narrative inquirers can feel that it is incumbent upon them to vigorously defend their methodological approach, in particular to those who persist in asking 'Is this research'? – as Green mentions in her chapter – or those, such as Wai Ming's colleague, who consider that narrative inquiry is a simple and thus less rigorous way to conduct an inquiry. Our original rationale in wanting to produce this edited collection was to foreground the value of narrative inquiry as a methodological approach in contexts that continue to eschew it for what seemed to us to be spurious reasons. Rather than consider the value and appropriateness of narrative inquiry for a broad range of research topics in the context, those who resist and reject it often do so because of the hegemony of positivism and quantitative methodological approaches. What we felt was crucial, therefore, was for us to be able to show not only why narrative inquiry is suitable for research in the Asia Pacific region but also how it needs to be problematised in order to render it so. Narrative inquiry can be interpreted differently by researchers and, in addition, can be informed by a range of philosophical perspectives that relate to the worldview(s) of the researcher. In compiling this collection, we were careful not to insist on a particular philosophical or methodological reading of narrative and, moreover, urged contributors to ensure that they critiqued the form of narrative inquiry that they used. We considered it important for them to be able to explain their approach, to articulate why it was suitable for research in their context and how it was congruent with that context. In addition, we conceptualised educational research as being any endeavour undertaken in formal and informal learning contexts that strives to further intellectual enrichment, social justice and equity (Ladson-Billings & Donnor, 2005; cited in Mertens, 2010).

Aside from Australia and New Zealand, where, as indicated earlier, narrative inquiry has a stronger presence, there are several powerful examples in the literature of the use of narrative inquiry in the Asia Pacific region. Yip's (2013) account of her methodological journey, told creatively through a fictionalised conversation with her masseur; Tsui's (2007) richly described narrative of a Chinese English as a Foreign Language (EFL) teacher; Craig *et al.* (2012) in their use of narrative inquiry in their comparative study of physical education research in South Korea and the US; Shu's (2010) narrative account of using drama to develop innovative teaching approaches with marginalised students in Hong Kong and Craig *et al.*'s (2014) use of narrative to explore experiences of a China study abroad programme in Shanghai. In reading this writing we, as editors, may feel vindicated. Narrative inquiry, together with its affordances and limitations, is clearly an appropriate methodological approach to use in these locations and for myriad topics. Yip and Tsui provide rich descriptions of the contexts so that the reader can understand both researcher and participant's narratives and their analysis. It seems to us, however, that the suitability of narrative inquiry for research in a particular location is not always foregrounded. Unless this is articulated, there is a danger in adopting an approach – and approaches – developed in one context and using them in contexts with different social, cultural and historical dimensions without critiquing their suitability and/or illustrating how they may need to be adapted in order to be more appropriate. Moreover, in addressing this complexity, we feel sufficiently confident to propose the use of narrative inquiry for many areas of research and to have people consider it rather than reject it for reasons that may be spurious and that reside in unfamiliarity with the approach.

There are other complexities in putting together a book such as this. The first one was that everyone needed to write in English, the first language of only a few of the contributors and of one of the editors. This requirement presented us with a quandary. To what extent do we proofread the chapters? In doing so, how much of their original meaning do we lose because of the lack of cultural equivalence between the writer's first language and English? Narrative inquiry is often evaluated on its aesthetic merit and proofreading can lose some of the original lyricism of the writing. We have striven not to lose meaning and to retain locally relevant metaphors by checking any changes with the writers – but this has been a complex and painstaking process. Second, a key question for narrative inquiry as, in our view, it should be for any methodological approach but perhaps in particular any other qualitative methodological approach is 'why in the particular moment of the telling, that unique story is told to the researcher in that particular way' (Gemignani, 2014, p. 129)? We would add 'why to that particular researcher in that particular context?' The contexts within which narratives are told and listened to are, therefore, 'a crucial dimension of this methodological approach' (Trahar, 2013, p. xi) and, as indicated earlier, we wanted contributors to focus on their use of narrative in their local environment, in particular to articulate its strengths in conducting research in it. This is not always easy to do, as it requires one to be able to stand outside one's locality and to look in, to make the familiar strange through intense and critical reflexivity, to determine the particularities and how they can be reflected and researched using narrative inquiry. In reading narrative accounts, while critical reflexivity is very often a key component, a critical analysis of the suitability of the methodology for the context can be a missing dimension, in our opinion and experience, hence it being foregrounded in each chapter in this book. If the use of narrative inquiry is to be extended to those contexts where people continue to be sceptical about its value for research into the particularities and complexities of people's lives, then its appropriateness needs to be considered carefully. In each chapter, writers, in their different ways, are mindful of this crucial element as they seek to inform, to persuade and to invite the reader to reflect on her/his own experiences and perceptions as s/he reads.

The chapters

The first two chapters by Adisorn Juntrasook and Wendy Green focus on using narrative inquiry in higher education. Both authors use their research into different dimensions of higher education – Juntrasook into leadership and Green into academics' movement between cultural and disciplinary boundaries – as vehicles with which to challenge the paucity of higher education studies employing narrative methodological approaches. Both authors identify themselves as outsiders – Green as a relative newcomer to research in higher education in Australia and Juntrasook as a Thai man researching in New Zealand. Narrative inquiry often begins with an autobiographical story or an event that was significant to the researcher – or took on significance as the research developed. In Juntrasook's case, an angry outburst at a conference provoked him to ask questions differently about leadership in higher education. In doing so, he came to understand that the ways in which people construct themselves as leaders are situated within their broader society and institutional cultures. Such realisation caused him to eschew a more realist approach to narrative and to locate himself within social constructionism, a philosophy that resonated with his Buddhist values and beliefs. In doing so, Juntrasook does not accept, uncritically, a predominantly 'Western' philosophical perspective and one that commonly informs narrative inquiry, but considers how it is reflected in Buddhist teachings. Juntrasook's reflections on his anxieties at conducting unstructured interviews raise questions about the importance of problematising the narrative interview; indeed, the importance of theorising any form of interview. Juntrasook muses on whether he was positioned as 'less privileged' by his academic participants, noting that, although it is becoming more common for researchers from 'non-white ethnic backgrounds' to conduct research with 'participants who are white', in a 'white-dominant context like Aotearoa New Zealand', this process has not been documented to any great extent. His diary entries after each interview illustrate how he gained in confidence but also reveal how he realised that he was both researcher and researched. People participate in research for their own reasons and can disrupt an interview in order to say what it is that they want to say. As Juntrasook attests, this would obtain in any interview situation but narrative inquirers write about it as a way of enabling the reader to see transparently how the interactions between researcher and participant help to structure and shape the text. On the other hand, he also recognises that his positioning as an outsider meant that his participants had to explain culturally specific terms to him. This, in turn, enabled him to understand the range of discursive practices that we all draw on in constructing accounts of our lives but that can remain invisible, until we are invited to make them visible to 'outsiders'. Narrative inquiry is not well known in Thailand, a context that, in common with many in this book, is dominated by positivism and quantitative approaches to research. Juntrasook ends his chapter on an optimistic note, however, sharing that he has given several public seminars on narrative and that many of his students are interested to use narrative inquiry in their research.

Narrative inquiry is not uncommon in social science and education in Australia but, as in other contexts, its presence in higher education research – what Wendy Green refers to as an 'unhomely' field – is rarely felt. Green, in her chapter, traces her own route to becoming a narrative inquirer, paralleling this with the methodology's fledgling emergence in higher education, asking why research using narrative inquiry is barely present in higher education journals. Green's main area of research has been the mobility of academics and students driven by the monumental changes in higher education that have occurred throughout most of the world, changes that have left many academics experiencing 'pressures to cross disciplinary and geographical borders in search of an intellectual home'. Green claims that narrative provides the means to listen to and analyse these stories of shifting and messy identities, and how they are produced in order to render them intelligible 'in ways that other methods cannot'. A reason for eschewing narrative inquiry can be that it is less favoured by policy makers, who tend to want large, statistically analysed data sets that are generalisable to wider populations. Green provides an example of how a narrative inquiry influenced local policy making within her university. This research into Australian students, who study abroad, illuminated ways in which dimensions of privilege work together to enable a minority of students to participate in this opportunity, while the majority remain excluded. Insights gained through this study have enabled the researchers to 'begin imagining ways that universities could enhance the mobility capital across the whole student cohort', thus initiating important policy changes. Learning and teaching and curriculum development are intrinsic to higher education and Green proposes that if more researchers were to risk turning to narrative inquiry in this area 'we could better interrogate, evaluate and reflect on the narrative construction of the messy work of teaching and learning in universities'. Narrative inquirers, in common with most other qualitative researchers, do not set out to claim generalisability in their research but, in recognising that 'stories don't fall from the sky' (Riessman, 2008, p. 105), they are composed and received in contexts, Green challenges narrative inquirers to consider ways in which they can theorise their work without losing its richness. Finally, in further celebration of success in raising the profile of narrative inquiry, Green describes how she and her colleague Paula Myatt started a narrative research network in 2008 with the aim of building an interdisciplinary, narrative community of practice across the universities in their city, a network that has grown, developed and extended outside Australia.

In the first two chapters, the authors make their case for developing narrative inquiry, in a field of research, rather than a specific geographical milieu. The subsequent chapters pick up on this theme, adding this particular component.

'The creative and aesthetic dimensions of narrative inquiry add to the transparency of textual re-presentation, enabling the reader to understand and resonate with the meanings of the experiences described' (Trahar, 2013, p. xiii) – and to understand them in different ways. The next three chapters use forms of fictionalisation for particular purposes. Fictionalisation is a device used by many narrative inquirers to communicate co-constructed narratives, or to bring to the awareness of readers complex situations that may be difficult to do otherwise. Renée Tan has constructed an imaginary conversation between a Singaporean woman and her Filipino domestic helpers; Crystal Cheung places her research participant, Fan, in dialogue with the Chinese Kungfu hero, Bruce Lee; and Jane Horan juxtaposes extracts from an interview with a Japanese businesswoman, re-storying them in the style of Ernest Hemingway.

The fictional construction of experiences can be a persuasive form of research writing, in particular where the writer wants to tell a story that is based on 'real' events to produce a version of the 'truth' as she or he sees it. In Tan's case, the conversation never took place, although conversations with her own domestic helper contributed to the fictionalised account. Tan is here providing an example of how narrative inquiry can be used in what she terms the 'education of the citizenry', to disrupt a powerful national narrative, the portrayal of the relationships between the major ethnic groups in Singapore as harmonious. She uses the fictionalised narrative to uncover a darker side of Singapore, one that discriminates not only against domestic helpers but also against 'foreign talent'. Such discrimination is not limited to Singapore but, in a country not known for its anti-government protest, challenging a dominant narrative of harmony in a creative way can speak to people's emotional sensitivity and thus be more productive. This is also an example of the political dimension of narrative inquiry. The fictionalised representation operates on many levels and thus provides us with glimpses of different narratives. We meet Rachel, the Singaporean businesswoman, witness her haughty treatment of her helpers and are enabled to recognise, as she does, that her children relate to the helpers more closely than they do to her. The conversation between Vilma and Gracia provides a rich and poignant insight into the lives of these Filipino women, but, as a pebble causes ripples on the surface of water, so too this conversation resonates more widely, causing us to reflect on the global inequities that force many women to leave their families and to endure such humilities in other countries.

One could argue that had Tan interviewed two Filipino women and a Singaporean she may well have gathered equally rich narratives – certainly different narratives – but, by having the fictional characters speak to each other in an 'uncomfortable script-like structure', she allows them to express raw emotions and to make discriminatory and racist comments that may be suppressed in a research interview. Moreover, we are provoked into thinking about the broader global structures that have created this society where Rachel is so reliant on her helpers to care for her family so that she can pursue her career in comparison with the Filipino women and their subsistence level existence. As Tan indicates towards the end of the chapter 'narrative inquiry need not be positive in content' and, in this case, its political edge foregrounds the need for greater social balance by highlighting these painful issues of diversity and social inequity.

In contrast to Tan, Crystal Cheung's use of creative fictionalisation, places Fan, a participant in her research into lifelong learning in Hong Kong, in a fictional relationship with the Chinese Kungfu hero, Bruce Lee. Cheung extrapolates from the narrative interviews that she has conducted with Fan to construct accounts in which he converses with his hero. Fan has expressed his admiration for this Chinese martial arts legend in conversations with Cheung. Her curiosity about his admiration leads her to investigate Lee's life, where she discovers that the philosophy that drove him is congruent with Fan's beliefs about lifelong learning. The construction of the fictionalised conversation between Fan and Lee, that takes place in Cheung's imaginary dream, enables us to understand how Fan conceptualises himself as a lifelong learner, providing us with rich insights into the struggles and opposition that he encounters in striving to be creative in his work as an educator. This is an example of how 'the creative act of remembering situates the teller in relation . . . to the listener and larger contexts of discourses, collectivities, and possible construction' (Gemignani, 2014, p. 132). Cheung reminds readers that they were not able to witness her conversations with Fan and so, in a sense, these conversations may be perceived to be 'fictions'. But, Bruce Lee existed; Fan exists and the creative use of fictionalisation is an invitation to readers to enter Fan's world and to experience, how, through the imaginary relationship Cheung creates between the two of them, she is able to deepen her understanding of Fan. At the beginning and the end of her chapter, Cheung recounts how, as a clinical psychologist, she was attracted to narrative therapy. She writes of how she has started to integrate elements of this therapeutic approach into her own work as a clinical psychologist. Narrative therapy positions the person in ways that are fundamentally different from her own much more positivist training as a psychologist. She now encourages her clients to re-author their stories to challenge the dominant narratives through which they live and which are unhelpful to them(White & Epston, 1990). In doing so, she reveals the similarities between the changing principles of her therapeutic practice and her research. Many clinical psychologists in Hong Kong are sceptical about narrative therapy, mainly because they consider that it does not have a strong empirical research base. But, Cheung is 'learning to accept and to tolerate uncertainties and unresolved issues' in her work as a therapist; and feels 'empowered to accept that the unresolved things created in narrative inquiry are, in fact, rich resources to value'.

Jane Horan's use of fictionalisation is positioned as creative non-fiction; in other words, the conversations and events described took place but the style used to present them to the reader has a particular purpose, that of drawing her/ him into the relationship that was constructed during the narrative inquiry. In her chapter, Horan re-presents extracts from research conversations held with Ms Ito, a Japanese businesswoman, but rather than transcribing them verbatim, she re-stories them in the style of Ernest Hemingway. She recreates the café in Singapore, one of the places where she met Ms Ito, and through the evocative style of Hemingway draws us into a steamy Singapore, where we can feel the suffocating heat and humidity; yet shiver in the café's freezing air conditioning. Ms Ito's accounts of her experiences in many different countries do not proceed in the way that Horan is expecting and she shares her surprise when Ms Ito tells her that nobody has influenced her in her life. This unexpected response challenges Horan to begin to interrogate her own cultural positioning and how this mediates her expectations of how people will respond to her. Her claim is that by imitating 'Hemingway's clear communication style and masterful use of dialogue' she was able to separate herself from her fixed opinions, to step outside of her relationship with Ms Ito and to see their conversations from many perspectives. In doing so, she was able to relate to Ms Ito – and to her own preconceptions – differently, thus engendering new learning. Horan starts to appreciate the complexities of Ms Ito's life, its turning points and her rejection of a traditional Japanese narrative for a woman. She reveals how she had been mired in her own cultural stereotyping and thus unwilling to accept Ms Ito's counternarrative.

Using creative non-fiction enabled Horan to 'see Ms Ito as an individual, devoid of the cultural constructs in which I originally placed her', a brave acknowledgement from a woman who has lived and worked in various parts of the Asia Pacific for many years. Horan's central argument is that creative non-fiction can enable the researcher to 'move beyond self and explore entrenched beliefs'; crucial when one is conducting research with those from very different contexts. Not all readers may identify with the Hemingway style of writing but a lack of identification does not reduce the impact of the narrative.

A field of research where the use of narrative inquiry is used quite commonly is that of identities. Mabel Shek used narrative inquiry to investigate her curiosity about the changing professional identities of school counsellors brought about by the many educational reforms implemented in Hong Kong. Shek is a teacher educator and a former school counsellor and, throughout this chapter, she shares how the narratives of the school counsellors resonated with similar experiences of her own. In sharing these resonances, she is able to articulate and to deepen our understanding of elements of Confucian heritage culture and how these elements inevitably impact the changing identities of the counsellors. Hong Kong has adopted, uncritically, policies on guidance and counselling that were developed in the UK and the US, two very different contexts. By surfacing the discomfort caused in professional counsellors by having to work with policies that do not reflect their Confucian values and beliefs, she artfully draws our attention to the importance of context sensitivity when implementing policies and practices developed elsewhere. In addition to narrative interviews, Shek uses the collaborative practice of a reflecting team; a practice that originated from family therapy but is less well known in her context as a research method. The chapter is a substantive discussion of her experience of a reflecting team and the complexities of its use in Hong Kong where there is a strong likelihood of people in the same profession, such as school counselling, knowing one another. For her participants, initially, the invitation to participate in such a practice, as a part of the research, raised anxieties, such as the potential risks of self-disclosure in a group with people that they may not like. Shek relates such anxieties to the importance of harmony for Chinese people and, after obtaining their permission, revealed the identities of all of the participants to each other. Shek then shares extracts from the reflecting team conversations that indicate, poignantly, how the counsellors hearing how their narratives resonate with their peers, gain comfort and strength. Shek concludes her chapter by attesting to how narrative inquiry has created space for these school counsellors in Hong Kong to tell their stories of how the policy changes have impacted their identities. There is, therefore, potential for policymakers to reflect more carefully on contextual factors in any future policy borrowing.

Towards the end of her chapter, Shek comments on how she has started to use narrative inquiry in her teaching. The next three chapters focus on using narrative inquiry in teacher education in Hong Kong and Macao. Yu Wai Ming writes about a course that she developed in 2010 in Hong Kong. 'A Narrative Perspective on Stories in Life' was aimed, originally, at undergraduate students.

More recently it has been opened up to people from the Elderly Academy of the Hong Kong Institute of Education. Yu's chapter, therefore, focuses on using narrative inquiry in teaching in a unique learning community – one in which students in their twenties learn together with people aged over 60. The course's aim is to employ narrative inquiry concepts and practices to enable students to understand their life experience and to construct and reconstruct meanings from such insight. Based on these new understandings, the students develop a firmer foundation on which to chart their unknown futures. The inclusion of older people in the course is a bonus to all participants and has become a precious forum for people from different generations to learn about each other's life experiences.

The approach and methods Yu uses are simultaneously commonplace and innovative. Many people in their day-to-day lives use chronicles and interviews but their use as course assignments is not common in Hong Kong higher education. Participants chronicle their life experiences and reflect on them from a narrative perspective. The purpose is to encourage and to develop an ability to find meanings in their daily life encounters. First, participants are required to review their upbringing by constructing and presenting a chronicle in class with the theme 'How did I become who I am?'. Many students admit afterwards that this is the first time they have ever looked back on their upbringing, to discover new meanings in their relationships with their parents or siblings, or to find out how their years of schooling have affected how they are as young adults. In the second assignment, students conduct an in-depth interview to learn about the life experience of people who are significant to them in some way. Through these assignments and sharing in class, participants have valued opportunities to listen to their own and other people's life stories and discover meanings in them. Alternative understandings of each other are gained and course participants begin to see how stories circulate through cultures and how stories that are passed from generation to generation, help us to understand our lives and constitute us as human beings. Yu's chapter exposes how narrative inquiry can be used to enable people to reflect on their lives and their perceptions of others and how, through the inquiry process, see how those perceptions can change.

Drawing on the inspiration of a typical form of Portuguese music – Fado – that Sou Kuan Vong and Matilda Wong heard when they travelled together in Lisbon, their chapter is arranged as if they were composing a piece of music, using musical terms such as overture, composers, Cantopop and finale as subtitles to structure it. Fado adds another important meaning to their writing, as Macao is a former Portuguese colony with many of the Portuguese influences still visible. The Portuguese heritage and culture continue to interact harmoniously with those of the Chinese even though Macao was returned to the Peoples' Republic of China in 1999.

Vong and Wong describe their previous narrative research as 'travelling a long way on a broken road in Macao', being narrative inquirers in a context where this methodological approach is less well known. In common with other contexts described in this book, Macao is dominated by quantitative research in the field of education, and in teacher education in particular. Such approaches tend to generalise educational research practices that are, in fact, very diverse. Teachers have been complaining about the many educational reforms for several years, but their voices are not heard. Vong and Wong attribute this silent grumbling to Macao people being passive recipients of change, influenced by the Confucian beliefs of tolerance, patience and respect.

As teacher educators, Vong and Wong resonate with the difficulties that front-line teachers experience because of the many school reforms, sharing their vulnerability and challenges to their profession. The authors desire to make teachers' voices heard, and to enable their own voices to be heard, and so they tell their stories and help teachers tell theirs by using narrative inquiry. The life story told by Elsa, an experienced primary school teacher, reveals the unfavourable and unjust situations some of the teachers are undergoing. Through Elsa's story, the authors want us to see how personal and institutional narratives form two sides of a coin. They enable the teacher's voice to be heard and to become distinctive, rather than remain buried. Vong and Wong criticise certain academic conventions as 'boundaries of elitism', seeking to break through these boundaries by adopting an alternative approach to research, narrative inquiry. They believe more work has to be done to encourage teachers to make a noise. The answer to the question they ask in the beginning – 'Is the silent mode on?' – is obviously 'Yes'. What Vong and Wong attempt to do in Macao, however, is to change this mode and let the silenced voices be heard.

With its history as a British colony situated at the southern tip of Mainland China, Hong Kong is well known for its mixed culture of East and West. Local people in Hong Kong nurture the next generation by retaining Confucian virtues but, at the same time, encourage them to experience education influenced by the West. Thus, Chinese learners in Hong Kong learn to become critical and reflective, but also to conform and be obedient. In the next chapter, Esther Chan illustrates how story telling helps both the teacher and the learner to make meanings from their experiences of these possible cultural tensions in her context. As an experienced teacher in the field of early childhood studies, Chan uses narrative inquiry as an innovative pedagogy to teach topics such as child and human development. She gives detailed descriptions of the ways in which learning and teaching are conceptualised in Hong Kong. Through her analysis, she emphasises the tensions that can exist in her desire to promote approaches to learning that involve the student teacher taking a more active role in her/his learning and thus, ultimately, to integrate such approaches into her/his teaching. Such tensions arise because she is challenging the stereotype of Hong Kong learners as being 'examination robots who lack critical thinking and self-reflection'. Chan chooses to share critical incidents of the students and herself to show us how deep reflections can be made from stories told. Sandy and Esther have had a traditional Chinese upbringing with their strict fathers, while Kate has had a more lenient mother. In the process of re-telling childhood stories, Sandy and Esther share how they were silenced. Sandy learnt to be silent from being criticised by her father when she insisted on wearing her hair long. Esther also learnt to be quiet and submissive but this came about from her mother's Confucian way of thinking and desire for her to be a good daughter, wife and mother. Kate is the only participant who has been supported by a caring affectionate mother to find her own voice. Chan improves her own professional practice by using narrative inquiry and, in doing so, helps student teachers to improve their learning by using it. She attempts to break through the traditional teaching methods of lecturing and memorisation, employed in her own training to be a teacher, to be more open and experiential by using narrative inquiry. She advocates the importance of teacher knowledge being constructed through story telling, reflection and meaning making of student teachers' own learner experiences, thus foregrounding the value of narrative inquiry in examining how culture mediates learning.

Ethical considerations are imperative in all social research but they can be especially complex in narrative approaches. This complexity arises because the relationship between participant and researcher is continuously developing and shifting and also because narrative is often used in research with people who feel that they are on the margins of a society. Such people want their voices to be heard; their stories to be read and they want to own those stories by being named. In research that is conducted across cultures, these ethical complexities can be even more pronounced as Shijing Xu recounts in the next chapter. Xu focuses on her exploration of Chinese newcomers' family narratives of schooling in Canada and of how she found herself at the boundary between narrative and formalistic inquiry. She articulates the ethical struggles encountered when such a close and trusting relationship is developed between research participants and a researcher, that the purposes of the research, which is what brought them together, become less significant for the participant than the more intimate aspects of their relationship. Xu recounts the story of Zhi Gao and his family in their transition from China to Canada. As newcomers, they encounter many difficulties. Life is especially problematic for the adolescent Zhi Gao as he faces both language and cultural barriers. Yet, through the research relationship that Xu creates, he and his family develop a special kind of trust with her. Xu helps the family in many different matters, both at home and school, finding herself adopting different roles, from that of a researcher. She becomes a reliable friend of the family, offering help as an interpreter, a teacher and a social worker.

The main focus of the chapter is the importance of attending, continuously, to the different ethical concerns that emerge as the narrative inquiry progresses. These concerns are complicated further by the ethical demands of the Canadian context within which Xu works and the different values that are held by her and by her Chinese participants. In addressing these tensions, Xu identifies three types of ethical consideration; namely, procedural ethics, situational ethics and relational ethics.

Procedural ethics refers to ethical considerations in the procedures required to obtain approval from Ethics Review Boards in universities. If Xu followed the procedural ethics protocol, she would not have allowed herself to become involved in Zhi Gao's life. Situational ethics refers to the sensitivity a researcher needs in making decisions about what to tell, what not to tell, who tells whose stories and how. In obtaining consent for doing research in the school community, some of the participants, such as Freeman, an active volunteer, feel proud to be part of the research and want their given name to be used. However, revealing Freeman's identity risks other people being identified. Relational ethics is ethics in practice, or thinking about ethics in terms of relational matters. Xu takes on additional roles that involve her in helping the families in need and finds this essential in the process of negotiating relationships with her participants. As she concludes, 'ethical issues and their defined or imagined boundaries ultimately merged with the inquiry'.

In the next chapter, Lau Chun Kwok shares his experience in using narrative inquiry while doing his doctorate in Toronto some 15 years ago. In deciding that his own family will be the site of his research, he weaves together, skilfully and insightfully, his interests in culture, learning, life and education, his doctoral journey and his family life. Studying his own family raised questions about the value of such research. This first question came not only from his academic colleagues, but also from his wife Daphne, who may be seen to represent the deep rooted understanding about conducting research in Hong Kong. In thinking about research, the majority of people immediately think about questionnaires and statistics. Furthermore, what is the value of research based on the stories from only one family? Lau's chapter demonstrates that significant questions can be asked and thoughtful insights gained from such an in depth narrative study. Researching on and living closely with his participants, Lau has to gain consent from his wife and two children to appear in his study. He concludes that such close relationships could be a hurdle or a blessing in research, depending on whether one has a strong belief and passion for the significance of narrative in understanding life circumstances.

Carrying his curiosity and passion for education, Lau carefully observes and chooses two episodes from his children's learning experiences in a Toronto public school to represent his observations and reflections on Hong Kong and Canadian cultures and educational philosophies. He shares his joy in seeing the change in his own children's learning in a different culture despite their language difficulties as new immigrants. Lau is amazed to see how a Canadian teacher notices Andy's potential after having known him for only three months; Fanny's fast grasp of African American history enables her to teach her father as he encounters questions in his graduate class. In other tiny but carefully observed examples, Lau prompts us to realise how different messages can be revealed from different styles of student report cards and how daily homework can be given to children for many reasons.

He also chooses three vivid images about his life in Toronto to capture the little stories that prompt us to think and rethink some of the most simple and fundamental concerns about education for our next generation. How do we teach our children? What is valuable in education? How does a person become cultivated? These questions resonate for all those who are parents and educators.

In the penultimate chapter, Eunice Pui-yu Yim makes a breakthrough in her academic department in Hong Kong by adopting narrative inquiry in her research. Her colleagues are not familiar with this methodological approach and consider the use of I as more appropriate in fiction or other non-academic writing. In spite of this fervent opposition, Yim insists on writing in the first person in her research, considering this form of writing to be more congruent with her use of narrative inquiry into the identities of people newly arrived from Mainland China as well as Hong Kong locals as they participate in a parent education programme. Her encounters with this group of people and her witnessing of their stories cause Yim to reflect on her own experiences as a new arrival when she immigrated with her family to Canada as a teenager. She becomes a new arrival again when she returns to Hong Kong several years later. As a working mother with two children, she feels connected to the unpleasant feeling of being labelled as a new immigrant or an outsider in an unfamiliar social context that those from the Mainland describe in the parent education group.

Yim's chapter reveals the strong emotions that are experienced by the new-comers to Hong Kong, as they are labelled lazy, dependent on social welfare, as a 'second wife' intruding in others' families, unfashionable in their dress and lacking social manners. Yim's depictions of her participants' experiences provides useful insights into the grand narrative of the current social conflicts between the local and national cultures and identities, a phenomenon that not only appears in Hong Kong but, unfortunately, in many other parts of the world. Yim explores how the identities of her participants are negotiated and constructed in their daily encounters. At the same time, she uses her own immigrant experience as a way to interpret and analyse the multiple perspectives and identities that are evolving as the parents interact and share their perceptions and stereotypes of each other.

In her study, Yim observes how parents are helped to establish a platform for self-representation and reflection through their participation in the parent education programme. New arrival parents not only narrate and reflect on their past lives, but also reveal the underlying motives for their current behaviours and attitudes. Similarly, the Hong Kong locals are supported to challenge their stereotypical views of their Mainland cousins. By understanding what kind of story can be told, how, why, for whom and the influence of context, Yim makes sense of the participants' experiences and thus, gains insights about multiple identity formation that traditional empirical research may not be able to bring about.

In the final chapter, Chan Nai Kwok Francis explores issues of identity and identity education of Hong Kong Chinese people at a particular time in history. This chapter demonstrates the unique strength of narrative inquiry for research in which a rich and detailed description of the context is essential. Identity is not only an official status on one's passport or identity card but also a personal answer to fundamental questions such as 'Who am I?' and 'Where do I belong?' These questions are particularly vital for people in Hong Kong who have lived in a 'borrowed time and borrowed place' for the past 150 years and are now living in a society where these issues are still intensely contested every day.

Our personal lives are always closely tied to the social and historical contexts in which we live. Chan aptly employs narrative inquiry in a self-study of his own experience of two episodes: the world-shocking June 4 Incident in China in 1989 and a controversial debate held in 1994 on the inclusion of the June 4 Incident in history textbooks in Hong Kong schools. The first episode shows how the identity of Hong Kong people was intimately linked to the history of contemporary China and the tragic 1989 Tiananmen Incident amid the political unrest in the transition period of Hong Kong's return to China from British rule. Chan's chapter shows how these significant social and historical events have painfully disrupted ordinary people's lives and sharply called into question their identity and belonging. The second episode, in which Chan was involved as a history curriculum officer in the government, shows the strong undercurrent in the debates on shaping the national identity of school children and how these young people should understand and love their country. These two episodes happened over two decades ago, but their significance has indeed become more evident in the current struggles and heated debates over the political future of more than 7 million people in one of the most dynamic cities in the world. Chan's rich description of these social and historical events and his deep personal reflection as a history scholar is as timely today as two decades ago, providing clear evidence of narrative's ability to reconstruct 'personal and collective meanings of past events and their relevance to the current day'. Given the ongoing turmoil in Hong Kong to secure the right to govern itself, narrative inquiry will, as he indicates, 'undoubtedly have a place in the continuing story'.

Finally . . .

In writing this Preface, we, as editors, have tussled with how to present each chapter so that it honours the effort of the writer; not only the effort in writing the chapter, but also the effort that each one has made – and continues to make – in using narrative inquiry and in promoting its use locally. We ourselves have different perspectives on narrative inquiry and these differences have led to healthy and rigorous discussion between us. We recognise that we are influenced by our different histories, cultures and social contexts and that, being from Hong Kong and the UK, those differences can be complicated further by Hong Kong's colonial history, as mentioned by several writers in their chapters. On the other hand, we share a fervent belief in the value of narrative inquiry and the way in which it draws attention to context and detail, crucial in any study of social phenomena, whatever the location and irrespective of the background of the researcher. Narrative inquirers do not claim that the insights gained from their research are conclusive or universal but rather they set out on the journey of unravelling the puzzles faced by all human beings in ways that are plausible, creative, accessible and rigorous. We hope that, as you read the myriad contributions to this book, they may stimulate you to reflect on your own lives and to consider narrative inquiry's value in investigating the complex, lived experiences that occur in every context.

References

Andrews, M., Squire, C. & Tamboukou, M. (eds) (2013) *Doing narrative research*, 2nd ed. London: Sage.

Craig, C.J., You, J. & Oh, S. (2012) Why school-based narrative inquiry in physical education research? An international perspective. *Asia Pacific Journal of Education* 32(3), 271–284.

Craig, C.J., Zou, Y. & Poimbeauf, R. (2014) Narrative inquiry as travel study method: Affordances and constraints. *Asia Pacific Education Review* 15, 127–140.

Gemignani, M. (2014) Memory, remembering, and oblivion in active narrative interviewing. *Qualitative Inquiry* 20(2), 127–135.

Mertens, D. (2010) *Research and evaluation in education and psychology: integrating diversity with quantitative, qualitative, and mixed methods, 3rd ed.* Thousand Oaks, CA: Sage.

Riessman, C.K. (2008) *Narrative methods for the human sciences.* Thousand Oaks, CA: Sage.

Shu, J. (2010) Return of the ghost – to discipline and/or to teach? *Asia Pacific Journal of Education* 30(1), 105–120.

Trahar, S. (ed.) (2013) *Contextualising narrative inquiry: Developing methodological approaches for local contexts.* Abingdon, Oxon: Routledge.

Tsui, A.B.M. (2007) Complexities and identity formation: a narrative inquiry of an EFL teacher. *TESOL Quarterly* 41(4), 657–680

White, M. & Epston, D. (1990) *Narrative means to therapeutic ends.* New York: Norton.

Yip, P.L. (2013) A conversation with Ah Leung. In S. Trahar (ed.) *Contextualising narrative inquiry: Developing methodological approaches for local contexts.* Abingdon, Oxon: Routledge, pp. 122–139.

Acknowledgements

Many thanks to all of the contributors for sharing our vision for this book – and then making it possible. Thanks to Christina Low at Routledge Singapore for her positive response to our idea and for her support throughout. Special thanks to CK Lau for walking an extra mile. Finally, thanks, as always, to Barry who lives, patiently, with the piles of paper!

1 A journey in the land of the long white cloud

A Thai academic doing narrative inquiry in Aotearoa New Zealand

Adisorn Juntrasook

Prologue

My parents never read me bedtime stories. I didn't even realise that this was a thing that parents might do for their children, until I saw it in American films. I'm sure it would be easier to present such a romantic story about growing up with these rituals to help me explain why I became interested in stories. But that is not my story. Life is never simple – often things do not unfold like they do in the (American) films. To tell you the truth, I don't know why I became interested in stories. As a child, I recall myself enjoying books and watching films; and later, listening to people's life stories became one of my passions. It was through stories that I began to recognise other perspectives that were different from, or seemingly in opposition to, my own – sometimes with doubt, and other times with acceptance. Stories have enabled me to imagine what it might be like for someone to experience a certain thing, in a certain way, within a certain situation. It is through stories too that I became interested in narrative inquiry. This chapter is about my becoming a narrative researcher in a 'foreign' context. I am going to tell how I encountered my research topic, leadership in higher education, and my methodology, narrative inquiry. My research focussed on how academics at one university in Aotearoa New Zealand experienced and understood themselves as leaders in their everyday contexts (Juntrasook, 2013, 2014; Juntrasook *et al.*, 2013). I will share my reflexive account of how my thinking and practice of narrative inquiry shifted during my fieldwork. Finally, I will conclude this chapter with a narrative of my own dilemmas and illustrate how I negotiated them. By the end, I hope to engage you, the reader, to imagine what it might be like for a researcher with an ethnic minority background to use narrative inquiry in a white-dominant context like Aotearoa New Zealand.

But before I tell you these stories, let me introduce myself.

Me, myself and the researcher

I grew up in a Thai family where both of my parents were 'leaders' in their work. My mother worked as a director at an international higher education institution and my father was a deputy managing director at a large government agency.

Their positions often required long hours of work and generated a lot of stress that I could not fully appreciate as a child. The story I have told myself and others is that this background influenced my disinterest in pursuing positions of leadership, let alone working in a large organisation. I did not want to be like my parents – I did not want to be a leader.

Throughout my teens and young adult life, I continually positioned myself as an outsider who did not belong to the system. When I began my undergraduate degree at the age of 16, I decided to study theatre and journalism, believing that cultural work would not require the same kind of responsibilities as larger organisations. However, after I graduated my interests shifted toward education and social development. I 'accidentally' became a secondary school drama teacher and had an opportunity to work with many 'at-risk' teenagers both in and out of the school context. I learned that the work I wanted to do with young people required more than passion – I needed knowledge and skills. This experience inspired me to further my education in counselling psychology and expressive arts therapy, in Thailand and later in Switzerland. After gaining two postgraduate qualifications, I began my work as an art therapist with young terminally ill patients at a hospital in South Africa. Although this work was only for one year, it sparked a deep interest in social justice and transformation.

Upon returning to Thailand, I became involved in a social movement centred around transformative education and was invited to take a leading role in the establishment of a new higher education institution in Bangkok. Despite my desire to have a different life to my parents, as a 26 year old, I ended up working as a mid-level 'leader' at this institution. At that time, I had to learn about how to lead and manage and I turned to scholarly and 'self-help' books for advice. But I was dissatisfied with these resources. First, they were boring, and second, they usually failed to speak to my situation as a 'young leader' working in a cultural context where seniority was considered of utmost importance. Alongside this experience, I also started recognising that many of my academic colleagues, especially those who did not hold formal leadership positions, often acted like 'leaders' in their work. Conversely, many people who were in formal leadership positions did not necessarily act like 'leaders' themselves all of the time. My observation seemed at odds with the majority of literature on leadership in higher education, where there are both the leaders and the led.

Among existing studies of leadership in higher education, two foci seem to be most prevalent. First, researchers tend to focus on what works, asking questions such as, 'What is effective leadership?' and, 'How can we develop an effective leader?' (Simkins, 2005). These questions seem to be embedded in the assumption that knowledge situated in one context can be generalised and replicated in others. The second focus has been associated with formal positions including institutional and departmental headships or managers (Middlehurst, 2008). Within this focus, to be considered a leader, one needs to hold one of these positions within the institution or department. As a result, many individuals in academia – who do not hold formal positions – may remain overlooked and, to a certain extent, 'marginalised' by mainstream leadership researchers.

Ultimately, my professional experience, along with the results from reviewing the existing literature, attracted me to study higher education leadership in a more nuanced and critical way. I chose to conduct my doctoral study in Aotearoa New Zealand, primarily because I was interested to learn about an academic culture different to my own and partly because it was more practical to stay in the country where I was studying. I did not realise at the time that my decision would create a number of dilemmas for me, as a Thai academic conducting narrative research in a Western country.

My initial doctoral proposal sought to explore how academics at a university in Aotearoa New Zealand experienced and understood their leadership – whatever it meant to them – with a particular focus on how institutional, socio-cultural and political contexts may have shaped their sense-making. It attempted to disrupt taken-for-granted premises about leadership in higher education, questioning what we have come to know and accept as 'reality'. In other words, I explicitly challenged the dominant understandings of leadership that render certain ways of thinking, practising and 'becoming' intelligible within the context of higher education and not others. Early on in my research I believed that, by collecting academics' stories of their leadership experiences, I would be able to give 'voice' to those who are rarely recognised as leaders in public or scholarly spaces. In searching for a methodology that would allow me to follow this interest, I came across narrative inquiry, which seemed to be a perfect fit for both my research and for my own background, as a person with an abiding interest in the life stories of individuals.

Contemplating narrative inquiry

During the past 30 years, there have been an increasing number of studies in the social sciences that deploy narrative as a method of data collection, a tool for methodological analysis and a mode of representation. Scholars working within this 'narrative turn' have broadly come to agree that we live and make sense of our lives through stories (Clandinin, 2007). Narrative, in this sense, is an ontological condition of social life:

> [I]t is through narrativity that we come to know, understand, and make sense of the social world, and it is through narratives and narrativity that we constitute our social identities . . . that all of us come to be who we are (however ephemeral, multiple, and changing) by being located or locating ourselves (usually unconsciously) in social narratives rarely of our own making.
>
> Somers, 1994, p. 606, original emphasis

Despite the notion that identities are narratively constructed, scholars may still find themselves disagreeing about the nature of narratives and how they should be studied (Smith & Sparkes, 2006, 2008). Recent overviews of narrative studies suggest scholars approach the conceptions of narrative differently, depending on their theoretical orientations and foci. For example, scholars may view narrative identities through a (neo)realist perspective wherein narratives have the capacity to represent unique, coherent, authentic and trustworthy experiences of our selves in the world (Bochner, 2001; Crossley, 2000; Polkinghorne, 1988). On the contrary, social constructionist scholars often view narrative identities as multiple, fragmented, discursive, emerging, incomplete, performative and contextual (Gergen, 1991; Holstein & Gubrium, 2000; Sparkes & Smith, 2008). These contrasting views have also sparked ongoing debates across continents and disciplines in recent years, particularly over the issues of voice, authority and representation (see Atkinson & Delamont, 2006; Atkinson & Silverman, 1997; Bochner, 2001; Bochner & Ellis, 1999).

When I began my study, I found myself drawn to a more realist perspective as I saw an ethical imperative for me, as a researcher, to create space for the experiences of my participants who, by virtue of their position or identity, tended to be marginalised in thinking about leadership, by both their institution and also scholarly literature. However, not long after I submitted my proposal, I came to realise that my understanding of narrative was rather naïve. One particular incident contributed to the major change in direction of my study. I was presenting my research proposal at a national conference in my first year as a doctoral candidate. After my presentation, I asked the audience, most of whom were seasoned academics from different universities and polytechnics in New Zealand, to share stories about their leadership at work, stories that reflected their beliefs and values of professional life. One of the audience members commented towards the end of session that she thought leadership was 'bullshit'. She said it did not really mean anything to her and that she believed people simply used it for their own advantage. When I heard her say this, in the heat of the conference presentation, I was angry and unsure how to respond. Nevertheless, the time was up and my audience had to depart for the next session. Despite receiving encouraging feedback from some of the audience members later, the comment stuck with me, and I rehearsed possible answers in my mind for many weeks afterwards. Once I was able to move on from my negative thoughts and emotions, I began to recognise that her comment may offer some insights for my study. If leadership is 'bullshit' as she suggested, why are institutions still expecting it from their staff? Why do many academics not refuse it, but instead take it seriously as part of their identities? Indeed, what makes it possible for them to think and talk about themselves as leaders in academia in the first place? Asking these questions completely changed how I viewed my topic and took me in a direction that I never anticipated. Instead of taking people's stories of their experiences at face value, I became more interested in how individual academics tell their stories of leadership, how they construct themselves as leaders and how these identity constructions are located in the broader contexts of their institution and society. With this in mind, I adopted a social constructionist perspective as one of the major theoretical resources for my study. This perspective is not only relevant to my research focus but also similar to my worldview as a researcher and a human being.

Generally speaking, social constructionism is based on an understanding that what we come to account for in the world is relationally and socially constructed

(Gergen, 1985). This resonates with my own worldview, which is deeply rooted in Buddhism. In Buddhist teaching, everything is understood as being in a state of constant change and meanings are mentally and socially constructed by human beings (Payutto, 1995). A number of scholars have pointed out that, as a core value, Buddhism shares some significant commonalities with social construction-ism (Gergen, 2009; Sinclair, 2011). Both share a similar understanding that indi-viduals actively construct the meaning of their everyday lives through language, which does not reflect, but constitutes, their reality.

Alongside social constructionism, I also drew on poststructuralist and Bakhtin-ian scholarship to conceptualise my study, especially my analytical approach. Poststructuralism pays attention to language and its embedded power that consti-tutes individuals' ways of thinking and becoming. Bakhtinian conceptions direct a focus to the dialogic tensions within language, especially the coexistence of multiple values and points of view in social contexts. Together, social construc-tionism, with added layers of poststructuralism and Bakthinian concepts, made it possible for me to undertake critical research that understands leadership as relationally and socially constructed, discursive and dialogic, always incomplete and always unfinished.

By adopting a narrative approach to research, I was aware that my study and I, as a researcher, might be positioned as *the other* within the dominant discourse of leadership studies. Despite a growing number of qualitative researchers in this field, qualitative research, especially narrative inquiry, continues to remain less visible, and somewhat marginalised, in comparison to quantitative research (Bry-man, 2004). Historically, the status of qualitative methods in leadership stud-ies has been 'either subsidiary to the quantitative component in mixed methods research or mimics some of the features of quantitative research . . . but without numbers' (Bryman, 2011, p. 26). Despite a growing interest in the use of narra-tive inquiry in educational research within Western contexts, including Aotearoa New Zealand, narrative inquiry in the field of leadership, especially in higher edu-cation settings, remains marginal because the majority of leadership researchers tend to work within essentialist and instrumental paradigms as I discussed earlier. This may not be a surprise, considering that the field of leadership studies, both in the context of higher education and elsewhere, has been eclipsed by quantitative methods over the past century (Avolio *et al.*, 2009). What quantitative research promises is an ability to predict and prescribe the phenomenon, offering practical advice to 'leaders' and their organisations (Bolden *et al.*, 2011). This approach has informed the dominant discursive practices of leadership researchers from past to present.

Learning in the field: Collecting narrative data

Aiming to disrupt the dominant studies of leadership, I employed a narrative approach including narrative interviews and narrative analysis as the principal strategy for producing and analysing the narratives of my participants. Follow-ing Clandinin and Connelly's (2000) advice on three-dimensional narratives,

I devised the interview questions encompassing temporality (past, present and future), personal and social interaction and place (situation) in relation to leadership from my participants' experiences. Despite advice from narrative scholars to employ a non-structured interview, I found the idea of doing that frightening, especially for a novice researcher like myself. Being a non-native English speaker also made me nervous about my communication with native speakers. I was (and am) always conscious that my English is never good enough, and that my participants would not be able to understand me or, perhaps worse, that I would not understand them. Having a set of interview questions, even though I might not use them, helped me gain some confidence and prepare myself before facing the challenge of interviewing academics.

Even though most of my interview questions centred on producing stories, as is often suggested by narrative researchers (see Chase, 2003; Polkinghorne, 1995), I also asked a number of questions focusing on rationales (including, 'What do you mean by . . . ?' and, 'Why do you do that?'). Both types of data, I argue, are usually interwoven in human conversation, including research interviews. When individuals tell stories, they not only talk about their experiences but also justify, revise, repair or strengthen these stories by drawing on general knowledge (or socially established resources) in their talk.

Moreover, coming from a different cultural background, I also found it important to ask my participants to clarify some culturally embedded terms that are not obvious to an 'outsider' like me. One example was when I heard my participant talked about his experience of 'tall poppy syndrome', where he was reluctant to display his success openly in public. This social phenomenon is known to be common in Australasian contexts, shaping certain ways of thinking, talking and practising leadership (Trevor-Roberts & Ashkanasy, 2003). Even though my culture shares a similar virtue of humility, this term itself was foreign to me. Asking him to clarify the term while giving me some examples of his experiences both produced narrative data and also helped me understand the meaning he attributed to the term. Asking both kinds of questions was important for me as a foreign researcher, because I could not assume that these terms and phrases had universal meanings. Collecting both narrative and rationale data enabled me to gain insights into how my participants made sense of their lives, and the variety of discursive resources that they drew on in constructing their narrative accounts.

Another lesson I learned while conducting narrative interviews with my participants was how researchers often take for granted the relational dynamics between interviewer and interviewee (Scheurich, 1995). Scheurich (1995) warns us that researchers and their participants usually have different motivations, consciously or unconsciously, for being involved in the study. Their power relations are always at stake and constantly negotiated during the interview session (Scheurich, 1995). 'The language out of which the questions are constructed', he argues, 'is not bounded or stable; it is persistently slippery, unstable, and ambiguous from person to person, from situation to situation, from time to time' (Scheurich, 1995, p. 240). For that matter, participants' self-narratives produced during the interviews should be understood as co-constructed accounts between two speakers – the interviewer and interviewee.

During the interviews, I was attentive to how participants perceived me as their audience and interviewer, which contributed to the ways in which they constructed narrative accounts with, and for, me (see discussion in Alvesson, 2003; and also in Brannick & Coghlan, 2007). Perhaps I seemed like an insider (somebody who understood the context of higher education in general and their institution in particular) and/or an outsider (a foreign doctoral researcher who was located outside of their department) – perhaps, most likely, I was a complex mixture of both. The issue of insider and outsider identities is an important one because it did not only affect my participants – how they might respond to my questions during the interview – but also myself as a researcher. For example, my ethnic identity as a Thai person, or for most Westerners, an Asian, who was interviewing local academics in Aotearoa New Zealand might have positioned me as less privileged. This position contrasts to what many white researchers have identified, where the 'researcher' is often placed in a socially privileged position in relation to their non-white research participants. The reversal of conventional power between a researcher from a non-white ethnic background and their participants who are white is not uncommon, yet it has been infrequently documented by non-Western scholars who conducted research within white dominant contexts (Hoong Sin, 2007; Tang, 2002). These researchers reported experiencing some racist remarks from their 'white' research participants, for example, about the way they speak and write in English. Fortunately, I did not experience any racist comments from my participants, but I was aware that my identity and appearance may have affected the way they interacted with me prior to, and during, the interview. Nevertheless, Hoong Sin (2007) argues that besides ethnicity as social signifier, there exist other identities such as age, gender and class that may also come into play in how individuals interpret others.

Taking this notion into consideration, I understand that the ways I expressed sentences, the ways I dressed and the ways I responded and moved were inevitably unique to each interview context (or as I mentioned earlier, my ethnic identity). Here are two examples of entries from my research diary, which reflect on this.

Reflection from the first interview:

[T]he interview today was not as bad as I feared although there were some moments where I felt frustrated with myself especially the way I asked questions. Perhaps, I was a bit nervous since this was my first interview and I could hear myself talking with a louder-than-usual voice. I wonder whether she noticed that or not. I was also a bit distracted at the beginning, not sure what was going on in my mind. I think I was worried if I would be able to ask all the questions that I'd prepared. But after a while, I felt more comfortable and more able to concentrate, which helped a lot. What annoyed me the most, however, was that I observed myself wanting to ask more questions to generate stories, yet in reality I asked a lot of 'why' questions that required her to do the opposite.

Research diary, 8 March 2010

Reflections from the tenth interview:

> [T]oday I felt very relaxed and was able to become more open during the interview. I asked him some reflexive questions, questions that I think challenged him to see contradictions between the story he'd just told and the story he told earlier in the interview. Perhaps, it's the experience I have gained throughout these interviews that has made me feel more confident to engage in a reflexive moment with my participants. I was also able to question some of his experiences about leadership, and was then surprised when he said he enjoyed reflecting on those stories as well. Today I felt like I was not only a researcher but a conversation partner in a genuine dialogue. Being able to do that did not only give me a good feeling but also generated some good stories and responses that were also interesting and important for my research.
>
> Research diary, 29 April 2010

These reflections exemplify the uniqueness of what happened, at least for me as a researcher, in each interview. What I remember from the very first interview was my anxiety about communicating in English with my participants, as mentioned earlier. Such anxiety prompted me to become more prepared before meeting with my participants. I tried to familiarise myself with the interview questions so that I knew what I wanted to ask and would feel more confident with the direction I wanted to follow.

After each interview, I often asked the participant to reflect on their experience of being interviewed. The manner of my question was very informal as we were concluding our conversation. Some participants said the interview provided them with space to articulate ideas and reflections about their work and life. Some said it opened up an opportunity for them to express their thoughts and emotions, to regain their dignity, to recall their special memories and to remind themselves of why they chose to become academics. Of all these reflections, the words of one participant struck me the most:

> [I] often participate in research projects by students or other researchers because I'm more curious about the questions. That is, in part, how I learn. I'm always curious about what people are doing and how they're doing it and, of course, you're very interesting because I see you very rarely refer to your question sheet. You know most of your questions, so obviously, you've done it before. You know how to guide them. You know where you're going. You know roughly what you're looking for.
>
> Participant's reflection, the fifteenth interview, 28 May 2010

This reflection illustrates how the researcher's subjectivity, as well as the participant's, is always implicated in the interview process. Interestingly, this reflection suggests two important aspects of the interview process. First, it underlines that researchers are not the only ones in the interview interaction who observe; in my interviews with academics, I was simultaneously researcher and researched. From this participant's comment, it seemed that the questions I asked were as important as the way I asked them. My appearance and efficiency could be perceived and interpreted by participants in many different ways, which may have shaped how they responded to my questions. Second, my research participants were not naïve; they had their own agendas for choosing to participate in the research. The researcher can never know precisely what is going through each participant's mind during an interview (Schostak, 2006). It is important to note that these aspects of the interview process are not only present in narrative inquiry, but in all kinds of research interviews. Many narrative inquirers believe that it is important to be transparent about such interactional dynamics because these are crucial to understanding the production of the narrative between researcher and the researched (Trahar, 2011).

Reflecting on narrative writing and representation

Writing about research findings is not a straightforward process. It involves not only a researcher's interpretive act but also their construction of narratives and their positioning within the broader fields of knowledge (Bogdan & Biklen, 2007). In this process, researchers are themselves narrators as much as their participants:

> [A]s narrators, then, researchers develop meaning out of, and some sense of order in, the material they studied; they develop their own voice(s) as they construct others' voices and realities; they narrate 'results' in ways that are both enabled and constrained by the social resources and circumstances embedded in their disciplines, cultures, and historical moments; and they write or perform their work for particular audiences.
>
> Chase, 2005, p. 657

Understanding writing in this way, I do not claim to give 'voice' to my participants, as researchers working with narrative data often do (Atkinson & Delamont, 2006). The narratives of my participants, as well as my own, do not represent the coherent identities of individuals. Adopting a social constructionist perspective, I view narrative identities as multiple, fragmented, discursive, emerging, incomplete, performative and contextual (Gergen, 1991; Holstein & Gubrium, 2000; Sparkes & Smith, 2008). Because of this, I chose to focus my study on the narratives rather than the person who speaks, given that I understand a person's identity as fluid, incoherent and always in the process of 'ongoing construction and negotiation in talk' (Taylor, 2010, p. 7). This decision was also made as part of my ethical considerations in relation to researching narratives of academics from one university in Aotearoa New Zealand.

Considering the small size of the academic community in Aotearoa New Zealand, it might not be too difficult to identify a participant from details given in the interviews. Tolich (2004) distinguishes 'external confidentiality' from 'internal confidentiality', the former as more conventional and the latter as less apparent. He points out that 'external confidentiality' refers to preventing participants from being identified by outsiders of the study during research presentations while 'internal confidentiality' refers to preventing them from being identified by other participants in the same study (Tolich, 2004). I was therefore mindful of ensuring participants' confidentiality and deployed various strategies to prevent identification.

These strategies included removing any details that could identify a participant's institution, department, discipline or specific identification. I also had to consider, on a case-by-case basis, whether I needed to omit information or stories told by participants in order to avoid potential damage towards participants or others implicated in their stories. But as Tolich (2004) himself admits, it is impossible to achieve absolute confidentiality of participants because of unanticipated situations. Nevertheless, I did my best throughout my study to handle participants' information respectfully, in order to protect them from any disadvantage. Indeed, I take responsibility and claim authorship in the selection, organisation and transformation of participant narratives into one comprehensive story – the story of my research as a whole.

As a result, there remain many narratives that I did not include in my thesis. The choices I made about what was included or excluded, although guided by my theoretical framework and analytical method, were inevitably subjective. The way in which I conducted my research was always already informed by my cultural assumptions and the context of my life, as well as by my knowledge of the field and my theoretical position in this study (Alvesson, 2002). Accordingly, some stories had to be omitted because they might have jeopardised the confidentiality of my participants. The narratives I presented in my thesis, while contributing new accounts to the field of leadership in higher education, do not, and cannot, include all the possible narratives. Reading through my participants' accounts, I recognised many other narratives that seemed to be significant to their lives but contained some identifiable materials that might implicate others outside my study. These narratives largely concerned departmental politics, including possible accounts of corruption, bullying and scapegoating. Future research could be undertaken to further explore these issues – ideally in a way that avoids pathologising individuals involved as the source of a problem.

Epilogue

Upon revisiting my own journey as a narrative researcher, I have also recognised changes in myself, as both an academic and a person. Growing up in a country where a strong hierarchical structure is normative, dictatorship is acceptable, and our national leader is often considered a joke, I had little faith in leadership. Yet, listening to academics' stories helped me realise how important leadership is for many individuals in making sense of their professional lives (Juntrasook, 2014). My learning enabled me to see the potential of stories for individuals' growth and their power to transform society.

Some stories have unpredictable plot twists. While I began this chapter with a story which emphasised my disconnection from the idea of being a leader, I appear to have come full circle. Following my graduation I have returned to Thailand, where I am now the co-director of a new national leadership education and development project which is drawing together academics, activists and private sector stakeholders to consider emerging social issues and how to respond as collectives. This is a large project and an interesting opportunity for me, a relatively young scholar, to take up a formal position of leadership. Part of my plan in this project is to collect my own stories about my journey into and through this new position. Building on my research experience in Aotearoa New Zealand, I am excited about the possibility of applying my understanding of, and skills in, narrative inquiry in the context of my own country. Given the hegemony of positivism in Thai scholarly communities, I know that taking up narrative inquiry in this country will not be easy. For many of my colleagues, it would seem that stories are simply not research-worthy, and I anticipate that it will be hard to convince funding organisations that stories can be just as meaningful as numbers. However, there is hope. After a number of recent public presentations, I have been heartened by the responses of audiences, who have expressed curiosity about narrative's potential. Many people remarked that they had not known that such an approach even existed and wanted to find out more. I am particularly excited about the projects my own students are pursing, several of whom are about to embark on narrative research journeys of their own. This is a promising sign and I am hopeful that our fledgling community of narrative inquirers will continue to grow and deepen here in Thailand.

Acknowledgement

I would like to thank James Burford for his feedback on an earlier version of this chapter.

References

Alvesson, M. (2002). *Postmodernism and social research*. Buckingham: Open University Press.

Alvesson, M. (2003). Methodology for close up studies – struggling with closeness and closure. *Higher Education, 46*(2), 167–193.

Atkinson, P. & Silverman, D. (1997). Kundera's Immortality: The interview society and the invention of the self. *Qualitative Inquiry, 3*(3), 304–325.

Atkinson, P., & Delamont, S. (2006). Rescuing narrative from qualitative research. *Narrative Inquiry, 16*(1), 164–172.

Avolio, B. J., Walumbwa, F. O. & Weber, T. J. (2009). Leadership: Current theories, research, and future directions. *Annual Review of Psychology, 60*(1), 421–449.

Bochner, A. P. (2001). Narrative's virtues. *Qualitative Inquiry, 7*(2), 131–157.

Bochner, A. P. & Ellis, C. (1999). Which way to turn? *Journal of Contemporary Ethnography, 28*(5), 485–499.

Bogdan, R. C. & Biklen, S. K. (2007). *Qualitative research for education: An introduction to theory and methods* (5th ed.). Boston: Pearson Education.

Bolden, R., Hawkins, B., Gosling, J. & Taylor, S. (2011). *Exploring leadership: Individual, organizational & societal perspectives*. Oxford: Oxford University Press.

Brannick, T., & Coghlan, D. (2007). In defense of being "native": The case for insider academic research. *Organizational Research Methods, 10*(1), 59–74.

Bryman, A. (2004). Qualitative research on leadership: A critical but appreciative review. *The Leadership Quarterly, 15*(6), 729–769.

Bryman, A. (2011). Research methods in the study of leadership. In A. Bryman, D. Collinson, K. Grint, B. Jackson & M. Uhl-Bien (Eds), *The Sage handbook of leadership*. London: Sage Publications, pp. 15–28.

Chase, S. E. (2003). Taking narrative seriously: Consequences for method and theory in interview studies. In Y. S. Lincoln & N. K. Denzin (Eds), *Turning points in qualitative research: Tying knots in a handkerchief*. Walnut Creek: AltaMira Press, pp. 273–296.

Chase, S. E. (2005). Narrative inquiry: Multiple lenses, approaches, voices. In N. K. Denzin & Y. S. Lincoln (Eds), *The Sage handbook of qualitative research* (3rd ed.). Thousand Oaks: Sage Publications, pp. 651–679.

Clandinin, D. J. (Ed.). (2007). *Handbook of narrative inquiry: Mapping a methodology*. Thousand Oaks: Sage Publications.

Clandinin, D. J., & Connelly, F. M. (2000). *Narrative inquiry: Experience and story in qualitative research*. San Francisco: Jossey-Bass Publishers.

Crossley, M. L. (2000). *Introducing narrative psychology: Self, trauma and the construction of meaning*. Buckingham: Open University Press.

Gergen, K. J. (1985). The social constructionist movement in modern psychology. *American Psychologist, 40*(3), 266–275.

Gergen, K. J. (1991). *The saturated self: Dilemmas of identity in contemporary life*. New York: Basic Books.

Gergen, K. J. (2009). *Relational being: Beyond self and community*. Oxford: Oxford University Press.

Holstein, J. A. & Gubrium, J. F. (2000). *The self we live by: Narrative identity in a postmodern world*. New York: Oxford University Press.

Hoong Sin, C. (2007). Ethnic-matching in qualitative research: Reversing the gaze on 'white others' and 'white' as 'other'. *Qualitative Research, 7*(4), 477–499.

Juntrasook, A. (2013). *Narratives of leadership in academia: A discursive-dialogic analysis*. Unpublished doctoral thesis, University of Otago, Dunedin.

Juntrasook, A. (2014). 'You do not have to be the boss to be a leader': Contested meanings of leadership in higher education. *Higher Education Research & Development, 33*(1), 19–31.

Juntrasook, A., Nairn, K., Bond, C. & Spronken-Smith, R. (2013). Unpacking the narrative of non-positional leadership in academia: Hero and/or victim? *Higher Education Research & Development, 32*(2), 201–213.

Middlehurst, R. (2008). Not enough science or not enough learning? Exploring the gaps between leadership theory and practice. *Higher Education Quarterly, 62*(4), 322–339.

Payutto, P. A. (1995). *Buddhadhamma: Natural laws and values for life* (G. A. Olson, Trans.). New York: State University of New York Press.

Polkinghorne, D. E. (1988). *Narrative knowing and the human sciences*. Albany: State University of New York Press.

Polkinghorne, D. E. (1995). Narrative configuration in qualitative analysis. *Qualitative Studies in Education, 8*(1), 5–23.

Scheurich, J. J. (1995). A postmodernist critique of research interviewing. *Qualitative Studies in Education, 8*(3), 239–252.

Schostak, J. (2006). *Interviewing and representation in qualitative research.* Berkshire: Open University Press.

Simkins, T. (2005). Leadership in education: 'What works' or 'what makes sense'? *Educational Management, Administration & Leadership, 33*(1), 9–26.

Sinclair, A. (2011). Being leaders: identities and identity work in leadership. In A. Bryman, D. Collinson, K. Grint, B. Jackson & M. Uhl-Bien (Eds), *The Sage handbook of leadership.* London: Sage Publications, pp. 508–517.

Smith, B. & Sparkes, A. C. (2006). Narrative inquiry in psychology: Exploring the tensions within. *Qualitative Research in Psychology, 3*(3), 169–192.

Smith, B. & Sparkes, A. C. (2008). Contrasting perspectives on narrating selves and identities: An invitation to dialogue. *Qualitative Research, 8*(1), 5–35.

Somers, M. R. (1994). The narrative constitution of identity: A relational and network approach. *Theory and Society, 23*(5), 605–649.

Sparkes, A. C. & Smith, B. (2008). Narrative constructionist inquiry. In J. A. Holstein & J. F. Gubrium (Eds), *Handbook of constructionist research.* New York: The Guilford Press, pp. 295–314.

Tang, N. (2002). Interviewer and interviewee relationships between women. *Sociology, 36*(3), 703–721.

Taylor, S. (2010). *Narratives of identity and place.* East Sussex: Routledge.

Tolich, M. (2004). Internal confidentiality: When confidentiality assurances fail relational informants. *Qualitative Sociology, 27*(1), 101–106.

Trahar, S. (2011). *Developing cultural capability in international higher education: A narrative inquiry.* Oxon: Routledge.

Trevor-Roberts, E. & Ashkanasy, N. M. (2003). The egalitarian leader: A comparison of leadership in Australia and New Zealand. *Asia Pacific Journal of Management, 20*(4), 517–540.

2 Enabling narratives in the 'unhomely' field of higher education research

Wendy Green

Introduction

In her 1993 Nobel Lecture, the Black American novelist, Toni Morrison, described how dominant narratives work to 'sanction ignorance and preserve privilege'. 'Like a suit of armour, polished to shocking glitter, a husk from which a knight departed long ago', such narratives 'excite reverence' while summoning 'false memories of stability, harmony among the public'. Reading recent surveys (Haggis, 2009; Tight, 2008, 2013) of my field of research – higher education (HE) – I cannot help but recall Morrison's words. Since its birth as a new hub of inquiry some four decades ago, HE has defined itself through one dominant (positivist) narrative. Seemingly intent on creating 'false memories' of legitimacy, it has 'shored up certainties' (Haggis, 2009) by relying on a narrow range of well-worn theories and methods. For researchers with an interpretivist bent, HE has been an 'unhomely' field indeed (Manathunga, 2006). The terrible irony is that in this field, we all confront messy, 'wicked', ill-defined problems (Trowler, 2010), problems of students' learning, academic development, knowledge and curriculum and institutional change within universities, problems that have grown all the more messy in our 'turbulent epoch of globalisation' (Trahar, 2013a, p.301), problems that call on us not so much to know more, but to 'know differently' (Shay *et al.*, 2009, p. 373).

Narrative research can help us 'know differently' by 'illuminating how individual identities are connected, inextricably, with the social, cultural and historical landscapes' of universities (Trahar, 2013a, p. 302). Yet until very recently, narrative has been one of the most marginalised methodologies in HE. Now it seems, narrative, along with other interpretivist methodologies, is coming in from the cold. In recent years there have been a number of special issues of HE journals, which are fostering critical conversations about '*what we know* and *how we come to know*' (Shay *et al.*, 2009, authors' emphasis). In this chapter I aim to provide a critical account of the place of narrative in the story of HE research, from its marginalised beginnings to its recent emergence as a methodology of interest. Taking snippets from my own research about/with academics crossing cultural and disciplinary boundaries, I hope to reveal some of the richness narrative research can bring to our understanding of problems that confront us. I also hope to explore some of the barriers narrative researchers have experienced, and still experience, in

HE, before finishing with some thoughts about how we might sustain narrative research and narrative researchers in my still 'unhomely' field. By criss-crossing between personal stories (my own and others') and the discursive and material conditions which shape our lives, I hope to reveal some of the 'radical' potential of narrative that Morrison also alluded to in her Nobel Lecture: the potential to 'creat [e] us at the very moment it is being created' (Morrison, 1993).

A narrative researcher in the 'unhomely' field of higher education

I was not always a HE researcher. The story of how I came to be one is a disorderly tale, full of disruptive moments – quite a post-modern narrative, in fact. When I look back over my life I see that one constant is my passion for stories. In my first degree I majored in literature and studied the big, beautifully crafted stories of the Australian and British Canon. Realising that this was unlikely to lead to a job, I then trained as a social worker and so found myself listening, not to canonical narratives, but to other people's 'small stories' (Bamberg, 2006) and in the process, hopefully enabling them to re-tell them. But, when I decided to do my PhD, I felt drawn back to my first love – literature – and the powerful stories therein. Once I had begun, I expanded my field of vision to include film, media and cultural studies. Significantly, these are all disciplines that are at home in what Jerome Bruner (1985) calls 'the narrative mode' – a point I will return to in a moment.

My time as a PhD student offered me an interdisciplinary and very good apprenticeship into academe, a way of becoming a scholar in the humanities, as I took on rolling teaching contracts in the same school as well as the odd contract as a research assistant for more senior colleagues. In the process I began to imagine myself as an emerging teacher and researcher. Well, my life did not unfold as I had imagined it would back then. The year my PhD was awarded, my school was 'restructured', leaving no place for some of my well-established colleagues, let alone newcomers like me. Around the same time, another one of the three universities in my home city shut down their large humanities faculty, pushing yet more humanities scholars into the labour market. For me, the writing was on the wall: I needed to change direction. To cut a long story short, I saw the still-emerging field of HE as a place where I could at least pursue my intellectual curiosity and my passion for teaching and learning. And, it promised stability, job security and ultimately that holy grail of academic life – tenure.

So, that is how I came to find myself in HE. Actually, I have been moving in for ten years now, but I still do not feel quite at home. Depending on the day you ask me, I will tell my story as a migrant or as a refugee. On a good day, as a migrant, I might still feel somewhat bamboozled by some of the customs in this strange land but nevertheless feel welcome and very grateful for the opportunities I have been offered. But on other days, the not so good days, I feel more like a refugee – alone and here out of sheer desperation, pushed by circumstances beyond my control, uncertain if I will ever make a home for myself in this new country.

One of the differences between migrants and refugees is that the former usually come with a substantial amount of carefully packed luggage, while the latter flee their homelands almost empty handed. Like Francis Kelly (2013, p. 70), another 'émigré' from literary studies, I had 'a consciousness of and critical approach to language' stowed in my luggage as I made the crossing into HE. My doctoral thesis analysed dominant and subversive narratives of the mother–daughter relationship in Anglo-European cultures and the way they shaped, and were shaped by, the public and private lives of women. In the process of writing it, I became well-practised in the art of closely reading and (re-reading stories). I developed an ear for the dichotomies, silences and contradictions in narratives, as well as an acute awareness of the ways that stories, story-tellers and context shape each other. Using deconstructive analytical methods, I learnt how other stories might surface (Barthes, 1993/1957). In the interdisciplinary world of my academic apprenticeship, the narrative 'mode of thought' was seen as a particularly valuable form of human knowledge. This apprenticeship enabled me to understand, like Bruner(1985), that 'narrative cognition' is fundamentally different from, but equally valuable to the scientific (positivist) way of thinking valorised in many other disciplines. According to Bruner (1985, p. 11), there are two 'distinctive ways of ordering experience, of constructing reality'. The logical-scientific mode of thought, which dominates the Western academic tradition, he termed 'paradigmatic cognition'; this approach is concerned with universal truths irrespective of context. The narrative mode, on the other hand, deals with 'vicissitudes of human intention' (Bruner, 1985, p.16). It is these vicissitudes that scholars in my original disciplines found fascinating, and few ventured into the paradigmatic realm of seeking generalisable truths.

Crossing the disciplinary border into HE with my carefully packed intellectual possessions, I was surprised and unprepared for what I found: a new world operating very much in the paradigmatic mode. My initial sense of alienation, of speaking the wrong language, was something I shared with Catherine Manathunga, another humanities scholar who found herself in the field of HE. Drawing on Homi Bhabha's (1994) concept of 'unhomeliness', Manathunga observes that for some, HE can be an 'unhomely' place, populated by citizens from other, vastly different disciplinary backgrounds (Manathunga, 2006). In drawing this analogy, I hasten to acknowledge, as Manathunga does, that it is just that – an analogy. It should not be taken literally. I acknowledge the very real suffering of migrant workers and refugees and my own privileged place in an Australian university. Still, if we think about disciplines as cultures, or communities (of practice) (Trowler & Knight, 2000) and universities as a kind of world, there is a certain resonance between Bhabha's description of the 'cultural displacement' experienced by migrant workers forced by 'transnational capitalism and the impoverishment of the Third World' to undertake an endless search for work and the kind of unhomely experience I have had in higher education. With Manathunga, I have found that HE's disinterest in methods and theories we bring from our backgrounds in the humanities produces something like the refugee's vision that, according to Bhabha, is as 'divided as it is disorientating'. And, like a refugee searching for a new home, making myself at home in the new land of HE has necessitated a 're-creation of self in the world' (Bhabha, 1994, pp. 8–9).

Of course, I am not alone in feeling divided and disoriented as a researcher in a university. My personal story of reinvention is illustrative of wider pressures felt across the higher education sector, as well as within the field of HE research itself. As I will explain next, HE research makes particular demands on all of those who enter the field, precisely because we are so immersed in the subject of our research that it is impossible to get outside it. Our research both produces, and is a product of, HE. Hence, we cannot help but find aspects of our personal stories writ large in the wider world of our research and vice versa.

Beyond the personal

Many academics feel the same pressures I have to move, change and reinvent themselves. Disorientation and displacement are almost a given in academic life. The factors which have contributed to this state of affairs, at least in the Australian university context in which I work, are well-rehearsed: increasing pressure to compete in a global 'market place', significant loss of public funding, increasing managerialism at the expense of collegial governance, massification, the development of audit cultures and the building tensions between the university's civic responsibilities and creeping neo-liberalism. In this climate, border crossing, metaphorical as well as physical, is now commonplace. While international travel, particularly for sabbaticals, has long been a feature of academic life, the flow of university staff and students across national and linguistic borders has increased dramatically in recent decades due to the expansion and contraction of different national HE systems around the world (Green & Myatt, 2011). Even those who remain at home are not immune to disorientation and displacement. In the modern, 'enterprise' (Marginson & Considine, 2000) university, academic identities are continually contested, especially when disciplines – once a central feature of academic identities – are lost or diluted through 're-structuring' into large interdisciplinary faculties or subsumed into new fields of study in response to labour market demands (Trowler, 2012).

Nowhere is this more evident than within the field of HE, where the career pathways into it are extremely diverse (Hanson, 2013; Kelly, 2013). The centre where I work, for example, is peopled with academics from a range of disciplines – the sciences, social sciences and humanities – who like me, have experienced pressures to cross disciplinary and geographical borders in search of an intellectual home. In this post-modern landscape, marked by 'fragmentation and diffusion', where one's sense of self and place in the academy is not a given, the construction and exchange of stories is what enables us to form and re-form relationships to people and place (Kraus, 2006). It is through the production and circulation of some narratives and the exclusion of others that we co-create the university in our constantly shifting landscape. Listening to and analysing these stories and the processes of their production can make the experiences of mobile students and staff 'intelligible' in ways that other methods can not (Byram & Feng, 2006).

Given my acute awareness of my 'refugee' status in HE, it is perhaps not surprising that I have developed a scholarly interest in stories of mobility. Yet my research aims to unsettle the obvious by reflecting on experiences of displacement through various theoretical lenses – for example, post-colonial as well as narrative. Cultivating reflexivity in this way can be a powerful antidote to what some have called the unquestioning adoption of dominant ways of thinking in HE (Ashwin & Case, 2012; Kelly & Brailsford, 2013). As a field of study that has emerged as a response to critical social changes, it shares some characteristics with other domain-based studies. However, unlike many of those other domain based studies – women's studies, for example – HE does not 'draw from a number of disciplines' in order to understand complex problems in new and more nuanced ways (Trowler, 2012, p. 10). In her comprehensive review of research published in three key HE journals, Tamsin Haggis (2009) found that, in contrast to developments across the social sciences more broadly, HE draws on a narrow range of theoretical and methodological resources.

Narrative research is one case in point. The 'narrative turn' in the social sciences in the Anglophone world occurred in the 1980s and has been gaining ground ever since (Riessman, 2008). In the discipline of education more broadly, narrative research is seen as a particularly appropriate way to explore the production of curriculum and 'knowledge landscapes' (Clandinin & Connelly, 1995) by those engaged in forming and re-forming their identities through new practices and in response to new demands in the educational environment. Indeed, the narrative turn has a long history in educational research, dating back at least to John Dewey, who observed, 'the study of education is the study of life' which he argued, necessarily entails 'the study of epiphanies, rituals, routines, metaphors and everyday actions' (cited by Clandinin & Connelly 2000, p. xxiv). Yet, in HE journals, narrative research has barely merited a mention, until very recently.

In saying this, I hasten to add that I have enjoyed some success in having my narrative research published in mainstream HE journals and as book chapters. But it is the *rejections* – or the reasons given for rejections – that are more telling, I think, of entrenched attitudes and understandings of narrative research in my new field. For example, a common complaint of editors and reviewers is that narrative methods do not allow me to make a 'significant contribution' to our understanding of the phenomenon in question, or to assert the 'robustness of the results' because they rely on too few participants. Another bone of contention is my explanation of the methodology itself, of which I say too much, or too little, it seems – sometimes in the same review. For example, one reviewer found 'far too much attention given to methodology', yet the methods were 'opaque and lacking detail'. Some reviewers simply ask, 'Is this research'?' or assert bluntly, as was the case with a research grant application I wrote, 'Narrative "methodology" isn't research'. Colleagues who have submitted narrative research to HE have experienced the same, or worse: one was told her autoethnographic research might be accepted if it were written in the third person!

The recurring themes in these rejections suggest miscognition or cultural dissonance (Festinger, 1957); that is, it is difficult for the reviewers to make sense of narrative practices within their own (more or less conscious) 'schema' or epistemological and methodological framework. Misunderstandings arise because reviewers and writers hold different assumptions about knowledge and reality, the role of the researcher and how to evaluate rigour. We might say that narrative researchers trying to publish in mainstream HE journals seem to be speaking to reviewers living on the other side of Bruner's logical-scientific/narrative divide. But, instances of miscognition in HE extend beyond narrative research. Other qualitatively inclined researchers have had their work dismissed as 'non-reliable and inconclusive' (Oancea, 2005, p. 167). Fundamentally, we might characterise the problem in terms of the quantitative/qualitative (interpretivist) divide well-known to researchers in the social sciences. Crudely put, on the quantitative side, knowledge is viewed as objective truth; reality is 'out there' able to be contained and the role of researcher is to objectively observe that reality and findings are rigorous when they are generalisable. On the qualitative/interpretivist side, knowledge is constructed, relative and embodied, reality is socially constructed, culturally mediated and inter-subjectively shared, with diverse lived understandings. Researchers are understood as always bringing certain assumptions and values to their research, which affect all stages of data collection and analysis and are judged to be rigorous if they appear credible and trustworthy (Sandberg, 2005). The 'narrative turn' in social science research made four moves, which placed it clearly on the interpretivist side of the divide. These moves were: the acceptance of narrative as a particular way of knowing, distinct from the logical-scientific mode; a move from numbers to stories as data; a shift from a focus on the universal and disembodied to the local and specific; and a shift in the relationship between the researcher and the people participating as subjects (Clandinin, 2007, p. 9). The misrecognition of interpretivist approaches to research – narrative among others – is what makes HE an 'unhomely' place for many new arrivals.

But, why has not the disciplinary mélange that makes up HE produced a more diverse and lively intellectual climate, enriched by multiple ways of knowing? Who and what have been the structuring influences on the field? As Sue Clegg (2012, p. 667) reminds us, 'the trajectories and genealogy of the field is always a question of power . . . in the Foucauldian sense'. Genealogical explorations can 'provide insight into the contested contexts in which research takes place . . . and into the 'structural possibilities . . . associated with particular historical moments' (Clegg, 2009, p. 412).

Why is it, then, that narrative research, so well-established in the social sciences (at least in Anglo-European countries), is barely present in HE journals? To address this question adequately, I think we need to examine how this field has been constructed as a domain of research. What are the dominant narratives that define its scope, the questions it asks and the questions it does not ask?

The emergence of higher education as a research field

HE began to emerge as a field of research in Europe and the Anglophone countries such as the United Kingdom, United States and Australia in the late 1960s.

It has continued to grow in response to significant changes in the sector, such as massification, widening participation and increasing concern for the quality of the learning experience (Macfarlene & Grant, 2013; Tight, 2013). More recently, it has emerged as a field of study in other countries, particularly in the Asian region. Sue Clegg (2009, p. 404) suggests that, despite our differing national histories and contexts, the 'global nature of economic pressures, practices and policies' mean that the ways of doing HE research in the global 'north' are likely to find resonances in the HE research conducted in the global 'south'. To date, HE journals are predominantly British and North American in terms of editorial boards, contributors and places of publication (Tight, 2008), but it will be interesting to see what path(s) HE research takes as the field develops into a truly international enterprise.

Malcolm Tight's comprehensive analyses of submissions to key HE journals (2008; 2012; 2013), along with Haggis' (2009) analysis of three key higher education journals, clearly shows the current epistemological (as well as geographical) boundaries of the field. Tight's first analysis of 406 articles in 17 HE journals, which were published in 2000, revealed an 'a-theoretical community' operating within a narrow range of theories and methodologies (Tight, 2004, p. 395). In a second analysis of 567 articles in 15 journals, which were published in 2010, Tight (2012, p.732) found that, although the 'community' had become somewhat more engaged with theory, it was still methodologically narrow. Throughout its history, HE has been dominated by four methods: documentary analysis, surveys, multivariate analyses and interviews. Although there are slight regional differences, with more multivariate analyses found in North American journals, the field overall remains tied to 'fairly basic forms of these method/ologies [or] there may not be any discussion of method or methodology at all' (Tight, 2013, p. 149). Moreover, the ubiquitous interview in HE research tends to be under-examined, 'under-theorised and mis-described' (Clegg & Stevenson, 2013, p. 5).

In discussing the hegemony of HE, Tight notes a paucity of contributors from the humanities in the field. Manathunga (2006) takes this point further, arguing that the dominance of educational psychology and, more recently, phenomenography has produced a field disinterested in questions of power in universities and how it shapes practices and identities of those who work and study therein. Instead, the tendency is to construct pedagogical knowledge as homogenous and generalisable across disciplinary and geographical borders. This mindset, Manathunga (2006, p. 20) argues, is what enables HE to 'narrate its practice as a field that is "celebratory, progressive and positively change driven"' – in other words, narrating itself, as Morrison suggests, like a 'suit of armour' that 'preserves privilege'. Considering that all 22 of the most cited authors in journals analysed by Tight (2008) were men, Morrison's pointedly gendered metaphor of the knight seems all the more apt.

As a consequence of HE's epistemological and methodological armoury, research into learning cannot 'deal well with "the fleeting", the "disturbed" the "multiple" and the "complex"' (Haggis, 2009, p. 389). Nor does HE deal well with the complex, non-linear and necessarily contextual processes of teaching of curriculum development. Fraught with contradiction, and often 'messy' (Jones, 2011), 'curriculum' has been defined as 'an account of teachers' and [students'] lives together' – in the process of curriculum making, 'teachers, learners, subject matter and milieu are in dynamic interaction' (Clandinin & Connelly, 1995, p. 3). From this perspective, story telling is crucial to the formation of both (disciplinary) teacher identity and curriculum practices. If HE were to take the 'narrative turn' (Riessman, 2008) evident in the social sciences, we could better interrogate, evaluate and reflect on the narrative construction of the messy work of teaching and learning in universities.

Another good reason for making room for narrative research in HE is this: a good deal of HE's research is conducted by 'academic developers' (also known as educational developers, faculty developers and staff developers), the very people who are also charged with implementing recommendations from this research. The centralised units in which academic developers work have become a 'significant site in the reconstitution of higher education systems' (Clegg, 2012, p. 667). Hence, it is 'difficult to analyze the trajectory of higher education research without considering the trajectory of academic development' (Clegg, 2012, p. 667). That academic development straddles 'the fault line of academic identity' (Clegg, 2009, p. 407) can be seen in its nomenclature. With its colonial connotations of paternalism, 'development' implies a privileging of generalisable, 'professional development knowledge' over more 'context sensitive' local, disciplinary knowledge about ways of teaching and learning within particular disciplines (McWilliam, 2002, p. 289). On the other hand, we could acknowledge that both sides are simultaneously powerful and powerless (Green & Whitsed, 2013; Manathunga, 2006). From this perspective, academic developers are not in a position to colonise disciplinary-based academics through 'development'; rather, their contradictory positioning in centralised units, as both handmaidens of, and critical advisors to, university management invests them with an insider/ outsider status which is difficult to negotiate. 'Entwined in the micro politics of the institution', caught up in the 'tension between compliance and contestation' (Rowland, 2006, p. 73), it is not surprising that some academic developers at least are preoccupied with defining themselves (c.f. Hanson, 2013; Rowland, 2006). This preoccupation is evident in the questions of institutional power and identity, which run through the contributions to the *International Journal for Academic Development*, yet it is strangely absent in key HE journals (Tight, 2008, 2012). Understanding academic development – the way it accounts for its practices, the questions it asks and the questions it does not ask – is important not just to academic developers themselves but to the sector as a whole because its discourse of teaching and learning has 'insinuated itself into the pores of institutional life' (Clegg, 2009, pp.403–404). A broader acceptance of narrative research in HE could help here: it would give us some tools to explore 'the complex nature of subjectivity and agency' in the way we tell the story of HE research (Scutt & Hobson, 2013, p. 18), as well as the role academic developers play within it.

Happily, there are signs that HE as a field is opening up to new ways of knowing. Recently, several special issues of well-ranked HE journals have unsettled the habitual adoption of dominant ways of thinking in the field. The first, in *Studies in Higher Education* (Shay et al., 2009) challenged the 'too-familiar repertoire of concepts, theoretical frameworks and methodological approaches'. *Higher Education Research & Development* (*HERD*) followed with three issues: the first focussed on 'the dialectic between methods and theories' (Ashwin & Case, 2012, p. 271); the second explored the possibilities and challenges of opening the field to a wider range of approaches (Macfarlane & Grant, 2012); the third highlighted the potential of methods used by other disciplines, particularly the humanities to grapple with the 'messiness' of our field (Kelly & Brailsford, 2013). This third *HERD* special issue presents 'a re-evaluat[ion] of narrative and story telling in higher education' in order 'to explore the "unsayable" aspects of university life overlooked by other methodologies' (Kelly & Brailsford, 2013, p. 1). This re-evaluation continued with a special issue of the *European Educational Research Journal*, which focused entirely on narrative inquiry, authoethnography and collective biography. As the issue's editor, Sheila Trahar (2013a, p. 301) observes, a special issue of a HE journal devoted to narrative and related methods is somewhat of a milestone, in that it highlights the variety, as well as 'the value and richness' these methods bring to the field. Let us not feel too celebratory, however. As the two contributors to the third *HERD* special issue argue, in order for the field to benefit from methodological expansion, it will need to make room for those who come from the disciplinary backgrounds that celebrate 'rare tales . . . strangely shaped and reversed accounts, and stories that ultimately morph back round into questions' (Scutt & Hobson, 2013, pp. 18–19). In other words, room for the likes of me.

Doing narrative research in higher education

My own research concerns the 'rare tales' of university students and academics in our highly mobilised, globalised world. To date, I have used narrative research methods to explore the experiences of new international academic staff (Green & Myatt, 2011), students studying abroad (Green, 2012; Green *et al.*, 2014), and members of a faculty-based community of practice, developed in the wake of a painful process of institutional 're-structuring' (Green *et al.*, 2013). In co-creating, recording and analysing these stories I have sought to understand something of the complex processes of identity formation and re-formation within the context of new communities and the ways these narrator-participants negotiate the 'complex dialectic' between their professional selves and 'other aspects of identity' (Clegg, 2008, p. 336), rooted in family, gender, ethnicity, class, culture(s) and the disciplines/schools, institutions and countries in which they work or study.

Narrative methods have enabled me to dig beneath the dominant, 'romantic' (Tarp, 2006) myths about the ease with which academics and students move between cultures in a 'flat' world (Friedman, 2005), in a particularly rich, sensitive and reflexive manner (Trahar, 2011). To take one example: Australian students who study abroad for part of their degree. These students' personal histories, cultural traditions, professional aspirations and cultural experiences impact on them 'in ways that are neither uniform nor predictable' (Rizvi, 2005, p. 81). To date, research in this area has been predominantly quantitative, focussing on raw participation levels and leaving other many questions unanswered. Just two of these questions – who goes, and what enables them to go – were addressed in a paper I co-wrote with colleagues recently (Green *et al.*, 2014). Numerous quantitative studies have suggested that participation is far from equitable; in fact, they suggest that the typical exchange student from Anglophone countries is White, female, with mid- to high socio-economic status (SES) and professional parents (e.g., Olsen, 2008). In Australia, she is also likely to be private school-educated and come from the 'sandstone' (research-intensive) universities (Daly, 2011). In spite of the numerous studies revealing these inconvenient facts, little attention has been given to understanding how these multiple dimensions of privilege work together to enable some students to study abroad while excluding the majority from the experience. In view of considerable public funding available for study abroad, I felt that this issue deserved more attention. Through narrative interviews, we elicited and analysed stories from students participating in our university's exchange programme prior to their departure. Our analysis elucidated how privilege works to make study abroad imaginable, affordable and do-able for some. Particularly revealing was the role of less visible forms of 'mobility capital' in fostering participation in study abroad. These new insights enabled us to begin imagining ways that universities could enhance the mobility capital across the whole student cohort.

Standing back and considering my narrative research as a whole, I can see that one of its most significant implications concerns the value of story telling itself within universities. Narrative is critical to individual and collegial (well) being. It is fundamental to the process of identity re-formation, individually and communally. In a post-modern, globalised world, marked by increasing mobility, 'fragmentation and diffusion', one's sense of self and place in the world has to be continually constructed as 'a story without closure'. Telling or 'performing' one's story is 'the "doing" of identity' (Kraus, 2006, p. 104, p. 107). Community, too, is constructed through narrative. For better or worse, schools/faculties operate as communities of practice 'where culture is both enacted and constructed and where personal identity coalesces, is shaped and reshaped' (Trowler & Knight, 2000, p. 30). Story telling is integral to this process; it is the means by which individual members both absorb and become absorbed in the culture of practice (Lave and Wenger, 1991) – or are alternatively marginalised, or excluded from it. Understanding how this occurs through the stories we tell and silence can help us make universities a richer, more inclusive place to be.

Concluding remarks

In his analysis of HE journals, Tight (2008) suggests we might productively consider the field of HE as a community of practice (CoP), in that it has acted as a 'social container', binding together members through 'joint enterprise', 'mutuality' and 'shared repertories'. From this perspective, HE can be seen as a normative project. Yet, CoP literature also opens up possibilities for exploring the boundary crossing which is occurring more frequently now between the various disciplines contributing to the field, and 'achieving a generative tension' between them (Clegg, 2012, citing Wenger, 2000, p. 233). In a field now interested in exploring these generative tensions, it seems that narrative research, along with other interpretivist methodologies might find a home.

What, then, are the major issues facing narrative researchers in HE as the field 'comes of age' (Clegg, 2009)? First, let us not be overly optimistic. As noted by the editors in one special issue of *HERD*, the large number of submissions received suggests that while multiple theoretical and methodological perspectives '*are* out there they are possibly not finding a vehicle for publication outside of the special issue format' (Kelly & Brailsford, 2013, p. 4). Articles on HE published in non-HE journals currently use a wider range of method/ologies than those found in HE journals (Haggis, 2009; Tight, 2013), and this is likely to continue for some time.

One rationale for maintaining a methodologically narrow field is that HE's four methodological staples are well-known throughout the academy (Tight, 2013). This is an important consideration for those like me who want their research to speak to those who read HE journals: teaching academics across all disciplines, academic developers, educationalists, university managers and students. This suggests to me that narrative researchers must find ways to educate their readers about the 'narrative mode' without becoming strident. This means avoiding 'paradigm fundamentalism' by acknowledging the limitations as well as the possibilities of narrative inquiry within specific contexts (Trahar, 2013b) and explaining this in ways that are intelligible to a wider audience. It means avoiding a tendency to view narrative as 'truth-telling', explaining instead how it functions as 'method', as 'a place to begin inquiry', to represent rather than pin down meaning (Gallagher, 2011, pp. 49-53). It also means confronting a perennial problem for narrative researchers: what sense can we make of the rich, nuanced and highly contextualised accounts we construct? 'How do we advance to the level of theory without reifying or losing the richness of the narrative database? [As studies] accumulate, how do we add them up'? (Josselson, 2006, p. 4).

Making the possibilities and limitations intelligible to a wider audience is essential if narrative inquiry is to become a viable approach to research in academe. Governments in many countries have a large say in what research gets funded, effectively privileging or marginalising different approaches to knowledge production (Trowler, 2012). For example, the UK's Research Excellence Framework and Australia's Excellence in Research for Australia valorise quantitative methods over others – a trend that is mirrored in the proclivity for quantitative methods in HE journals, such as *Studies in Higher Education* (Scutt & Hobson, 2013, p. 17). We need to be mindful that contesting this hegemony comes at a cost, perhaps more so in HE, considering that the bulk of research conducted in the field is conducted by academic developers who are themselves in particularly precarious positions inside/outside the faculties.

Well aware of both the systemic privileging of HE's well-worn methodological 'suit of armour' through publications and research grants and the uncertain position of the field's foot soldiers in academic development units, my colleague Paula Myatt and I started our own narrative research network in 2008. Our aim was to build an interdisciplinary, narrative CoP across the universities in our city. Since our first meeting in 2008, our members have engaged in countless discussions about their narrative research projects from a range of theoretical perspectives. We have laughed and cried over successes and failures at our regular meetings and during our annual retreats. Our members have successfully completed doctorates and had articles, and even books, published. And all the while, we've been constructing our selves, 'performing' our identities as emerging narrative researchers (Kraus, 2006). Story telling has been integral to this process; it is the means by which each of us absorbs and becomes absorbed in narrative ways of knowing, doing and being (Lave & Wenger, 1991).

This community has enabled me to avoid the trap of seeing HE as an impenetrable methodological 'monolith', and instead be more alert to 'the significance of *multiple* narratives and *conflicting* narratives' within, and about, HE (Trowler, 2012, p. 23). Through membership in this community, I have come to appreciate, even enjoy, the 'unhomeliness' I feel in HE's 'borderlands' (Manathunga, 2006) and to celebrate my capacity as a narrative researcher 'to transform the familiar "into something rich and strange" '(King, 2013, pp. 96–97).

References

Ashwin, P. & Case, J. (2012). Questioning theory–method relations in higher education research. *Higher Education Research & Development*, 31(3), 271–272.

Bamberg, M. (2006). Stories: Big or small? Why do we care? *Narrative Inquiry*, 16(1), 147–155.

Barthes, R. (1993/1957). *Mythologies*. London: Vintage Press.

Bhabha, H. (1994). *The location of culture*. London: Routledge.

Bruner, J. (1985). *Actual minds, possible worlds*. Cambridge: Harvard University Press.

Byram, M. & Feng, A. (Eds) (2006). *Living and studying abroad: research and practice*. Multilingual Matters: Clevedon, Buffalo and Toronto.

Clandinin, D. J. (2007). *Handbook of narrative inquiry: Mapping a methodology*. Thousand Oaks, CA: Sage.

Clandinin, D. J. and Connelly, F. M. (1995). *Teachers' professional knowledge landscapes*. New York: Teachers College Press.

Clandinin, D. J. and Connelly, F. M. (2000). *Narrative inquiry: Experience and story in qualitative research*. San Francisco: Jossey-Bass.

Clegg, S. (2008). Academic identities under threat? *British Educational Research*. 34(3), 329–345.

Clegg, S. (2009). Forms of knowing and academic development practice. *Studies in Higher Education*, 34(4), 403–416.

Clegg, S. (2012). Conceptualising higher education research and/or academic development as 'fields': a critical analysis. *Higher Education Research & Development*, 31(5), 667–678.

Clegg, S. & Stevenson, J. (2013). The interview reconsidered: Context, genre, reflexivity and interpretation in sociological approaches to interviews in higher education research. *Higher Education Research & Development*, 32(1), 5–16.

Daly, A. (2011). Determinants of participating in Australian university student exchange programs. *Journal of Research in International Education*, 10(1), 58–70.

Festinger, L. (1957). *A theory of cognitive dissonance*. Stanford University Press: Redwood City, CA.

Friedman, T. (2005). *The World Is Flat: A Brief History of the Twenty-First Century*. New York: Farrar, Straus and Giroux

Gallagher, K. (2011). In search of a theoretical basis for storytelling in education research: Story as method. *International Journal of Research & Method in Education*, 34(1), 49–61.

Green, W. (2012). Great expectations: The impact of friendship groups on the intercultural learning of Australian students abroad. In M. Blythman & S. Sovic (Eds). *International students negotiating higher education: critical perspectives*. Oxfordshire, UK: Routledge, pp. 211–225.

Green, W. & Myatt, P. (2011). Telling tales: A narrative research study of the experiences of new international academic staff at an Australian university. *International Journal for Academic Development*, 16(1), 33–44.

Green, W. & Whitsed, C. (2013). Reflections on an alternative approach to continuing professional learning for internationalisation of the curriculum across disciplines. *Journal of Studies in International Education*, 17(2), 148–164.

Green, W., Hibbins, R., Houghton, L. & Ruutz, A. (2013). Reviving praxis: stories of continual professional learning and practice architectures in a faculty-based teaching community of practice. *Oxford Review of Education*, 39(2), 247–266.

Green, W., Gannaway, D., Sheppard, K. & Jamarani, M. (2014). What's in their baggage? The cultural and social capital of Australian students preparing to study abroad. *Higher Education Research & Development*. DOI: 10.1080/07294360.2014.973381 (accessed 14 November 2014).

Haggis, T. (2009). What have we been thinking of? A critical overview of 40 years of student learning research in higher education. *Studies in Higher Education*, 34(4), 377–390.

Hanson, J. (2013). Educational developers as researchers: The contribution of insider research to enhancing understanding of role, identity and practice. *Innovations in Education and Teaching International*, 50 (4), 388–398.

Jones, A. (2011). Seeing the messiness of academic practice: Exploring the work of academics through narrative. *International Journal for Academic Practice*, 16(2), 109–118.

Josselson, R. (2006). Narrative research and the challenge of accumulating knowledge. *Narrative Inquiry*, 16(1), 3–10.

Kelly, F. (2013). 'And so betwixt them both': Taking insights from literary analysis into higher education research. *Higher Education Research & Development*, 32(1), 70–82.

Kelly, F. & Brailsford, I. (2013). The role of the disciplines: Alternative methodologies in higher education. *Higher Education Research & Development*, 32(1), 1–4.

King, V. (2013). Self-portrait with mortar board: A study of academic integrity using the map, the novel and the grid. *Higher Education Research & Development*, 32(1), 96–108.

Kraus, W. (2006). The narrative negotiation of identity and belonging. *Narrative Inquiry*, 16(1), 103–111.

Lave, J. & Wenger, E. (1991). *Situated learning: Legitimate peripheral participation.* Cambridge: Cambridge University Press.

Macfarlane, B. & Grant, B (2012). The growth of higher education studies: From forerunners to pathtakers. *Higher Education Research & Development*, 31(5), 621–624.

McWilliam, E. (2002). Against professional development. *Educational Philosophy and Theory*. 34(3), 289–300.

Manathunga, C. (2006). Doing educational development ambivalently: Applying post-colonial metaphors to educational development? *International Journal for Academic Development*, 11(1), 19–29.

Marginson, S. & Considine, M. (2000). *The enterprise university: Power, governance and reinvention in Australia.* Cambridge: Cambridge University Press.

Morrison, T. (1993). Nobel Lecture. Available online at www.nobelprize.org/nobel_prizes/literature/laureates/1993/morrison-lecture.html (accessed 26 April 2014).

Oancea, A. (2005). Criticisms of educational research: Key topics and levels of analysis. *British Educational Research Journal*, 31(2), 157–183.

Olsen, A. (2008). International mobility of Australian university students: 2005. *Journal of Studies in International Education*, 12(4), 364–374.

Riessman, C. K. (2008). *Narrative methods for the human sciences.* California and London: Sage Publications.

Rizvi, F. (2005). International education and the production of cosmopolitan identities. In A. Arimato, F. Huang, K.Yokoyama & D. Hiroshima (Eds). *Globalization and higher education.* Hiroshima: Research Institute of Higher Education.

Rowland, S. (2006). The enquiring university: compliance and contestation in higher education. Buckingham: SRHE and Open University Press.

Sandberg, J. (2005). How do we justify knowledge produced within interpretive approaches? *Organizational Research Methods*, 8(1), 41–68.

Scutt, C. & Hobson, J. (2013). The stories we need: Anthropology, philosophy, narrative and higher education. *Higher Education Research & Development*, 32 (1), 17–29.

Shay, S., Ashwin, P. & Case, J. (2009). A critical engagement with research into higher education. *Studies in Higher Education*, 34(4), 373–375.

Tarp, G. (2006). Student perspectives in short term study programmes abroad: A grounded theory approach. In M. Byram, M. & A. Feng (Eds). *Living and studying abroad: Research and practice*, Clevedon, Buffalo and Toronto: Multilingual Matters, pp. 157–185.

Tight, M. (2004). Research into higher education: An a-theoretical community. *Higher Education Research & Development*, 23(4), 395–411.

Tight, M. (2008). Higher education research as tribe, territory and/or community: A co-citational analysis. *Higher Education*, 55(5), pp. 593–605.

Tight, M. (2012). Higher education research 2000–2010: Changing journal publication patterns. *Higher Education Research & Development*, 31 (5), 723–740.

Tight, M. (2013). Discipline and methodology in higher education research. *Higher Education Research & Development*, 32(1), 136–151.

Trahar, S. (2011). *Developing cultural capability in international education: A narrative inquiry.* Oxon, UK: Routledge.

Trahar, S. (2013a). Contemporary methodological diversity in European higher education research. *European Educational Research Journal*, 12(3), 301–309.

Trahar, S. (2013b). *Contextualising narrative inquiry: Developing methodological approaches for local contexts.* London & New York: Routledge.

Trowler, P. (2010). Wicked issues in situating theory in close up research. *Higher Education Close Up (5) Conference: Questioning Theory-Method Relations in Higher Education Research.* Lancaster University, United Kingdom, 20–22 July 2010. Available online atwww.lancaster.ac.uk/fss/events/hecu5/index.htm (accessed 26 April 2014).

Trowler, P. (2012). Disciplines and interdisciplinarity: Conceptual groundwork. In P. Trowler, M. Saunders & V. Bamber (Eds). *Tribes and territories in the 21st century: Rethinking the significance of disciplines in higher education.* London & New York: Routledge, pp. 5–29.

Trowler, P. & Knight, P. (2000). Coming to know in higher education: Theorising faculty entry to new work contexts. *Higher Education Research & Development,* 19(1), 27–42.

Wenger, E. (2000). Communities of practice and social learning systems. *Organization,* 7(2), 225–246.

3 Embracing new narratives in Singapore

Renée Tan

Introduction

Mention the term 'Sang Nila Utama', who was the Palembang prince who founded Singapore and named it 'Singapura' or 'Lion City', or speak about the 'Merlion', the mythical creature with the body of a fish and head of a lion which is the iconic representation of Singapore, and anyone who has been through the education system in Singapore would be able to tell you which part of the 'Singapore story', a term used officially in the national education curriculum, these icons inhabit. The Singaporean affinity towards narratives in education and nation-building is cultivated from a very young age. However, if questioned about the possibility of using narrative as a basis for research, responses are likely to be less enthusiastic, as a general understanding of inquiry criteria would include the need for hard data and evidence. This chapter aims to explore the reaction of the Singapore citizenry to the use of narratives in public and national education, to attempt to offer a possible alternative to such dominant narratives and to put forward an argument for the potential of narrative inquiry to be used as a tool in national education and offer a means to examine and reflect on a currently sensitive issue in Singapore – that of the treatment of, and relationship with, foreign workers.

National education as a context and setting for educational research

This chapter is framed within the claim that the education of the citizenry, which I name 'national', 'public' or 'citizen' education throughout, and which is under-taken through a range of means, is a legitimate context and setting for educational research. Although there are no visible walls to this 'school' and no persons designated as 'teachers', the purposes and dissemination of definite messages to shape mindsets of a citizenry would strongly constitute education. It is informal learning, which has been categorised into three recognisable forms: self-directed learning, incidental learning and socialisation (Schugurensky, 2000, p. 3). What the state undertakes is socialisation, which refers to the 'internalization of values, attitudes, behaviours, skills, etc. that occur during everyday life' (Schugurensky, 2000, p. 4). On the part of the learner, the education process is unconscious and unintentional, but on the part of the state, the messaging and means to trigger such tacit learning is highly deliberate.

Admittedly, informal learning contexts and settings remain a less popular choice of educational research context, as compared to formal education environments. Furthermore, the full educational potential of nonformal education in a positive sense, as an important and unique domain that is not just a substitute for, or a supplement to, 'real' education, is seldom recognised (Bekerman *et al.*, 2006, p. 2).

Still, interest in this area of educational research is growing, especially with the increasing impact of globalisation and immigration affecting communities across the globe. With many governments having to undertake more educative efforts to manage their entire citizenry, this area becomes a new and exciting context for educational research, especially in the means and modes employed by states, of which national narratives is one such, to transmit preferred values and attitudes.

National narratives

National narratives, or the stories that nations tell to connect their past, present and future, are powerful and necessary tools in shaping national identity. Within such narratives, the 'nation as a concept may often appear to rely heavily on an essentialised narrative that seeks to homogenise diversity as a strand of coherent unity. Yet, this is arguably a mere blanket over the differences that truly exist within and between communities' (Chin, 2009, p. 3).

The notion of a 'national' narrative that rallies a citizenry to a cause is not a new one, and thus far, such dominant, uni-directional narratives have been the norm, woven together and packaged by the state for the main purpose of citizen education. The narratives are used to increase receptivity to a particular mode of behaviour, thus 'educating' the citizenry to contribute towards building a community with the preferred social norms and values. One purpose of the use of such a narrative has been to pull together the different ethnic groups in Singapore, to such an end that 'racial harmony' is now something the majority of Singapore citizens would be happy to point out as a defining trait in Singapore. Such public education efforts where these catchphrases are emphasised are undertaken via mass media and through compulsory school programmes such as 'Citizenship and Community Education', which is worked into the national curriculum. The traditional narratives consciously and carefully portray the major ethnic groups in Singapore (Chinese, Malay, Indian, Eurasians and 'Others') in cooperative and collaborative circumstances, with respect and tolerance for each other's cultural and religious differences. However, as the earlier quotation illustrates, the homogeneity that such dominant narratives portray is problematised by the environment of diversity and difference that marks the Singapore of today. Singapore's racial mix has changed greatly in the last decade or so, with globalisation and the relaxation of rules regarding 'foreign talent' in the local economy. Singaporeans have become markedly less tolerant and more vocal in expressing their discomfort against these foreigners, with their vociferous reaction against a white paper on the continued influx of foreigners into the country causing the government to admit that more discussion on the issue would have to be initiated. Newer narratives in the public education space have started to manifest and to resist the "us versus them" mindset which seems to have set in. The most popular storyline now constructed by the state would be that of successful integration between locals and foreigners from different communities. These newer versions of the national narratives today run alongside differential policies to manage the local–foreign divide. The obvious strategy involves dishing out more subsidies and benefits to Singaporeans relative to foreigners, which encourages foreigners to take up citizenship while at the same time reassuring Singaporeans that the policy-makers have their interests at heart (Leong, 2012, p. 4).

On 8 December 2013, Singapore witnessed her first ever 'riot' in her 48 years since independence. A fatal road accident involving a foreign worker victim sparked off large-scale mob violence amongst a sizeable group of mostly foreign workers, shocking Singaporeans who had never before witnessed such a scene. There was soul-searching and speculation on how things had come to this, as people looked beyond the immediate reasons given of the riot triggers being alcohol and anger over the accident. There was reflection on how Singapore had not quite come to terms with her uncomfortable relationship with foreign workers. Are national narratives, then, no longer working as a public education means? My argument is that they may continue to be as powerful a tool as ever, but the potential may have to be harnessed in a different way, appealing to the emotional sensitivity of individuals through greater subtlety and evocation. To this end, narrative inquiry may provide us with a way to do so.

Narrative inquiry and creative fictionalisation

Narrative inquiry is, as Susan Chase (2011, p. 421) asserts, 'still a field in the making'. However, narrative inquirers generally concur that

> the term *narrative* carries many meanings and is used in a variety of ways by different disciplines, often synonymously with *story* [. . .] the narrative scholar (pays) analytic attention to how the facts got assembled that way. For whom was this story constructed, how was it made and for what purpose? What cultural discourses does it draw on – take for granted? What does it accomplish?
>
> Riessman & Speedy, 2007, pp. 428–429;
> quoted in Trahar, 2009, p. 1

The questions which narrative inquiry lays open help to foreground the potential of narrative inquiry as a tool to be used in social research and ethnographic observation. I hope that I can capitalise on this and use it as an educational method in my attempt to offer a means to critically understand Singapore's new landscape, with many more nationalities from diverse cultures working and living side-by-side.

A means to represent the social observations made, in the hope of sensitising more Singaporeans to the areas of friction encountered within these new landscapes, is through producing an individualised and alternative narrative. In this instance, I will attempt to do so through creative fictionalisation, since Singaporeans have so far proven fairly open to the use of stories and narratives as a means to help them realise what needs to be picked up in the community. The fictional mode also has the advantage of being a gentle, persuasive and non-threatening way to deliver 'lessons' to be learnt in the building of community and nation.

Fictional representation, though, may sit uncomfortably with those unable to reconcile between fact and fiction in what is supposedly meant to be a form of inquiry and hence, unquestionably, the handling of facts. Despite Norman Denzin (2001, p. 22) articulating that 'the narrative turn in social sciences has been taken', many remain unconvinced. However, Pat Sikes has noted that researchers such as Peter Clough have 'suggested that fictional stories can make public those experiences and perceptions that other methodological approaches and research techniques are unable to reveal' (Sikes, quoted in Clough, 2002, p. xii).

More and more, the methodology has gained critical ground, and the call has even been strong enough to assert that

> we need to shop around more and encourage narrative ingenuity and novel interpretation [. . .] We need more, not fewer, ways to tell of culture. The value of ethnography from this standpoint is found not in its analysis and interpretation of culture, but in its decision to examine culture in the first place; to conceptualize it, reflect on it, narrate it, and, ultimately, to evaluate it.
>
> van Maanen, 2011, p. 140

I thus worked to offer an alternative narrative, focussing on the domestic helper, to fulfil the purpose of engagement and to hopefully offer an opening to dialogue about and a mode of educating our citizenry on our evolving landscape in Singapore.

A possible new narrative to be embraced?

Vilma

She hadn't been home in four years.

Each contract was two years long, and her fear was that the trip home would mean the immediate spending of all the money she had managed to save over the two years. It was a very small amount, but her salary did not amount to much – S$550 was about 19,000 pesos, a princely sum when she had contemplated it in Pangasinan, but earning it the way she did, it never seemed enough. Her children, the useless man at home and her extended family were always calling her for money – she was the only member in the family earning.

He could not find a job – none of them could. There were no jobs back home – the men could drive a *tricycle* if ever the family could afford one, or open a *sari-sari* at the front of their shack or run a roadside pushcart snack stall like she had done before coming here, but they could never manage to earn enough. Only those who had done a 'contract' overseas could afford anything better. He had not wanted her to go, not because he would miss her but because he was proud and could not take it. If he could get a construction job in the Middle East, like some of the other men, he would go instead, but he did not manage to pass the medical and so she went, leaving the four children behind in his care.

For they were growing older, needed more and she knew they could not go on this way. She took a loan from her aunt, already out in Hong Kong, to make the down payment to the agency and started the long journey to Singapore. The five-hour bus journey from Pangasinan to Manila left her limp and then the plane ride, her first time ever, terrified her.

✱✱✱

Rachel

She sighed in exasperation as she surveyed her large walk-in wardrobe – nothing seemed to fit her mood today, even though she had one of the largest wardrobes of designer wear she knew about. She finally selected an outfit – new, as most of her clothes were, many worn once or not at all. Calling out to Vilma, she instructed briskly, 'Change my bag – that one, second shelf, red and polish my red pointy-toe shoes – yah, Jimmy Choo right? Down there. . . . Hurry, or I'll be late.'

Walking out to the dining room, she saw her daughter picking at her breakfast and curtly told her to speed up. She then watched her younger son struggle with his shoes. 'Gracia, help him lah! What are you doing standing around?' She thought irritably, 'Maids nowadays are totally useless. What help am I getting? I still have to do everything!' Her husband looked up from his iPad, and without a word to her, shepherded the children into his car to drive them to school. She would drive herself to work in their second car later on, after she had had some coffee and left the maids their instructions for the day.

✱✱✱

Vilma

Left to themselves, Vilma and her work partner Gracia heaved a quiet sigh of relief, but not too discernibly, for they knew the cameras all over the house were whirring and working, so that they could be monitored throughout the day. Vilma hated it – she felt like a criminal under constant surveillance. The two of them started their daily litany of complaints against their employer in a torrent of Tagalog, unafraid of conversation as the cameras were without sound capability. They did their chores quickly, deftly and efficiently and Vilma's favourite task of the day was cooking their meal, for their employer was, thankfully, generous enough to allow them to cook their own food and take separate meals from the family. She was a proficient cook of Singaporean food, but frankly, she found the food either bland or overly spicy and steamed fish, their employer's favourite – horrible! Instead, Gracia and she had Filipino favourites daily – *adobo, siniggang, bangus, embutido* or *paksiw*. They were not, however, allowed to eat *tinapa*, as it was highly pungent and their employer drew the line there. Depending on how much meat or fish they were given, Vilma always tried to pack a small portion for the maid a few houses down the road who so missed Filipino food and who was not allowed to cook it.

Gracia and she chatted as they worked. They had not liked each other at first – Vilma was Pangasinan-born and bred, whilst Gracia was from Negroes Occidental. They spoke different dialects, but like all Filipinos, shared the common bond of Tagalog. Under the circumstances though, they had to work and live together as companionably as possible – they shared a room and it was too tight a fit to not at least be civil.

> '*Pare-pareho ito ay kaya mainit ang ulo.*' (The uniform is so ugly.)

> '*Siya ay may kaya maraming mga damit, kaya lahat mahal, at siya ay gumagawa sa amin magsuot ito.*' (She has so many clothes, all so expensive, and she makes us wear this.)

> '*Wala kaming choice, kailangan namin ang pera. Gusto ko ang mga bata ay mas mahusay sumusunod na.*' (We have no choice. We need the money. I wish the kids were better behaved.)

> '*Ang batang lalaki kick sa akin kahapon. Wala kaming isa sa magreklamo s.*' (The boy kicked me yesterday. Who can we complain to?)

The conversation went on, as they gossiped about their friends and all the employer horror stories they had heard. But some of their friends did have very good employers and the Caucasian employers were also highly regarded, although it was a matter of luck, since some Caucasian madams were very difficult to please and were suspicious that the maids would seduce their husbands.

***

Rachel

The day had proven a challenge – her colleague Daphne and she had been locked in a 'discussion' at the board meeting, but everyone knew Daphne was angling for the chairman's favour and had ruthlessly tried to bring down her unit's performance. The international economy was bad though, Europe being in the state it was, and she would have to drive her team even harder if they were to meet this year's KPIs. The thought of quitting when she was at the top of her game came to mind – she had just turned 40 but was already the fourth most powerful member in the large organisation. She dismissed the thought quickly though, there were many like Daphne nipping at her heels and she knew she was the subject of nasty gossip, but she thought about how her husband no longer really spoke to her anymore, and if anything happened to her marriage how would she take care of the children and maintain her lifestyle?

Her Samsung Galaxy phone lit up – it was her son – now what? She heard him whine in his babyish voice about how Auntie Vilma and Gracia had made him the meal he hated most, and he was not going to eat it. She clicked her tongue impatiently, must she really deal with everything?

'Vilma, did you give him the *tau yew bak* again?'

'Yes maam, he had the chicken wing yesterday already maam. But he wants again.'

'That's not healthy, but he won't eat now. Can you think of something else and make it for him? He must eat something, ok?'

'Ok, maam, I try.'

As she swiped the phone to turn it off, she contemplated that it was indeed difficult to be a working woman. Maybe she should just give up and become a *taitai*.

***

Vilma

Maam, in the Philippines
We don't do like this
In the morning, we eat rice
One sack – 50 kg, every month.
Maam, I like to sing
And wear shorts and jeans pants is okay for me
And our nails we do for each other
Ours is sharp, not round like you.
And we like sour and sweet together
Vinegar and sugar with fish
And bihon and fruit salad with condensed milk
When we have party maam.
And I like handphone maam
But you not allow
I want to talk to my kids maam
No handphone, no top-up how?
Our life like that maam
Philippines now so hard
I don't think so much maam
Just work and wait and see how.

Her thoughts were all jumbled up in her mind, as Gracia and she lay in their narrow beds in the warm night, with only a single fan working, whilst everyone else in the household slept comfortably with air conditioners. Still, it was a room – she had friends who had to share with the children in the house, some of them on a mattress laid on the floor. Both Gracia and she were texting with their mobile phones, which was against the rules, but they had to have a means of keeping in contact with the family at home. She was texting her children, lecturing her eldest daughter, 14 years old and already looking at boys – everyone in the Philippines started so early. She had been a mother at 17, and now, at 31, was younger than her employer who was already 40 but whose oldest girl was eight. They studied too much here; she smiled as she remembered how shocked her employer had been when she had found out the age of her oldest child, and the fact that she was not even married. Most of them, especially in rural Philippines did not formally get married; common law partnerships were the norm. Should a formal marriage result in divorce, they had to wait seven years before they could officially separate. That was just too much trouble. She thought of her employers – she had never seen them happy together, they either fought or completely ignored each other. What was the point really?

She frowned as she received a text from her daughter:

> '*Mama, Jen siya ay umuwi minsan, napupunta upang manatili sa bahay ang kanyang kaibigan.*' (Mother, Jen does not come home sometimes; she goes to stay at her friend's house.)

Jen was her second girl, 12 and already determined to drop out of school and leave Pangasinan as quickly as possible. She yearned to make it in Manila or some other city somewhere, but Vilma knew that 'making it' in the city often meant being a nightclub dancer or a prostitute. Sighing, she ended the text conversation with her older girl and turned to sleep. Her day would start early and she needed all the rest she could get.

***

Rachel

'These bloody *Pinoys* are everywhere!'

She bit her lip as she saw that Vilma had heard her low outburst, but was trying to act as if nothing had happened. They were at Orchard Road doing the shopping, and Lucky Plaza even on a weekday was full of Filipinos, who had recently come into the country on work passes to take on service jobs in the shops and restaurants, as well as IT maintenance jobs for the men. She heard the singsong but loud and rapid language that she sometimes heard Vilma and Gracia converse in all around her. When she had first suggested hiring Filipinos instead of Indonesian or Myanmar maids because they could at least speak some English, her husband had told her that he 'despised their accent' and that 'they were all crooks'. He had always operated on the premise that maintaining maids was her choice, but how else could they cope? She had selected Vilma and Gracia very carefully, they were not as young as some of the others and were not dressed as scandalously as the younger ones were. They did not seem like the type who would hang around the Blue Banana at Orchard Towers – where she knew some of her Caucasian clients went during the weekends to pick up maids soliciting on their off-days.

Vilma, especially, had been a saviour. She had a way with the children her son especially, could sometimes only be pacified by her and both children were attached to their 'aunties', sometimes more so than to her. She felt fleetingly jealous at times, but at others told herself not to be soft and to get on with it – the maids were just doing their job, and the better they did theirs, the better she could do hers.

***

Vilma

She had to go home.

Four years was a long time to be away. She was stuck here taking care of someone else's children, while hers were showing signs of neglect. Her youngest son, just one year old when she had left, had started refusing to answer her phonecalls – he did not know who she was.

***

Rachel

Vilma had gone home.

The children had cried so hard for so long, rejecting her when she had tried to comfort them – even the older girl! Thank goodness for Gracia for some familiarity. She had gone to the agency for another maid, and much as she dreaded the thought of inducting yet another person into the routine, it had to be done.

They were indispensable to her.

***

Glossary

Pangasinan:	province in the Philippines (in Western Luzon region)
tricycle:	a 3-wheeled motorised pedicab popular in the Philippines
sari-sari:	Tagalog for a makeshift retail stall hawking daily essentials
Tagalog:	primary language in the Philippines
adobo:	Tagalog for pork cooked in soy sauce and vinegar
sinigang:	Tagalog for a vinegar-based soup with meat and vegetables
bangus:	Tagalog for milkfish, often cooked in vinegar
embutido:	Tagalog for meat loaf
paksiw:	Tagalog for milkfish boiled in vinegar
tinapa:	Tagalog for smoked, preserved fish
Negroes Occidental:	province in the Philippines (in Western Visayas region)
KPIs:	key performance indicators
tau yew bak:	Hokkien (Chinese dialect) for pork stewed in soya sauce
taitai:	Cantonese (Chinese dialect) for a lady of leisure living in luxury

bihon:	Tagalog for fried rice vermicelli
handphone:	Singaporean slang term for mobile phone
top-up:	Singaporean slang term for a stored value card used in mobile phones
Pinoys:	derogatory Singaporean slang term for Filipinos

Embracing the new narrative as a national education tool

Putting forward the earlier creative piece has helped me to represent people's experiences in a way that Mair expresses perfectly when he says

> [I] want to suggest the importance of a poetic understanding of our experiencing of our world: poetic rather than prosaic [. . .] A poetics requires that you are deeply attentive to yourself and others, so that you become the meeting place of messages spoken and unspoken, the place of transformation of what is moving between and amongst you [. . .] You have to listen to the lilt and rhythm, to the use of words and phrases, the telling metaphor, the silence, and the moving spaces in between.
>
> Mair, 1989, p. 63

I thus paid great attention to the poignant call I heard from many Vilmas and Rachels, and made a form work for me by making the often prosaic details in the text poetic, thus enhancing the story that needed to be told. What resulted is not so much formal poetry (not even the verse form used to express Vilma's thoughts counts as that), but a dialogic-type of turn-taking structure deliberately chosen for its irony, since the two characters never actually communicate with each other, even though they are enmeshed in a routine of mutual dependence. The uncomfortable script-like structure also seems to give it a performative potential, but with the two characters not really in the same performance, so to speak. The form is thus a means of reiterating the main observation in this piece of social inquiry, thus strengthening and 'crystallizing' (Richardson & St. Pierre, 2005, p. 963) its impact and helping to shape the reader's response to the story.

The narrative is also ethnographic in nature with ethnography defined by van Maanen as

> a portrait of diversity in an increasingly homogenous world. [It] displays the intricate ways individuals and groups understand, accommodate, and resist a presumably shared order. These portraits may . . . develop from the more intimate contrasts of gender, age, community, occupation, or organization within a society.
>
> van Maanen, 2011, pp. xvii–xviii

This piece is ethnographic as it records authentic experiences of a group of foreign domestic workers (the official term for them, although in mainstream language, we do still call them 'maids') in Singapore. They are mainly from the Philippines,

Indonesia and Myanmar, and there were 214,500 of them here as of December 2013 (Ministry of Manpower, 2014, p. 1). This works out as one in every five households in Singapore employing at least one foreign domestic worker (Transient Workers Count Too, 2013, p. 1). This was a story which needed to be told to encourage the process of public, citizen or national education, attempting to take a step towards sensitising and socialising the public to a diversity issue which can no longer be ignored. How I sought to do this was through authentic representation of the place, cultures, vernacular and emotions of the subjects. Naming the cities, using native languages, capturing the cadences of the English as used by one of the characters and referencing cultural markers such as food and lifestyle helped to ground the work as narrative and ethnographic inquiry, as

> postmodern ethnographers seek to promote an understanding through recognition, identification, personal experience, emotion, insight, and communicative formats which engage the reader on planes other than the rational one alone. They seek to *evoke* the postmodern culture, moment and consciousness rather than to *describe* it.
>
> Gottschalk, 1998, p. 213

I worked to immerse the reader in the experience of being in Singapore, in the daily life of the Singaporean employer and the Filipino maid. Authenticity was also achieved in the verse sequence of Vilma's thoughts, as the lines are a collage of actual utterances by my helper and the many other Filipino helpers in my neighbourhood who often stop by. It had to be authentic enough to come across as a credible base from which one could learn. I am definitely not Vilma or Rachel, but we are all women and has what was going through their minds not gone through my own at some point or other? The form thus very powerfully highlighted the underlying feminist issue in the story as well; that in some situations, awareness of women's abilities (or desires) to support other women may be non-existent, and the contrast in the concerns of each woman and the lack of connection between the two characters all serve to echo the message. Thus, in writing this piece, I was 'committed to an actual world. A world of social relations and experience, of human practices and activities, of embodied joys, pleasures and pains' (Mykhalovskly, 1996, p. 143). This enhanced the validity of the ethnographic inquiry, thus bolstering its ability to sensitise the public to what is actually happening around them.

This honest representation of the actual world put forward as a public education tool was not a natural choice of mode to work with. In fact, my first instinct was to work against this honesty. Thus far, public education-type narratives have focussed on rosy and affirming portrayals of Singaporeans, with the messages concentrating on that of the inspiring and aspirational. I thus struggled with the impression given of the Singaporean woman here, as I viewed Rachel with a mix of dismay, shame and annoyance. As a matter of ethical consideration of respecting our narrative and research subjects, I also wanted to ensure that my characterisation of Vilma was not a patronising or stereotypical one or, worse, one where 'the topic of a family from a strata of society employing a foreign domestic worker from a lower stratum (becomes) one fraught with the potential for cheap emotional manipulation' (Lui, 2013, p. 3).

John Lui, a newspaper journalist, reviewed the film '*Ilo-Ilo*' (another province in the Philippines), which recently won Singapore's first-ever film award at Cannes and a string of other awards at various Asian film festivals. Its subject matter similarly covered a household with a Filipino domestic worker, something which would not have been thought of even ten years ago. I thus seized the momentum and went on to write the story which wanted to be represented and which 'could be true, they derive from real events and feelings and conversations but they are ultimately fictions: versions of the truth which are woven from an amalgam of raw data, real details and where necessary symbolic equivalents' (Speedy, 2008, p. 169).

This was exactly the way the data for the story had been collected, with keen observation, conversations with my helper and her many friends, my own acquaintances who were employers of foreign domestic workers and my personal feelings about being one myself. My helper was also an active participant in that she gamely translated the dialogue found in Tagalog in the text, repeating the words so I might capture them. The authenticity and detail was for a larger purpose though, and so I laid aside my misgivings and decided against my initial defensiveness and as Sparkes (2002), who quotes Coffey and Atkinson (1996), expresses: 'ethnographic fiction should be used to construct and convey analyses of social settings and social action that are given particular point or are impossible by other means [. . .] one must be clear that such exercises have an analytical purpose' (Coffey and Atkinson, 1996, pp. 128–129; in Sparkes, 2002, p. 179).

For this to be considered as a possible public or national education tool, I had to put aside my fear of being vulnerably exposed as the observer, and exposing 'those whom we observe' (Behar, 1996, p. 24). To work effectively as public education artefact, this should also elicit an emotional response, to affect enough people so that dialogue about the issues may begin.

Narrative inquiry need not be positive in content, and in fact, has the advantage of being able to tell it as it is, hence capturing authentic and real emotions which could lead to the evocation of strong responses towards an issue, increasing the impetus for possible dialogue. Such narratives can thus be significant when they are bold enough to tell the 'truth', since 'a social science worth having must at times be grim, documenting the pain of worldwide transformations' (Connell, 2007, p. 232).

Whilst not exactly a 'worldwide transformation', the story puts forward a version portraying the phenomena of global social relations resulting from a change in wealth and power relations in South-East Asia. More importantly, it focuses on a real issue in Singapore and a strong reaction to the story would heighten its potential to fulfil its educative role, as my version joins other similar efforts on different platforms and through different methods (such as the film *Ilo Ilo* mentioned earlier). The reflection and debate that arises from this story being circulated on public space could generate the beginnings of a national-level conversation necessary for such education to take place, as the careful drawing out of these experiences rendered in very real 'narrative environments' (Gubrium & Holstein, 2008, p. 252) convinces the citizenry to confront the issues at hand. The power of narrative inquiry is such that it lends a voice to, in this case, foreign domestic workers such as Vilma, who have thus far remained silent in the dominant national narratives of Singapore. Narrative inquiry as the means used to ignite this dialogue can then magnify its effect, as 'creat[ing] the conditions for dialogue . . . implies a research agenda that both revisits research methods and ethics, but also unmasks the inequalities of the global public sphere' (Gready, 2008, p. 147; quoted in Trahar, 2009, p. 11).

Comparing what I have put forward here with the traditional narratives of the past, an obvious difference which would require a measure of reconciliation would be in 'negotiating the top-down approach to the building of a national narrative with a bottom-up approach' (Chin, 2009, p. 7). The policy-makers would feel that their understanding of how national narratives should be used in the domain of mass education has already been defined, with substantial proof of their success in the earlier years. The approach presented here, though, relies on citizens drawing their own conclusions from a not-so pretty picture and appealing to their emotional selves, so to speak. For a country supposedly rated as the 'least emotional' (Hodal, 2012, p. 1) in the world, this is a tall order. However, the turn of the tide in recent events, and the very apparent local-foreign affective divide, signals the need to move forward in the way we understand the use of narrative in public education contexts.

Conclusion

'Today we understand that we write culture, and that writing is not an innocent practice. We know the world only through our representations of it' (Denzin, 2001, p. 23).

Putting names and flesh to the impulse of the stories to be told, with the voices of these characters committed to paper and released into public space, I understand that narratives are powerful and effective tools for public and national education. Narrative inquiry's political edge and the stark portrayal of reality as represented here all work to appeal to a person's sensitivity and emotion, so that a re-examination of the issue will be undertaken, and responses calibrated across the citizenry. I am aware that a single narrative by itself will not do it, that the collective power of a consistent set of narratives is required, but it is a small step towards us being better educated in, and thus better able to handle, our diversity and social issues so that we may achieve the social balance we urgently need.

References

Behar, R. (1996) *The Vulnerable Observer: Anthropology that Breaks Your Heart.* Boston: Beacon Press.

Bekerman, Z., Burbules, N., Silberman-Keller, D. (2006) *Learning in Places: The Informal Education Reader.* New York: Peter Lang Publishing.

Chase, S.E. (2011) Narrative Inquiry: A Field in the Making. In Denzin, N. K. & Lincoln, Y. S. (Eds). *The Sage Handbook of Qualitative Research*, 4th Ed. Thousand Oaks, California: Sage.

Chin, Y. (2009) *The Nation: Narratives and Community*. Singapore: S. Rajaratnam School of International Studies.

Clough, P. (2002) *Narratives and Fictions in Educational Research*. Buckingham: Open University Press.

Connell, R. (2007) *Southern Theory*. Cambridge: Polity.

Denzin, N.K. (2001) The Reflexive Interview and a Performative Social Science. *Qualitative Research*, 1(1), pp. 23–46.

Gottschalk, S. (1998) Postmodern Sensibilities and Ethnographic Possibilities. In Banks, A. & Banks, S. (Eds). *Fiction and Social Research: By Ice and Fire*. Walnut Creek, California: Altamira Press.

Gubrium, J.F. & Holstein, J.A, (2008) Narrative Ethnography. In Hesse-Biber, S.N. & Leavy, P. (Eds). *Handbook of Emergent Methods*. New York: The Guildford Press.

Hodal, K. (2013) Singapore is World's Least Emotional Country, Poll Finds. *The Guardian*. 21 November 2013. Available online at http://theguardian.co.uk, (accessed on 21 February 2014), p. 13.

Leong, C.H. (2012) The New Singapore Narrative. *Today*. 4 September 2012. Available online at http://today.com.sg (accessed 16 December 2013), p. 4.

Lui, J. (2013) Ilo-Ilo: A Heartland Tale from the Heart. *The Straits Times*. 28 August 2013. Available online at http://stonline.com.sg (accessed 16 December 2013), p. L3.

Mair, M. (1989) Towards a Poetics of Experience. In *Between Psychology and Psychotherapy: A Poetics of Experience*. London: Routledge.

Ministry of Manpower (2014). Available online at www.mom.gov.sg (accessed 4 July 20140.

Mykhalovskly, E. (1996) Reconsidering Table Talk: Critical Thoughts on the Relationship between Sociology, Autobiography and Self-Indulgence. *Qualitative Sociology*, 19(1), pp. 131–151.

Richardson, L. & St. Pierre, E. (2005) Writing: a Method of Inquiry. In Denzin, N.K. & Lincoln, Y.S. (Eds). *The Sage Handbook of Qualitative Research*. 2nd ed. Thousand Oaks, California: Sage.

Schugurensky, D. (2000) The Forms of Informal Learning: Towards a Conceptualization of the Field. *New Approaches to Lifelong Learning* Working Paper 19, pp. 1–8.

Sparkes, A. (2002) *Telling Tales in Sport and Physical Activity: A Qualitative Journey*. Champaign, Illinois: Human Kinetics Press.

Speedy, J. (2008) *Narrative Inquiry and Psychotherapy*. Houndmills: Palgrave Macmillan.

Trahar, S. (2009) Beyond the Story itself: Narrative Inquiry and Autoethnography in Intercultural Research in Higher Education. *Forum: Qualitative Social Research*. 10(1), pp. 1–13.

Transient Workers Count Too. (2013). Available online at http://twc2.org.sg (accessed 20 August 2013).

Van Maanen, J. (2011) *Tales of the Field: On Writing Ethnography*. Chicago: The University of Chicago Press.

4 Conversations with Bruce Lee

Capturing the richness and complexities of Chinese stories

Crystal Cheung

Introduction

This chapter is a journey; a journey taken by a positivist and clinical psychologist – me –towards becoming a narrative inquirer. In the first part of the chapter, I articulate some of the tensions that I encounter as a narrative inquirer in Hong Kong. In the second part, I discuss creative fictionalisation, a device that I used to allow me to 'thicken' a participant's stories in my research into lifelong learning in Hong Kong. I explain this narrative device, and share my rationale for presenting the stories in such a way so as to capture and sustain the complexities of Chinese storytelling. Through Fan (a pseudonym), one of the research participants, I describe how I resolved the problems in finding my position as an inquirer, in managing the conversations and in identifying the message that I wanted to convey to readers. I also discuss how narrative inquiry has helped me to understand Fan's experiences in a Hong Kong Chinese context. Fan is a higher education teacher who describes himself as a lifelong learner. He told his stories of lifelong learning at different points in his life, points that were full of difficulties. He believed that his life was similar to that of Bruce Lee, whose Chinese name is Jun-Fan Lee, a famous martial arts artist, who persevered in establishing a new form of martial arts and in developing his career in Hollywood, in spite of much opposition. In recalling narratives of his life, Fan made many connections with Bruce Lee, a life filled with mysteries and despair and yet also strength and perseverance. Using fictionalisation to create a relationship between the two lives enabled me to understand Fan's struggles and hardships and to be clearer about how he identified as a lifelong learner.

Developing an interest in narrative therapy

As a clinical psychologist, I have become interested in using narrative therapy in my counselling practice. The principles of narrative have influenced the clinical practices of some psychologists for more than a decade, with systematic application of the concepts in psychological interventions (Riessman & Speedy, 2007). I consider story as the basic unit of a person's life, no matter which therapeutic approach is being adopted. I usually invite my clients to tell me their life stories, which could be fragmented, chaotic and even distorted, at the start of every psychotherapy session. I encourage my clients to see their life in a 'multi-storied' way when they come to see me with 'problem-saturated' stories (White & Epson, 1990, p. 16). They are always surprised to discover that they can tell alternative stories, which reflect themselves as having more strength and resources to deal with problems in their lives. The goal of bringing in narrative ideas in clinical practices is to 'thicken' the thin and inadequate descriptions of human lives that tend to disempower people and to create new meanings and possibilities for living. The meanings that the stories carry, to the individuals and to me, as the clinician, become the rich resources that may facilitate self-discovery of their strength and resilience.

The lack of controlled outcome studies in the area of narrative therapy is, however, a major obstacle to its implementation in clinical psychological practices in Hong Kong, as clinical psychologists are committed to empirically-validated psychological interventions when working with clients. Unfortunately, narrative therapy is somewhat under-researched and many psychologists in Hong Kong are, therefore, reluctant to consider experimenting with a therapeutic approach that eschews positivism and concepts with which they are more familiar.

Adopting narrative inquiry as a methodological approach

I am striving for a reconciliation of the tensions induced by my positivist foundation in my psychology training and my beliefs in humanistic and hermeneutic ways of understanding people's lives. I always have questions or doubts about my 'identities' as a clinical psychologist and at the same time as a narrative inquirer. I experience tension between the positivistic practice of psychology and my belief in a humanistic way of understanding people's experiences everyday. Narrative inquiry is in the early phases of being accepted as a methodological approach in research in psychology. A basic course in research methods in psychology teaches us to evaluate a research paper using statistical validity and reliability. We learn about human behaviours through hypotheses testing and statistical inference. Believing in the 'storied nature of human life' (Crossley, 2003, p. 290), I learned about narratives as a method of knowing people's lives. I enjoy the flexibility in the narrative approach in which people's emotions, behaviours and lives can be reflected. Researchers are also free to use different narrative devices to facilitate their recording of human experiences. An example is Gilgun's (2004) use of fictionalised writing in reporting a case of sexual abuse. She reflected that,

> [T]his narrative is a fictionalisation of a story an informant shared during a research interview. The story was so compelling that standard social science formats did not seem to fit.
>
> Gilgun, 2004, p. 691

It is a pity that Gilgun did not elaborate on why she thought that the story could not fit into a standard social science format. One reason may be related to the strict empirical boundaries that many social science researchers believe that they have to work within. As a result, many aspects of human lives are excluded. As a new approach in psychology, 'narrative psychology' was introduced by Crossley (2003), with the intention of inheriting the 'sense of both psychological and sociological complexity and integrity' (Crossley, 2003 p. 288) to study the questions of self and identity. Crossley (2003) believed that 'through the use of such language, we constantly and perpetually interpret and change the meaning of our and other peoples' actions, in accordance with our everyday practical and moral tasks' (Crossley, 2003 p. 288).

Being influenced by the philosophy of narrative psychology – and, indeed of narrative therapy, as I indicated earlier – which emphasises the importance of individuals' meaning making within their own context, I began to adopt this as my personal attitude as well as my way of understanding the world. Following on from my developing interest in using some elements of narrative therapy in my counselling practice, it seemed appropriate to use narrative inquiry as my methodological approach in my research into lifelong learning in Hong Kong.

Creative fictionalisation: a device for capturing the complexities and avoiding the loss of richness

Fan told me how he had been influenced by Bruce Lee's life. Bruce Lee was a famous martial arts artist who was an important figure in the history of the development of martial arts and film. He inspired many people by his perseverance in establishing himself in Hollywood. Nevertheless, he had a miserable life and suffered from poverty in the early days of his career. His tragic death in July 1973, at a young age, shocked many people. Fan told me how he relates to Bruce Lee, with the intention of facilitating my understanding of the miserable life that he worried he would have if he insisted on pursuing his beliefs and dreams. Fan relates his experiences, however, only to particular aspects of Lee's character. For many people, Bruce Lee was more famous for his talent in martial arts.

Recently, there has been an exhibition titled 'Bruce Lee: Kung Fu·Art·Life' at the Hong Kong Heritage Museum (2013). The exhibition introduced Bruce Lee, saying that:

> [T]he legend of Bruce Lee's life is intertwined with his confidence and charisma as well as a personal background that married East and West . . . . A charismatic actor, he also found fame in both the show business and martial arts community through his role as "Kato" in the US TV series *The Green Hornet* . . . . His dynamism as a film star and his achievements in the field of martial arts took the world by storm and made him an international icon.
>
> Hong Kong Heritage Museum, 2013

The image of Bruce Lee portrayed in the exhibition is very different from the one that Fan talked about. Readers shape the characters of stories according to their interpretation and their beliefs. Given that most people see the glamorous side of Bruce Lee's life, for instance, his achievement in the TV series 'The Green

Hornet', they may not be able to see his miserable experience and the poverty that he suffered after acting in it. Freeman (2007, p. 138) mentioned that 'the interpretation and writing of the personal past . . . is . . . a product of the present and the interests, needs and wishes that attend it'. As a result, I am aware that I cannot take for granted that readers will interpret Fan's connection with Lee as I do. On the other hand, I appreciate that readers' understanding of the 'sense-making process' (Phoenix, 2008 p. 67) of Fan is also an important part of the narrative inquiry. Fan's identification with Bruce Lee reflected his insights into his life struggles and his life values. His emotions, his dilemmas and how he used his life and Lee's to enable my understandings are considered as the 'small' stories to facilitate our understanding of the 'unconscious motivations' in conversations (Phoenix, 2008, p. 65).

A way of conveying my understanding of the message and the possible meanings of Fan's experience, therefore, is to let Bruce Lee talk directly to Fan and to readers through a fictionalised conversation. In this way, readers can also experience the interactions between Fan, Bruce Lee and me. As Mattingly stated (1998, cited in Riessman, 2008, p. 22): 'narratives do not merely refer to past experience but create experiences for their audiences'. To me, my thoughts and emotions are authentic, my understanding of Fan's experiences is authentic and Bruce Lee was a real character. But, for readers who did not experience the process of the inquiry, as I did, our conversations were, in a sense, fictions, as they were not present when they took place. The fictionalised conversations give readers the chance to play a role in the relationship and to hear their own inner voice as they internalise the emotions and ideas of the two characters.

In the fictionalised conversation, I constructed the interactions in the form of a dream, which represented my understanding of Fan's struggles and the way that he identified with Bruce Lee in his lifelong learning experiences. I am also assisting readers to construct their understanding of Bruce Lee's life, with the new insights, which they may gain from the conversation. They may be aware of Lee's glamorous life as an actor, but not of the importance of Chinese philosophy in shaping his beliefs and development of martial arts. Through reading the fictionalised conversation, readers can visualise the interaction, co-construct the meaning of the experience of Bruce Lee and develop a deeper understanding of Fan.

The co-construction and reconstruction of narratives

I was not comfortable with my transcription of our interview conversations, even though I had transcribed and translated everything narrated by Fan. Something was missing. I failed to name what was missing until I read Clandinin and Huber's account (2010):

> [A] second dimension of the sociality commonplace directs attention to the inquiry relationship between researchers' and participants' lives. Narrative inquirers cannot subtract themselves from the inquiry relationship.
>
> Clandinin & Huber, 2010, p. 436

What was missing was my inner voice during our interviews. Fan's narratives had an impact on myself as the inquirer. I did not 'record' my inner voice and I could not present it in the transcription. However, Fan's narratives, especially how he related himself to Bruce Lee and how his philosophy of learning has been influenced by him, created a strong impression in my mind. I did not know very much about Bruce Lee's life before I spoke with Fan but I felt that I understood Fan's struggles from different perspectives and of the importance of Bruce Lee's life to him, through our social interaction in the interview. This testifies to the meaning of narratives being constructed within the context of the interviewer–interviewee relationship (Phoenix, 2008).

Furthermore, narrative inquiry is a process of reconstruction, i.e. the reconstruction of experience, 'There is a double poiesis at work in this process, such that the heterogeneous elements of a life a synthesized, drawn together via the narrative imagination, and the self in turn is reconstructed . . . ' (Ricoeur, 1991, 1992; cited in Freeman, 2007, p. 138). Fan reconstructed his experiences so as to let me see his learning and career path. The process of writing the fictionalised conversation allows me to reconstruct my knowledge of Fan's experience in lifelong learning and importantly, to hope that my readers will also open up their minds to see and sense how lifelong learning is manifested in individual experiences.

Illustrating creative fictionalisation: lifelong learning and Fan's narratives

Lifelong learning was adopted as the guiding principle of the education reforms that took place in Hong Kong in 2000. As we are now moving into the second decade of the implementation of these reforms, I am exploring how our policy makers and learners understand the implications of lifelong learning. Lifelong learning is often considered as government policy rhetoric and the general public understands it as the government's deployment to serve political agendas, i.e. to maintain the stability of the society during the changing 'post-1997' political situation (Kennedy, 2006). Gathering stories from my participants through narrative inquiry is enabling me to see new meanings of lifelong learning and 'thicken' the understanding of this important principle of education in Hong Kong.

The conversation with Fan . . . and my sleepless night

I have known Fan since I was pursuing my graduate degree in clinical psychology. He was a few years younger than me and he took psychology as his major subject. Later, he received his graduate degree in experimental psychology from the University of Oxford. Ever since I have known Fan, he has given me the strong impression that he is struggling along a path, a path full of uncertainties and challenges, a path to find himself and to find his life goal. He is very good at listening to people and reflecting on what they say at a deep level. He is committed to being creative and to making changes in his teaching. I would meet him from time to time and be fascinated by the stories that he told me about adventures that he had. It was for all of these reasons that I invited him to participate in my research into lifelong learning in Hong Kong.

I met Fan in a cafe in Causeway Bay, one of the busiest areas in Hong Kong, to listen to his lifelong learning stories. I picked a café, famous for its nice coffee, on a relatively quiet street. It was around three o'clock and the café was already serving afternoon tea. Fan told me he was hungry as he had not had his lunch yet and he needed to order a large portion of 'something'. I was not surprised as, ever since I have known him, he has always been busy, with a long to-do list and, as a result, he often forgot to eat. I ordered a cup of coffee, watched Fan eating his pasta and we started to talk about his experiences of lifelong learning. I was interested in how he represented the meanings of his experiences in the conversation. Fan mentioned how his ideas about learning have been influenced and are represented by the experiences of Bruce Lee, the martial arts artist. As I developed more understanding of the experiences of Bruce Lee, as explained by Fan, I found myself agreeing that they have many beliefs in common.

I did not sleep very well that night after the meeting with Fan, probably because of the strong coffee that I drank. It was already half an hour past midnight and, by coincidence, the television was showing 'The Big Boss' (唐山大兄), one of Bruce Lee's major films. It seemed like a good idea to watch this film as a way of understanding Fan's narratives. I could feel my eyelids drooping. I was drifting into sleep. . . .

The first encounter between Fan and Bruce Lee

It was an autumn day in 1968 in Seattle. Fan, who had just received his postgraduate degree in psychology from a university there and started his teaching career in a local school, was visiting Bruce Lee at the Lee Jun Fan Gung Fu Institute. The institute is a martial arts school founded by Bruce Lee a year previously. Fan was very excited about meeting Bruce Lee, a martial arts artist of a similar age to himself:

Fan: It is my pleasure meeting you, Mr. Lee and to visit your institute.
Bruce: It's my pleasure too. Just call me Bruce. The last word of my Chinese name is also 'Fan'.
Fan: Yes, I know.
Bruce: Let me show you around my institute. Tell me more about yourself.
Fan: I have just received my master's degree. I am still thinking about my career path. I am interested in teaching. I am teaching psychology in a university.
Bruce: What did you study?
Fan: I studied psychology. I wish to be a psychology teacher.
Bruce: Oh, I took a course in psychology when I was in college too. I like psychology and philosophy. Philosophy influences me a lot! If you notice the symbol of my Jeet Kune Do (the school of martial arts developed by

Bruce Lee), the arrows in the symbol represent the 'endless interaction between yang and yin'.

Fan: I am aware of that. You have transformed the techniques of Wing Chun (in Chinese 詠春, a school of Chinese martial arts). What is the meaning behind the transformation?

Bruce: I have been practising Wing Chun for a very long period of time. You may also see how I performed the fights in my movies. I found that the fight usually lasts too long and the traditional martial arts techniques are not practical when I perform in the movie scenes of street fighting. I think I need to break away from these rigid and formalistic ways of martial arts.

Fan: How do you achieve the 'breaking away'?

Bruce: I want to develop a martial arts system which is practical, flexible and efficient.

Fan: I cannot believe that you have the courage to challenge the traditional approach of martial arts!

Bruce: You are right. I need the courage. But that's what I need to do! I don't have a reason, but I just know that I need to be true to myself!

Fan: Have you made your breakthrough?

Bruce: I am developing "the style of no style"! I wish to perform martial arts outside any parameters and limitations.

Fan: How did you come up with your ideas?

Bruce: I studied philosophy when I was in college and I read extensively. My way of performing martial arts is influenced by my philosophical beliefs. The more I read, the more I understand myself and this eventually leads to my self-knowledge.

Fan: So, learning really helps you to develop yourself. I experience a lot of self-doubt, especially now when I am struggling with my career path.

Bruce: I understand that. I think it is a crisis stage that every one of us needs to go through. Be open-minded and keep learning. To engage in learning is my way of managing my struggles. I always learn something, and that is: to always be yourself.

Fan: I understand that. It is the meaning of lifelong learning. By engaging in learning, we develop our confidence to manage our life and adversities. By engaging in continuous learning, we have the courage to overcome our limitations and to actualise our dreams.

I woke up at four o'clock in the morning and found myself lying on the sofa with the television still on, wondering why I had dreamed of Fan and Bruce Lee. The interesting characteristics shared by Bruce Lee and Fan lingered in my mind. I felt thirsty and went to the kitchen to pour myself a glass of warm water. I could not stop thinking about the dream. I believe I am as inspired by Bruce Lee as Fan is! Bruce Lee was deeply inspired by Chinese values and philosophy. Martial arts and Chinese philosophy cannot be separated. When I am studying the issues of lifelong learning, one of the important aspects that I need to attend to is the place of Chinese values in learning. Bruce Lee explained in his writings that:

[G]ung fu (Martial Arts) is a special kind of skill, a fine art rather than just a physical exercise. It is a subtle art of matching the essence of the mind to that of the techniques in which it has to work. The principle of gung fu is not a thing that can be learned, like a science, by fact-finding and instruction in facts. It has to grow spontaneously, like a flower, in a mind free from emotions and desires. The core of this principle of gung fu is Tao – the spontaneity of the universe.

Little, 1999, p.15

As described by Bruce Lee, the beauty of martial arts is its property of spontaneity. It focuses on the continuous and spontaneous growing of knowledge (in martial arts) in one's mind. This idea coheres with the topic of my research, – lifelong learning. Further to that, Bruce Lee strongly believed that one needs to live 'outside a frame'. Fan, like Bruce Lee, is very mindful that he is limited by the frame of traditions. This leads to his continuous struggles in his teaching and learning whenever he feels that he is suffocated because of the limitations of traditional frameworks.

With these thoughts lingering in my mind, I went back to sleep . . . .

Fan: My teaching path has become a bit lost. I change jobs frequently. Many of my teachers told me that I need to live with the consequences of my learning . . . . Let me describe a breakthrough in my teaching . . . . I lined up many students to work on a project that I had wanted to do for several years. That is to produce some movie clips for the purpose of teaching psychology. . . . I lined up a professor to assist in encouraging the project. I have doubts about myself, whether I can continue on this. . . .

Bruce: What is your hesitation? It seems that you have some commitment towards this educational belief; that is, to promote innovations and creative practices in education.

Fan: Yes, I am struggling with whether I should continue with this, whether I could make this happen.

Bruce: Tell me about how your plan.

Fan: I received funding support . . . and the project was reported in the media. When I was working on these things, I did not really consider how my career path would be. I believed that something would 'happen' at some point. By the time there was an increase in the media exposure . . . I started to have self-doubts. I wondered whether there has to be a strong commercial angle in order for the concept to be actualised. I may have to compromise some of my values. I thought about you! I want to become a 'Bruce Lee'. A 'Bruce Lee' in education. In Hong Kong, teachers receive very little respect . . . . We lack a figure in the field of education. If we have this figure to actualise our educational beliefs in an innovative and fun way, the atmosphere of the education field may change positively. This is what I want to achieve by running my course in a creative way. . . .

Bruce: You want to be a 'Bruce Lee'? What do you know about me?

Fan: I read about your interviews conducted during the time when you were not very popular . . . . You intended to open a school to teach martial arts. Later, you found that film production might be a faster way to promote martial arts. You integrated the martial arts, education and movies . . . you gave us an image that you were very devoted to martial arts and you could spread your messages to people and influence people. You were innovative . . . . Your work was educational and attractive.

Bruce: My life was, in fact, miserable. There are a lot of sacrifices when you want to actualise a dream and a belief. . . .

Fan: Exactly. When my production team is formed and I move forward, I feel that I am becoming a revolutionary and that my parents and family will be miserable. Do I really need to do this to such an extent?

The alarm clock rang. It was six forty-five in the morning. I felt uncomfortable with the images of the two miserable faces that I saw in my dream. I see Fan is confronted with a lot of self-doubt and internal struggles. These struggles are neither because of being incompetent nor because of a lack of confidence. The self-doubts are, in fact, the outcome of his learning through his experiences, i.e. he has developed the capacity for 'critical analysis so that one can question taken-for-granted assumptions' (Gouthro, 2010, p. 466). Fan perceives the struggles as the consequences of his learning. His concepts of learning correspond with a recent definition of lifelong learning: 'the learning consists of a ubiquity of experiences in both formal and informal settings, and also involves unintended and incidental and unconscious learning' (Selkrig, 2011, p. 578).

Fan described the process of how his educational beliefs have become fine-tuned from his experiences of teaching and learning. This process involves a lot of self-reflection, critical self-challenge, and negotiation. Bruce Lee also described a similar process in his experiences of learning and teaching martial arts:

> the best way of learning is not through the computation of information. Learning is discovering, uncovering what is there in us. When we discover, we are uncovering our own abilities, our own eyes, in order to find our potential, to see what is going on, to discover how we can enlarge our lives, to find the means at our disposal that will let us cope with a difficult situation. And all this, I maintain, is talking place in the here and now.
>
> Little, 1999, p. 84

This philosophy is central to the principles of lifelong learning, i.e. a process of self-directed learning throughout life (Bolhuis, 2003). This self-directed lifelong learning allows us to fine-tune our values, beliefs and attitudes according to different experiences that we encounter in our lives. As we see from Fan, however, this process can give rise to feelings of discomfort.

The dilemma of *The Green Hornet*

A few days later, I visited Fan at his office, intending to borrow some books from him about Bruce Lee because I wanted to know more about his philosophy.

On our way to his office, I told Fan about my dream. I asked him what learning meant to him when it brought him so many struggles:

Crystal: How do you see your learning in everyday life? What does learning mean to you?

Fan: Learning . . . . From the perspective of 'Bruce Lee', it's 'be yourself'. As a human being, we need to be ourselves honestly . . . .

Fan introduced to me Bruce Lee's central concept of learning, i.e. be yourself. Later, I read about how Bruce Lee emphasised the importance of 'self' in his teachings of martial arts:

> In Jeet Kune Do (Bruce Lee's school of martial arts) we begin not by accumulation but by discovering the course of our ignorance, and oftentimes this involves a shedding process. Its core, however, lies in the individual mind, and until that is touched, everything is still uncertain and only superficial. Truth will not come until we have come to understand personally the whole process of the working of our being. Knowledge in martial art simply means self-knowledge, and Jeet Kune Do can become intelligible only in the vigorous and constant process of self-inquiry and self-discovery.
>
> (Little, 1999, p. 140)

I believe that the force that drives Fan's self-directed lifelong learning is his own desire to touch his self, to know what is working within his being and find out who he is. In psychological terms, this is known as the intrinsic motivation for learning (Ryan & Deci, 2000).

Crystal: You are fine-tuning yourself . . . your goal is to let people know your belief.

Fan: This thing is quite narcissistic. I am, in Bruce Lee's way, practising using the sand bag everyday so as to wait for the 'explosive' point of breaking through the barriers and limitations. . . . But the fact is I am now almost reaching the stage of *The Green Hornet*.

Crystal: What do you mean by *The Green Hornet*?

Fan: *The Green Hornet* was Bruce Lee's first TV series. This was when he started to be known by people. Bruce Lee was miserable after acting in *The Green Hornet*. He only had around ten dollars left and he returned to Hong Kong. The family was in financial crisis. He thought that he had reached a certain level, but it was not the case and nobody employed him to act. In my case, after I finished the project at the university, it seemed that it was cutting edge and an innovative case study of teaching and education in the area of Asia. Yet, I did not receive the attention as expected. Compared with having a stable life, I needed to sacrifice a lot. This is crazy. Besides, a lot of people would criticise me for being so revolutionary.

Fan seemed to be in a dilemma about whether or not he should sacrifice his stable life to actualise his dream. He explained the dilemma that he had been facing by talking about Bruce Lee's life. I am touched by reading one of Bruce Lee's poems entitled "The Silent Flute" (Little, 1999 p. 113) to understand more about his miserable life:

The Silent Flute

> I wish neither to possess,
> Nor to be possessed.
> I no longer covet paradise,
> More important, I no longer fear hell.
> The medicine for my suffering
> I had within me from the very beginning,
> But I did not take it.
> My ailment came from within myself,
> But I did not observe it
> Until this moment.
> Now I see that I will never find the light
> Unless, like the candle, I am my own fuel,
> Consuming myself.

Bruce Lee did not take a smooth and comfortable path. Fan worried that he would put himself in a similar position. I believe that it is not easy for Fan to give up his dream. After all, it is a 'calling'. I emailed the poem to Fan and we had the following conversation:

Crystal: Fan, I believe that there must be some people who will support you
Fan: Yes, those are people who think differently. They told me that it is not a problem of being idiosyncratic. A lot of idiosyncratic people manage to survive. Maybe they have compromised a bit so that they can earn money but they may not be happy about it . . . . People told me that I may not become a legend, but people around me would be happier. I can be a 'one-tenth Bruce Lee' and have a stable life in other areas. But a 'one-tenth' Bruce Lee' is not really Bruce Lee.
Crystal: Why do you need to take up this role?
Fan: I don't know. May be I am born to be like that.

Narrative inquiry in Hong Kong Chinese culture

Through using narrative inquiry as a methodological approach to understand Fan's struggles in his lifelong learning, I appreciate it as a way to integrate my voice and Fan's voice to create a 'narrative truth' (Spence, 1982; cited in Chan, 2003, p. 177), a term used by Spence (1982) to describe the outcome of psychotherapy as being 'the construction of a coherent and satisfying account of events' (Spence, 1982; cited in Chan, 2003, p. 177). Narrative inquiry allows me to reconstruct the tension that Fan experienced from his Chinese culture and as a person brought up in a context influenced by 'Western' educational concepts. The Confucian values of having a sense of shame, a respect for tradition, persistence, reciprocation and personal steadiness (The Chinese Culture Connection, 1987) conflict with the Western ideas of individualism that we acquired growing up in Hong Kong. The tension between Fan's wish to enhance himself, his dissatisfaction towards the teaching profession, his sensitivity towards the collectivistic values of Chinese culture, how his behaviours would affect people around him and his desire for an individualistic life are all elements that constitute Fan's lifelong learning experience. As a narrative inquirer, I understand how the cultural context, including its history and social experiences, is crucially important in enabling Fan to make sense of his experiences and emotions. Being from the same context, I am able to develop insights that may be more complex for those from other contexts, hence my use of fictionalisation to engender understanding in the reader.

Gubrium (2006, p.250; cited in Phoenix, 2008, p. 65) highlighted that 'if we take the time to understand how members of society use culture to interpret and represent their own and others' lives, we stand to diversify what it means to become who and what we are'. Through the presentation of Fan's narratives, I gain insights into my interpretation of my own lifelong learning experiences as a Chinese learner. I believe that through reading the narratives of Fan, readers will make their interpretation of their own learning experiences. All of these different interpretations make up the narrative truth of lifelong learning.

Epilogue: a sacred responsibility

It was the end of a workshop on cognitive behavioural treatment for generalised anxiety disorder by Professor Tom Borkovec. He said to us, 'Thank you for your sacred work of listening to hearts . . . .' I never think of my work being considered as 'sacred' but his comment reminded me of how lucky I am that my days are filled with stories. Clients come to my office with their stories and they leave my office with their stories of new learning and refreshed with new insights. My belief in the power of stories led me to the landscape of narrative inquiry. In this chapter, I have presented many of my unresolved struggles and questions during the process of inquiry into Fan's experiences in lifelong learning. For me, this is something new. I am learning to accept and to tolerate uncertainties and unresolved issues. I also enjoy the freedom of feeling that I do not need to wrap things up with the pretty wrapping paper of completeness. I am empowered to accept that the unresolved things created in narrative inquiry are, in fact, rich resources to value:

> [H]ermeneutic inquiry of this kind can never achieve a 'factual' or 'objective' explanation of a phenomenon. Its goal, instead, is to construct a representation of a slice of social reality that promotes a sense of an enhanced understanding, and contributes to new ways of seeing that reality.
>
> McLeod and Lynch, 2000; cited in Riessman & Speedy,
> 2007, p. 403

Narrative inquiry, used with careful attention to Confucian beliefs and values, is a powerful way to engage with the richness and complexities of Chinese stories, and thus a methodological approach worthy of closer attention in Hong Kong.

References

Chan, D. (2003). Multicultural considerations in counseling Chinese clients: Introducing the narrative alternative. *Asian Journal of Counseling, 10(2)*, 169–192.

Clandinin, D.J. & Huber, J. (2010). Narrative inquiry. In B. McGaw, E. Baker & P. Peterson (Eds), *International encyclopedia of education (3rd ed.)*. New York, NY: Elsevier.

Crossley, M. (2003). Formulating narrative psychology: The limitations of contemporary social constructionism. *Narrative Inquiry, 13(2)*, 287–300.

Bolhuis, S. (2003). Towards process-oriented teaching for self-directed lifelong learning: A multidimensional perspective. *Learning and Instruction, 13(3)*, 327–347.

Freeman, M. (2007). Autobiographical understanding and narrative inquiry. In D. J. Clandinin (ed.) *Handbook of narrative inquiry: Mapping a methodology*. Thousand Oaks, CA: Sage Publications, pp. 120–145.

Gilgun, J.F. (2004). Fictionalizing life stories: Yukee the wine thief. *Qualitative Inquiry, 10(5)*, 691–705.

Gouthro, P.A. (2010). Well-being and happiness: critical, practical and philosophical considerations for policies and practices in lifelong learning. *International Journal of Lifelong Education, 29(4)*, 461–474.

Hong Kong Heritage Museum (2013). Bruce Lee: Kung Fu. Art. Life.

Kennedy, P. (2006). The politics of "lifelong learning" in post-1997 Hong Kong. *International Journal of Lifelong Education, 23(6)*, 589–624.

Little, J (1999). *Bruce Lee: artist of life*. Singapore: Tuttle Publishing.

Phoenix, A. (2008). Analysing narrative contexts. In M. Andrews, C. Squire & M. Tamboukou (eds). *Doing narrative research*. Thousand Oaks, CA: Sage Publications, pp. 64–77.

Riessman, C.K. (2008). *Narrative methods for the human sciences*. Sage Publications.

Riessman, C.K. & Speedy, J. (2007). Narrative enquiry in the psychotherapy profession. In D.J. Clandinin (ed.) *Handbook of narrative inquiry: Mapping a methodology*. Thousand Oaks, CA: Sage Publications, pp 426–456.

Ryan, R.M. & Deci, E.L. (2000). Intrinsic and extrinsic motivations: Classic definitions and new directions. *Contemporary Educational Psychology, 25(1)*, 54–67.

Selkrig, M. (2011). Learning about ourselves from others: Transformation of artists' identities through community-based arts practice. *International Journal of Lifelong Education, 30(5)*, 577–589.

The Chinese Culture Connection (1987). Chinese values and the search for culture-free dimensions of culture. *Journal of Cross-Cultural Psychology, 18(2)*, 143–164.

White, M. & Epston, D. (1990). *Narrative means to therapeutic ends*. W.W. Norton & Company.

5 Creative non-fiction across cultures in Asia Pacific contexts

Jane Horan

Introduction

Since time immemorial we have learned through stories. Stories can teach, cutting across cultures and connecting individuals in unique ways. The evocative nature of storytelling drew me towards narrative inquiry as a research methodology. A few years ago I embarked on a cross cultural narrative journey, to better understand leadership from Asian women's perspectives. My research focused on four women's experiences on their journey towards leadership. In crafting each narrative from the stories that they shared with me, I combined historical elements, cultural traditions and personal reflections, and used creative non-fiction writing, the act of which offered space to silence my embedded beliefs and to listen from multiple perspectives. This chapter is intended to position fiction writing positively, as well as demonstrating its value in narrative inquiry and researching cross culturally. Although fiction can be found in social science research, the word, fiction, conjures up different meanings. For some using fiction denotes 'make believe', 'pretending' or 'acting.' For others, fiction is considered as informative research writing in social sciences. While fiction carries many definitions, this chapter explores the use of creative non-fiction in writing research and re-telling stories. I use the term creative non-fiction to tell a story based on interviews, events, conversations and feelings, re-formatting words into expressive, readable stories. The information used in creating this story is not 'made up or make believe' rather I have 'made something' (Speedy 2008:169) from data collected. In using creative non-fiction my intent is to engage the reader in the interpretive process from multiple perspectives including emotional, reflective and analytical.

The first part begins with a short, creative non-fiction vignette, 'In Another Country – Singapore', focussing on Ms Ito, a Japanese social entrepreneur and one of the four women leaders in my research. I use the term creative non-fiction – that is, data gathered from my interview notes –and place the story within a fictionalised setting. Our interviews took place over many years and in different venues; this story positions the interview in one setting. The story brings together conversations and the writing style of American author Ernest Hemingway in order for the reader to engage in the story. Using this style allowed distance from Ms Ito's story and enabled the conversations to be interpreted from many angles. The second part of the chapter explores other fictionalised techniques of imaginary interviews, (Speedy 2008), narrative fiction (Trahar 2011; Clough 2002; Sparkes 2002) and dream stories (Phillion 2004). These eclectic, research stories demonstrate the use of fiction in educational research and within multicultural settings. The chapter concludes with a discussion on story interpretation, an evaluation of the use of fiction and the implications for cross cultural narrative inquiry within the context of the Asia Pacific region.

In another country – Singapore

It was lunch time, and there we were, sitting beside the large glass windows over-looking a garden at a German restaurant in Raffles City Singapore. During the day, the streets outside the restaurant were busy, but at night the business profes-sionals favoured other places near the water and you could feel the difference. It was quieter in the evening. The restaurant was next to a large shopping complex and the sprawling subway system in the tiny city state that locals call the Red Dot. Ms Ito picked the place, believing it was quiet, clean and well-lit. Between the lunch crowds leaving, the music blaring and the background chatter of the staff, my tape recorder picked up everyone's conversation but our own. Luckily, I took notes, and the writing allowed me to reflect and comment on Ms Ito's story at the same time.

When the waiter saw us at the table close to the window near the back door of the restaurant, he walked over and brought two menus.

The interview begins. 'Ito-san, growing up, who were your influences?' I asked.

As she thought about the question, I added a few more clarifying points as I had done with other interviews.

'This could be your parents, teachers, sports coach – anyone.'

Silence ensued and she continued to think. At first her eyes gazed past me, and then after a long pause she looked right at me and said, 'No one.'

'What do you want to drink?' The waiter asked looking around the room as if he wasn't interested in our response or as if we weren't there. We asked for water. He returned swiftly and placed two glasses and a bottle of sparkling mineral water on the table.

'There,' he said.

I looked up in response to what Ms Ito said.

'No one?' I asked incredulously.

There were others, important leaders, quiet leaders and outspoken lead-ers, though none the same and for most this was a casual question. This ques-tion started conversations. Looking back, I had conducted several interviews in Hong Kong, China and Vietnam before this one. All of the previous participants answered with 'family', 'teacher' or 'coach.' When Ms Ito answered, I must have had a puzzled look on my face which gave off the impression that I had never heard anything like this before.

'No one,' she insisted and repeated.

Then a funny thing happened: silence. Time and silence crossed once more and then stopped. As I sat watching Ms Ito working out in her mind how to respond to the upcoming questions, the silence loomed. Living here, I am familiar with silence and what to some appear to be surprisingly, long pauses between responses. Yet for some reason with this particular pause, I felt the need to speak, rather than remain quiet. I started filling in the silence gap with unnecessary chatter. This may have been due to Ito-san's questioning look.

The sky darkened and it was now raining hard outside. Her response to my first question jolted me like the sound of thunder from the storm. I thought maybe Ito-san had made a mistake and, as she looked at me, I kept thinking, 'No one.' How could that be?

Then she revealed a story of difficulties, challenges and being an outsider in a homogeneous, conforming society.

Time passed and the waiter returned, 'Another bottle of water?' 'No, thank you,' we said and continued talking. The waiter took the empty bottle of water back to the bar and sat down with his colleagues on the bar stools in front of the kitchen.

'It is because of them, well, because I never liked any of them. These – the not liking anyone or anything – were the influences on my life.' Ito-san said.

A well-thought out response and one I had not expected.

'Growing up in Japan,' Ito-san said, 'I was different. My teachers didn't like me. I was afraid to go to school and afraid to talk. I didn't talk much. Until recently, I mean a couple of years ago, I was terrified of talking in front of a group; my hands sweated, my voice cracked and I started to cry.'

'Violence at school was quite common,' she said. 'Relationships were tightly controlled in my family, at school and in Japan.' She talked about being hit with a stick by her teachers and having a violent, alcoholic father who was cruel to her mother. 'There were rules to follow and you were punished if you didn't follow the rules,' Ito-san said.

'When I was little',' she said, 'I brought a caterpillar home and told my mother, "This is my best friend". My mother was upset.'

As I listened to the beginning of her story, I was hooked. I wanted to know how much more she had to tell.

'I do what I do now because I don't want to hurt anyone,' she said.

As she told her story she smiled and leaned back in the chair. 'I found primary school scary. I was afraid of being judged. I was very quiet. For a long time, I believed the scariest person has the rules and we had to follow.'

'I left Japan in my mid-twenties. I was hardened. I didn't want family and didn't want anyone. I wanted to pursue learning and creativity. I went to Europe after obtaining a semi-degree in architecture. I was inspired by the people, language and the buildings. I thought, "This is different".'

'I left and had no plans,' she said.

Hearing these words, I reflected on my journey in Asia. As Ito-san spoke, I made a note in the side-column in my notebook – China. In 1985, I left the US to study Chinese and teach English. Like Ito-san, I had no plans.

'I went to Canada to learn English first and then travel the world,' Ito-san continued. 'I lived with families, travelled and spent two years there. This was a special time for me because I lost my words, I couldn't speak. I learned everything from scratch. In Japan I couldn't speak because I was always framing questions, I never spoke from my heart. In Canada, I used children's language; using children's language felt good – simple, authentic and real.'

'I felt like I lost everything and started a new life. Canada was like a dream. I can't say it was one person who helped me; it was the entire experience. I was totally closed and became totally open.'

'I let go of stuff, my childhood and happiness came from rejecting everything,' Ito-san said.

'I now recognise values – giving, sharing and letting go,' she said. 'My travels in developing and developed countries provided the ground work for what I do today. I believe when we give we feel abundance; when we're not giving we feel or sense not having enough and that others have more. Not only in Japan but everywhere I went I saw this – people giving and sharing are the happiest and are surrounded by others that are loving.'

Leaning forward on the table, holding a glass in her hands, she continued. 'I found this to be particularly true in my travels to Guatemala and Costa Rica. I was completely stressed living in Japan and teaching English. That's when I decided to go to Guatemala and Costa Rica to study Spanish. I had very little money and spoke a little Spanish, not much.'

Standing on the street corner in Guatemala with backpack in hand, she had watched as people stood in line for a bus. She felt the desire to get on a bus and travel anywhere, with no destination in mind. 'I got on the bus and decided I would get off at some point.'

As she sat on the bus gazing out the window at the dirt road, she suddenly realised she'd lost everything: her passport, money and bank card, all gone.

'This was the first time I thought of life as a game.'

Sitting on the bus, 'I looked down at my well-worn map and found a name, Santa Rosa, the name of a saint. My family was not religious but I knew this name and decided to get off the bus there. Five or six hours later the bus stopped at a little village. The end of the ride. No one was there. The streets were empty. It was hot.'

'I put the backpack on and knocked on doors, explaining with the use of hand gestures that I had no money but I could cook and clean. There was no answer. By the looks on the faces of the people walking in the street, I knew this village had never seen a foreign face before. I moved from house to house and finally looked up to see a food place. I saw a big truck with a red cross,' Ito-san said.

She had seen this red cross before and felt a certain familiarity with it.

'The Red Cross rescued me.'

Leaning back in her chair, she put the water glass down on the table. 'This was crazy and not something I would do again but this was a very exciting time in my life. I was not a tourist in a big hotel. This was the time in my life I kept playing the game and enjoyed the fun. I remember asking myself, 'How can I maximise this game?''

The next few days she stayed with the Red Cross. They gave her money and brought her back to town, where she was dropped off at the Japanese Embassy, thinking they would help. The Japanese Embassy, however, was not as welcoming as the Red Cross or the people in the village.

Ito's story in Guatemala took me back to 1985 – my first trip to China and the first time I lived outside of the US. Like Ito-san, I travelled through China with very little money, little knowledge of the language and few concerns about where I was going.

As I listened to Ito-san, memories of China floated through my mind. I was on a train going from Beijing to Beidai He, a beautiful beach town where Mao and Deng Xiao Ping vacationed. Exiting the train, I walked out to the road, where 15–20 buses waited to take travellers to the beach. Unlike the quiet, small, Guatemalan town of Santa Rosa, I was standing in the middle of a busy intersection with thousands of people and buses. The problem was that I spoke very little Chinese, only a few words at best, and could not read it at all. I stood on the dusty street corner, looking around, amidst a cacophony of sounds.

Ms Ito continued, 'I spent time in an Ashram to learn Ayurveda. I went by myself. In India I watched street children playing. I started to connect things and discovered that I wanted to create a business about food and to connect with people who didn't have food like the children I watched playing in the streets.'

'I dreamed of the business I am now doing, connecting people, business and giving. I returned to New Zealand and created a fast food organic food business. I started the business with no money. The business took off, we had over 150 distributors, but my idea was to build soup kitchens in India to feed the poor. I was too busy with this business and no time to do what I wanted to do – give back.'

'We moved to Australia and I developed blisters on my hands. I couldn't work. It was very painful. I had to wear gloves and couldn't touch food. I had my hands covered for one year. I kept judging myself. I couldn't perform my duties as a cook in the business. Some things helped but my hands were continuously getting worse.'

'I was driving down the road and I looked at my hands and started to cry. I cried, and cried and cried. I realised I wasn't seeing the most important thing. I was sitting looking at my hands and they were giving me a message. All I knew is my hands were stopping me and I couldn't continue. My role is to help people and let people help me and not about cooking. I cried, and cried and cried.'

'Two weeks later my hands healed. In one month the virus was gone. The blisters died and left me alone. I changed the way I felt about myself. I would get out of cooking and start helping people. I was physically trying to build a cooking business but it wasn't about pushing myself, it was about letting go.'

The business was gone, that was what she needed and that was all that mattered. She would not look at this business again. It was finished.

'I look at this as a gift to learn something new,' she said. 'I started a business in transactional giving. It was not all my idea. I am the founder but the idea came from many people's inspiration. We are now a foundation. The foundation works for everyone and we are now in every country.'

'I am here to give value, nothing is scary anymore. Now things are simple and easy. Life is easy because it's just a game. Lessons happen every day because I don't live for a big reason, my goal is to live to be caring and open. Things happen continuously to remind me to be present. Me being the best, not external me but the internal me. I say, "Enjoy the game at the maximum level."'

The waiter appeared out of nowhere to hand us the bill and wait for payment. The rain stopped as Ms Ito-san ended her story.

Reflections on using creative non-fiction

Cross cultural narrative inquiry can disorient, as ambiguities test emotions, intellect and patience. Writing this story using this style forced me to take a step back from bookish cultural ideals and question my interpretations, and it took time for me to feel comfortable writing it. Using creative non-fiction reinforced the fine art of listening, particularly during quiet periods when neither I nor the interviewees said anything. These silent pauses, made explicit six times in this story, highlight the experience of the interview process. There were many silent episodes or elongated pauses in our meetings. I created this story to shift from my pre-conceived notions of culture and engage the reader in the experience, allowing the reader to formulate their own interpretation. Creative non-fiction not only shaped the potential for suspense but offered a new perspective on an old performance. Reflecting on this experience, connecting multiple life events provided a deeper understanding of Ms Ito and myself.

A story can either be an abstruse jumble of words or a riveting page turner of suspense. Reading through my interview notes, I was encased in a pile of words, fixated on the cultural circumstances surrounding the story. After every meeting with Ms Ito I ran full tilt into the writing process. I sat with my jar of words, waiting for nuggets of insight to spontaneously appear. This narrative inquiry was not a breezy journey; I struggled on many levels. Reflexivity challenged me, that is, my ability to balance personal experience and knowledge within the context of Ms Ito's story (Etherington 2009). I attempted to write reflexively, illustrating multiple layers of complexity of the story and cultural identity (Etherington 2004). I entered this research with multicultural experiences and knowledge, but this particular understanding was – subconsciously – almost crippling. I meandered through cultural ambiguities, many misinterpretations, blurred memories and confused feelings. Using creative non-fiction provided clarity and distance with which I shaped the story representation. I reviewed various formats in re-telling Ms Ito's story, from poetic representations, mystery writing and imaginary interviews, until I settled on creative non-fiction using Hemingway. Invoking the voice and spirit of Hemingway forced me to push back opinions and thoughts swirling in my head. Hemingway's clear communication style and masterful use of dialogue set the stage for this story. Settling into this writing style allowed me to better relate to the data collected, revealing deeper insights and new learning for me.

In this story, Ms Ito's responses reveal personal choices and complex motives, depicting differences from her Japanese peers in the same era and social context.

The painful sharing of family and school experiences, along with her lucid recollection of Guatemalan adventures, provided insights into her philosophy of life, her story visually blossoming on each page. Forced to stay in character by writing in Hemingway's style, I saw how pivotal life events (all of which she recalled) led her to become the leader she is today. I used this style of writing to engage the reader, to make her story clearer through dialogue and allow the reading experience of events, locations, silence and even noises to be tactile. I was able to step back and almost watch the story unfurl, although I had to concentrate on Ms Ito's words and listen unequivocally to her message. By listening without judgement, I started to see a different picture unfold. I began to connect the dots. I started to see the impact of life's complexities, personal choices and serendipitous events.

The journey of narrative fiction

JoAnn Phillion's (2002:536) work on narrative multiculturalism, multicultural research and multicultural education was the fillip to my learning journey. Her description, 'Narrative multiculturalism focuses on understanding derived from a starting point in experience rather than in theory' complemented my background. My interest was leadership experiences across cultures, industries *and* from a woman's perspective. Phillion shared her deepening awareness and transition into narrative multiculturalism through an imaginative dream-like story, '*Koto to Pan*', which captivated and disoriented me when I first read it. Subsequent re-reading gave a different perspective on the use of fiction and imagination in narrative. For Phillion (2002:545), this imaginary writing redefined narrative multiculturalism and 'helped show how intimately people must examine and know themselves in order to examine and know another'. That sentence resonated with me, epitomising my experience with narrative inquiry.

Reviewing narrative fiction

Exploring the many variations of how fiction is used in social science research, Jane Speedy's (2008) compelling use of imaginary interviewing in narrative research and psychotherapy was extremely valuable. Through an interactive dialogue with a whimsical alter-ego, Speedy delves into complex themes, ranging from feminism and poststructuralism to magical realism. Originally written in a slightly dry prose, these topics are now transformed into a more compelling and captivating story, covering narrative inquiry, philosophy, history and ethics, while actively demonstrating the collaborative process of story creation. Using this literary technique, Speedy (2008:7) blurs boundaries and 'troubles the edges between therapy and research practices,' showing that using fiction mixed with fact provides learning. The learning is not only for the reader as the researcher also learns much in the process.

For some, the use of fiction continues to raise questions of legitimacy (Spindler 2008). For others, the link between fiction and research has been made, the benefits provided. In his book, *Narratives and Fiction in Educational Research*, Clough

(2002) explores educational research through writing stories based on events which may or may not have happened (Badley 2003). For this work, Clough has received both accolades and criticism on his vacillating perspectives about truth. Yet it is not the veracity of the story that matters. What makes a difference is the evocative, emotional and at times gut wrenching narrative, pulling the reader into the experience. Like an abstract painting, the story draws us closer or makes us recoil. Whether sucked in or repelled from the raw emotions depicted in the stories, his persuasive technique and writing style forces us to think. We interpret these stories from our vantage point, triggering a personal memory or experiencing first hand the struggles of others. Rather than discuss Clough's pontificating or vacillating, the primary question needs to be, 'What have we learned?' These stories and Clough's re-telling of events provides learning and the evocative beauty of fiction draws the reader into the story. In this setting the writer shapes reality, the story informs and the reader interprets. Similar to Clough, using a fictional technique enabled unexplored events to rise to the surface. With Ms Ito's story, I used observations from our interviews and conversations through meetings, phone calls or emails to build an imaginative vignette. In this story, her mother's reaction to a pet caterpillar or elongated silence around early influences may have gone unnoticed. In writing this story, I started to reflect on the significance of these comments and events. I could have written the story as, 'Ms Ito responded with silence', full stop. Instead, I used this word repeatedly throughout the story and expressively wrote sentences with, 'silence loomed', 'silence ensued', or 'time and silence crossed once more . . . .'. I wanted to depict the experience of sitting through interviews listening to silence and to demonstrate that silence, like words, can teach.

As I continued reading, the boundaries between art, fiction and research overlapped. Fictional representation, creative non-fiction or narrative fiction are often couched in terms of ethical issues; specifically narrative fiction's ability to hide identity or keep research participants anonymous (Sparkes 2002). Beyond ethical considerations, fictional representation provides a voice for the unheard – women grappling with anorexia (Kiesinger 1998), the relationships between strip club workers and married clientele (Frank 2000) or surfacing racial tensions within a culturally diverse group (Trahar 2011). Trahar (2011) uses fictional representation to discuss ethical issues and at the same time to expose tensions within a multicultural community of students. Cleverly written, using the voice of Charles Dickens, Trahar pulls the reader into a cold, dark classroom on a winter evening. While we are welcomed into the setting, Trahar's description foreshadows gloom, conjuring up memories of a cold college classroom – damp, dark and dismal. We are not certain of the location but have been given vague logistics of a Northern European city. Trahar uses the classroom to allow each student a stage to share the challenges of studying and living away from their home country. Racial or cultural tensions that may be simmering beneath the surface are brought to the forefront in this fictitious setting, but Trahar (2011:272) states, 'in the 'real event' I did not challenge them about that racism'. Trahar is explicit in telling what happens, outlining reasons for using this fictional technique to explore ethics, tension and vulnerabilities. The clear voice and rational intent engenders trust in the reader. Following postmodernist philosophy, questions on truth in Clough's stories or with other narrative research are misaligned; the emphasis should be placed on trust. In these three very different examples, Speedy, Clough and Trahar all encourage the reader to be part of the performance, allowing her/him to derive her/his own meaning. By inviting the reader into the performance, exposing the tension and struggles, provides an avenue of trust.

The impact of creative non-fiction

In the book *Fields of Play*, Laurel Richardson (1997:1) asks, 'How does what we write affect who we become?' Contrary to the idea that writing impacts identity, I probed identity and how what the researcher brings into the study influences her writing outcomes. I understand Richardson's point, but found the question of identity across cultures a challenging one. Culture and identity can be false friends (Maalouf 2011). These common words used often are rarely defined or questioned. Both are a complex mix of disparate parts that make up who we are. I trusted my definition of culture formed through graduate school courses, cross-cultural textbooks and work experiences across the Asia Pacific region. Culture is one part of identity, not only defined by country of origin. In this story, Ms Ito was born in Tokyo to Japanese parents and spent her formative years in Tokyo and adult years studying in the UK, Canada and Latin America. At odds with Japanese traditions and beliefs, she left Japan in her early-twenties and worked in Australia, New Zealand, India and Singapore. On many occasions I tussled with cross cultural identity when interviewing Asian women leaders and in hindsight had too much attachment to a vague concept of culture, not paying enough attention to the fluid elements of identity. Unconsciously I held on to control the process. I held onto this vague notion of culture and far worse, I wanted my participants' responses to fit within my mental framework. In hindsight I was grappling with two issues: my narrow definition of culture and my reluctance to let the narrative process flow.

When starting my interviews, the questions were intended to engage in a dialogue and encourage participants' experiences and stories to unfold, often through an open invitation into each story, such as, 'Tell me about a time when . . . ' and to see the individual in the process. In my first interview with Ms Ito I found it difficult to grasp meaning, as it was in English but I struggled with questions of identity, culture and early influences. In my mind, these were simple questions, a good way to start. When I asked about early influences, Ms Ito responded with a long, protracted silence and then simply said, 'No one'.

Resisting her response, I asked again. Ms Ito's answer did not fit my cultural framework of what I thought someone from Japan would say. I started to believe (but not question) my ingrained beliefs and cultural generalisations. To wit, my American mindset and cultural awareness were at odds with one another. When I wrote her story, I finally removed my cultural strait-jacket and started to listen deeply, to see beneath the response. In doing so, I uncovered difficult and sensitive events in Ms Ito's early life. These pivotal events have significantly influenced her leadership and life's philosophy. As narrative is a collaborative process,

I asked about these pivotal events and connections in her life. She responded with, 'You know me better than I know myself'.

When Ms Ito's interview presented a convoluted maze of words, I read more on creative non-fiction. Richardson's poetic representation was intriguing to me, although writing poetry has never been my strong suit. I spent significant time creating an imaginary interview, following Jane Speedy's (2007) format but found my voice overshadowed my participants. Sheila Trahar's (2011) and Peter Clough's (2002) narrative fictions were captivating. Along with their writing, a previous expository college writing course provided guidance to experiment with fiction writing which required mimicking the style of a well-known author. I chose Hemingway and have tried to emulate his style for years in other writing. I have previously submitted short stories to literary journals and imitation Hemingway competitions. The choice of Hemingway was familiarity and simplicity of expression. In this chapter, the decision to use creative non-fiction provided a way to move beyond myself, a format to question embedded beliefs and a method to navigate the circumstances surrounding Ms Ito's story.

Narrative inquiry is neither bound by rigidity or strict definitions. Writing without rules provided freedom and facilitated creativity in representing these stories. Yet fiction and reflexivity have both received their share of criticism. To some, reflexivity is considered self-indulgent or worse, narcissistic (Etherington 2004). Fiction in academic research raises questions and sometimes disapproval. John Spindler's (2008) research in fictional writing in educational research questioned the narrow definition of fiction. He believes the lines between fiction and non-fiction in research remain hazy as the writers experience shapes meaning. 'Research texts are inevitably fictional since they have been fashioned and moulded by their writers and their quality depends at least in part on the skill and imagination with which they have been crafted' (Spindler 2008:3). Using Hemingway's voice places Ms Ito's story under creative non-fiction category. In terms of research impact, using creative non-fiction, I uncovered the rich, multidimensional aspects of cross cultural narrative inquiry. More than being reflexive, I argue that the use of creative non-fiction allows the researcher to move beyond self and explore entrenched beliefs, which are important for cross cultural narrative inquiry. Exploring leadership experiences of Asian women amidst Asian cultural complexities required fluid research method and unconventional writing to achieve this level of understanding.

Interpreting creative non-fiction across cultures

We are influenced by our culture and deeply rooted values. How we interpret a story rests with subjective conditions and social influences (Rorty 1991). These principles are not easy to suppress, yet each time we read a story, whether author or reader, our interpretations change and the mind play tricks on us. The same is true when writing a story. We review an event, re-read our notes, but something has changed. Memories can be fleeting. Siri Hustvedt (2011:38), American author and essayist, sums up this ephemeral nature, 'It is impossible to divine a story while you are living it . . . we never recover what was. Most of it vanishes'.

This transient feeling can obscure thinking, but hindsight has the advantage of recapturing or redefining events. We recall events and in doing so, see something new. Our mind reshapes the story offering a new perspective.

Reflecting on my experience of writing stories about women across the Asia Pacific region, Hustvedt's words ring true. For three years I interviewed Asian women to understand their experiences in multiple industries and professions. The vast cultural differences added to the richness of their stories and complexity of my journey. As I write this chapter, exploring creative non-fiction in narrative, these memories resurface: a rainy café in Hong Kong, a freezing office in Singapore and a cavernous conference hall in Bangladesh. The places are real, the words genuine but through time and distance memory fades, the story shifts and interpretations change.

Narrative inquiry is a shared process providing insight into self, others and (simultaneously) narrative itself. My stories in multicultural settings become a tangle of shared experiences and complicated interpretations. Reflexivity helped undo the knots and bring awareness of self into the research process. Creative non-fiction reproducing interviews and re-formatting words into expressive stories brought awareness on many levels and multiple audiences. Reflexivity was valuable from a personal perspective, but using creative non-fiction produced remarkably different interpretations of cross cultural understanding and identity of participants and their stories. Writing this story using creative non-fiction provided distance, granting the mental space to delve deeper into the individual story and cultural complexities. Transposing experiences mixed with fiction writing provides a freedom in which to explore ideas (Ketelle 2004).

Challenges and evaluation

Writing fiction allowed me to step away from my identity and into the other person's story. After completing Ms Ito's story, I realised the challenges of maintaining Hemingway's voice. Although enlightening, I felt disoriented trying to maintain myself and emulate Hemingway. The writing process was too taxing to use for the stories from the other women in my research. I was also not certain the same style should even be used, as each story required a different voice and perspective. Fortunately, narrative offers many ways to tell a story. Henning Mankell (2011:9) maintains that narratives have entirely different structures across cultures, as 'Western literature is normally linear; it proceeds from beginning to end without major digressions in space or time'. I did not agree with this statement until I noticed my preference to write in this linear fashion. I soon relaxed into a more lateral style, allowing Ms Ito's story to unfold, moving back and forth in time through various life events. All of the stories I gathered and re-told traversed time, blended history and explored culture through fact and fiction.

When I began my research, I did not have a written framework, but soon realised my personal plan was very much a part of it. Hemingway's voice provided a way to see the world from Ms Ito's perspective rather than to fit her into my 'mental plan'. Tangled in words, the chaos of researching across cultures tested my patience, but ultimately the learning became visible. The defining moment was putting aside what I thought I knew about cultures,and adapting(or relaxing), which enabled new perspectives.

Concluding thoughts in evaluating creative non-fiction

How do we evaluate creative non-fiction? A story can be evaluated on many dimensions-from clarity, credibility and communication, to contribution (Finlay 2006). The aim of my research was to expand knowledge on cross-cultural leadership and narrative inquiry, not only for myself but for the reader as well. Drafting stories using creative non-fiction allowed me to recognise actions and insights representing Ms Ito's life and leadership journey. In this sense, writing became a method of inquiry (Richardson 1997) and creating this story provided clarity. I hope the reader will interact with the content to discover something new.

I followed Finlay's (2006:12) perspective of evaluating qualitative research on the ability to 'draw the reader into the researcher's discoveries, allowing the reader to see the worlds of others in new and deeper ways'. As lives are not lived in a linear fashion, neither are stories. A story changes with each reading. Reading from start to finish, mixing fictionalised voice and fact allows the reader to draw their own conclusion and agree or disagree with ideas presented. Credibility combined with trustworthiness rests with the reader's interpretation. Being reflexive, defined as the ability to look back on myself and understand what I brought into this research, coupled with the use of fiction, unveiled hidden meanings. Writing, telling and re-reading Ms Ito's story became a source of wisdom for me (Coles 1989). Stories, like research, are personal journeys. Doubt remains on how to evaluate fiction in research, but perhaps some answers can be found in the questions asked of Clough's (2002) work: 'What have we learned?' Jonathan Wyatt (2007:326), writing on Clough's research, added more questions: 'Does it engage me? Is it well written and does it have aesthetic merit?' Evaluating creative non- fiction, I would add one more question to this list: 'Does good research writing disturb, influence or impact us?' A well-written story pulls us in, triggering emotions and incites reactions. The answers to these evaluation questions are open to the reader's interpretation. From a multicultural perspective, a challenging question is, 'Does the reader identify with the writing?' (Ketelle 2004:459). I ask this question because Hemingway may be viewed as the quintessential American. Some readers may not identify with this writing style but the story based in an Asian Pacific context has impact nonetheless. Creative non-fiction provided clarity for me to see Ms Ito as an individual, devoid of the cultural constructs in which I originally placed her. The use of creative non-fiction offers possibilities, paradoxes and multiple truths for the reader and writer to interpret (Vickers 2010). Using this style and re-writing Ms Ito's story from multiple angles offered a new perspective on my participants, myself, narrative inquiry, culture, identity and leadership. Stories teach – and other people's stories help us learn about ourselves. Using creative non-fiction in narrative inquiry with people from different contexts has enabled these processes for me.

References

Badley, G. (2003) The Truth of Stories: Graham Bradley Reviews, Narrative and Fiction in Educational Research by Peter Clough, with a rejoinder by the author. *Research in Post Compulsory Education*, 8(3), 441–452.

Clough, P. (2002) *Narratives and Fictions in Educational Research Philadelphia*. PA: Open University Press.

Coles, R (1989) *The Call of Stories: Teaching and the Moral Imagination*. Boston: Houghton Mifflin.

Etherington, K., (2004) *Becoming a Reflexive Researcher: Using Our Selves in Research*. London: Kingsley Publishers.

Etherington, K., (2009) Reflexivity: Using our 'Selves' in Narrative Research. In S. Trahar (Eds) *Narrative Research on Learning: Comparative and International Perspectives*, Oxford, Symposium Books, pp. 77–92.

Finlay, L., (2006) 'Rigour, 'Ethical Integrity' or 'Artistry'? Reflexively Reviewing Criteria for Evaluating Qualitative Research. *British Journal of Occupational Therapy* 69(7), 319–326.

Frank, K. (2000) The Management of Hunger: Using Fiction in Writing. *Anthropology Qualitative Inquiry* 6(4), 474–488.

Hustvedt, S. (2011) *The Summer Without Men*. London, England: Hodder & Stoughton.

Ketelle, D. (2004) Writing Truth as Fiction: Administrators Think about Their Work through a Different Lens. *The Qualitative Report*, 9(3), 449–462.

Kiesinger, C. (1998) Portrait of an Anorexic Life. In A. Banks & S. Banks (Eds) *Fiction and Social Research: By Fire and Ice*. Walnut Creek, CA: Alta Mira Press, pp 115–136.

Maalouf, A., (2011) *In the Name of Identity: Violence and the Need to Belong*. New York: Arcade Books.

Mankell, H. (2011) The Art of Listening. *New York Times*, 13 December 2011, 9.

Phillion, J., (2002) Becoming a Narrative Inquirer in a Multicultural Landscape. *Journal of Curriculum Studies*, 34(5), 535–556.

Richardson, L., (1997) *Fields of Play: Constructing an Academic Life*. New Brunswick, NJ: Rutgers University Press.

Rorty, R. (1991) *Objectivism, Relativism and Truth: Philosophical Papers*. Cambridge: Cambridge University Press.

Sparkes, A. C., (2002) *Telling Tales in Sports and Physical Activity: a Qualitative Journey*. London: Human Kinetics.

Speedy, J., (2008) *Narrative Inquiry and Psychotherapy*. Hampshire: Palgrave Macmillan.

Spindler, J., (2008) Fictional Writing, Educational Research and Professional Learning. *International Journal of Research & Method in Education*, 31(1), 19–30.

Trahar, S., (2011) *Developing Cultural Capability in International Higher Education: A Narrative Inquiry*. Oxon: Routledge.

Vickers, M. H., (2010) The Creation of Fiction to Share Other Truths and Different Viewpoints: A Creative Journey and an Interpretive Process. *Qualitative Inquiry*, 16(7), 556–565.

Wyatt, J. (2007) Research, Narrative and Fiction: Conference Story. *The Qualitative Report*, 12(2), 313–331.

6   Riding the wave of education reform

Using a reflecting team to explore the professional identities of school counsellors in Hong Kong

Mabel Shek

Introduction

Professional identities develop through an understanding of oneself in relation to the environment. The development process is never fully internal or external but is constructed holistically by individuals interacting with the environment and creating stories within themselves (Appiah, 2005; Conyne & Cook, 2004; Miller & Garran, 2008). In complying with the education and curriculum reform programme launched in 2002, the Education and Manpower Bureau in Hong Kong has borrowed a theoretical framework from the US to implement a new school counselling policy – the Comprehensive Student Guidance Service (CSGS) – in all primary schools (Education and Manpower Bureau, 2003). Within this framework, the traditional role of the school counsellor as a caseworker taking a remedial approach has shifted. As a result, counsellors have struggled with their internal value system and contextual constraints that require them to renegotiate their inherited professional identities.

In this chapter, I start by explaining the changing context of school counselling in Hong Kong, where professional identities are being shaped and reshaped. I then discuss the suitability of using narrative inquiry to explore the professional identities of school counsellors and my reflections on the complexities that I encountered in applying this methodology in the local context. Through the counsellors' narratives, constructed through the collaborative research process of a reflecting team, I set out to understand the stories they lived by and how they negotiated their professional identities within the particular context of current educational reform. The chapter concludes with suggestions for ways of creating a space for the methodological development of narrative inquiry in Hong Kong and in the wider Chinese community.

The changing context of school counselling in Hong Kong

Since Hong Kong was a British colony for more than 150 years (1842–1997), it is not surprising that the UK ideology and practice of school counselling, based on the concept of pastoral care, was embedded in its educational system. The goal of promoting the whole person development of students (Watkins, 2001; Watkins & Wagner, 2000) has greatly influenced the formulation of school counselling policy in Hong Kong. In the 1990s, due to a growing demand for such services, and in response to the recommendation of the Education Commission Report No. 4, the Education Department formally adopted the UK model as set out in the *Whole School Approach to Guidance* as its first formal policy on school counselling (Education Commission, 1990). To implement the policy effectively, a number of experienced primary teachers were recruited as school counsellors. They were trained and certified by the government to offer a counselling service to students in need and to organise programmes in schools; this was a crucial part of their functions and responsibilities (Hue, 2008).

Over the last few decades, the speedy advancement of information technology (IT) in the US has initiated an almost fanatical reform movement in education systems all over the world. Educational borrowing from a foreign country is customary in the Hong Kong education system and has influenced policy formulation. Aligned with such educational reforms, school counselling began to take on the role of facilitating students to acquire competencies in the domains of personal, social, academic and career development (Gysbers & Henderson, 2012) in order to close the achievement gap. Soon, the concepts of comprehensive and developmental guidance also came to the fore. The Education and Manpower Bureau borrowed a theoretical framework from the US to formulate the second school counselling policy, the CSGS, which has been implemented in all primary schools since 2002. The CSGS aims to 'strengthen the development of guidance policies and personal growth education' (Education and Manpower Bureau, 2003, p. 1), with the intention of repositioning the service to be geared towards a preventive and developmental approach that would form an integral part of education.

Even though models from the UK and US have been adopted in Hong Kong over recent decades, many educational practices still reflect embedded Chinese traditions. For people in Asian countries, ideologies of egalitarian participation, paternalism, and duty, organisational collectiveness and collective identity are social values that are instilled and reinforced throughout the educational process (Watkins, 2001; Zaffuto, 2005). Luk-Fong (2010) argues that the culture of Hong Kong is hybridised, mixing and interacting Western tendencies with Chinese traditions. School counselling is concerned with individual personal growth, whereas Chinese societies emphasise collectiveness, discipline and harmonious relationships (Cheng & Wong, 1996). Therefore, some teachers in Hong Kong perceive a disciplined culture which stresses uniformity as dominant and powerful, and counselling as weak and isolating (Hue, 2007). As in other Asian countries, Hong Kong students have to undertake highly competitive and stressful public examinations. School counselling is often expected to assist them to attain the highest levels of educational achievement and promote the school's prestige (Romano *et al.*, 2005).

Evolution of the professional identities of school counsellors in a shifting context

Professional identity is not singular or unchanging; it is continually informed, formed and reformed as individuals interact with others over a period of time (Day *et al.*, 2006). Professional identity has both intrapersonal and interpersonal dimensions (Gibson *et al.*, 2010). In the former, an individual shapes her/his professional identity from within to conceptualise the professional role through acquiring professional skills, values, roles, attitudes, ethical beliefs, thoughts and decision-making styles. This is a process whereby the inner self creates a meaning for one's professional role. In the interpersonal dimension, professional identity develops through one's relationship to the immediate social and cultural context. In this ongoing process, the school counsellor moves from an external to internal locus of evaluation and from a dependence on external experts to a reliance on her/his own experience and training (Auxier *et al.*, 2003; Gibson *et al.*, 2010; Howard *et al.*, 2006). Thus, the development of the professional identity of a school counsellor begins with counselling training and continues throughout the career life span as a dynamic and interactive process.

The personal construction of professional identity is significant to school counsellors' readiness and commitment to perform effectively in leading school counselling. Self-labelling as a professional is a major theme of professional identity and is dependent on the congruence between the personal worldview of the self and a view of oneself as a competent professional (Gibson *et al.*, 2010; Reisetter *et al.*, 2004). The school counsellor's role is not articulated explicitly in the *Whole School Approach to Guidance* policy document, which emphasises the involvement of all staff in school counselling. Without a clear definition, role confusion may result (Studer, 2007), which may impair the counsellor's ability to function professionally (Gibson *et al.*, 2010). In reality, professional practices are not directed by the letter of written policy documents, but are also guided by counsellors' personal conceptualisations and external realisations of their role within their immediate social and cultural context (Chong *et al.*, 2011). In a dynamic process, the school counsellor will compare new input with her/his internal views, evaluate the comparison, then internalise or reject the new information (Auxier *et al.*, 2003; Reisetter *et al.*, 2004).

Situational and social factors also influence the formation of an individual's professional identity (Dobrow & Higgins, 2005; Pratt *et al.*, 2006). Under the rationale of the CSGS model, school counsellors are not only required to render a remedial counselling service but also to be responsible for programme design and advocacy, development of the guidance curriculum and fostering collaboration with other subsystems (Adelman & Taylor, 2002; Baker, 2000; Bemak, 2000; Herr, 2002). Such a change requires a fundamental alteration of the mindset of counsellors and how they use their internal resources to initiate new practices in the school system. In addition, the perceptions of the principal and other teachers will affect the counsellor's professional decisions and practice.

From the ecological perspective, a school counsellor's professional identity is embedded in and connected to a multilayered network that influences her/ his inner and outer worlds (Lewis & Hatch, 2008). The inner world consists of a set of beliefs and values and a self-defined meaning of oneself that develops one's worldview. The outer world denotes the external social structure, such as the school system, policy, and culture, within which school counsellors seek to be recognised and validated as professionals. Although Hong Kong has often been described as a place where East meets West, our educational system is deeply rooted in Eastern traditions. The philosophy of Confucianism in a Chinese society continues to influence counsellors' values and beliefs, their interactions with other staff and the implementation of school counselling. For instance, the counsellor must exercise professional autonomy under the prevailing Confucian ideology of cardinal human relationships in our school system (Luk-Fong, 2006). In a Confucian heritage society, the construction of a school counsellor's inner self and how she/he interacts with the social context in order to implement a counselling model that has been borrowed from a very different society, is worthy of exploration and is a focus of this chapter.

Using narrative inquiry to explore the professional identities of school counsellors

Narrative is used in a variety of ways by different disciplines, and is often synonymous with story. Story is first and foremost a way of thinking about *experience* (Connelly & Clandinin, 2006). Narrative inquiry is a human-centred approach to research that involves the construction and reconstruction of personal stories and which delves beneath external behaviour to explore thoughts, feelings and intentions (Webster & Mertova, 2007). In this study, I conducted individual interviews with four school counsellors to encourage them to relate their experiences from the commencement of their teaching careers to becoming counsellors in primary schools, and to discuss how they were carrying out their work during a period of education reform. After I had collected their individual stories, I invited all the school counsellors to participate in a reflecting team process (RTP) to share the challenges they had encountered in implementing the school counselling service as an outcome of educational reform. Storytelling created spaces for these participants to tell their diverse stories, which may differ from those narrowly shaped by policymakers. From their narratives, readers may understand the self-defined meanings, perceptions and self-in-situation meanings that they attributed to their professional role from both the personal and social aspects. Their insider lens reveals the complexity of their lived experience along with the social structure in which they are situated and which is conceived as a source of important knowledge and understanding.

Differing from other methods used to study certain aspects of subjects or phenomena, narrative inquiry captures the whole story to unfold the complex interrelationships in a particular context (Webster & Mertova, 2007). If professional identity is an ongoing process of maturation, narrative inquiry is a suitable methodology through which to understand the professional journey of the school counsellors over time. For the school counsellors, this has provided a precious opportunity for them to look backward and forward on their professional trajectory as well as to discover the inner meaning of this role in relation to the external social context. In doing so, they have been able to recall where they came from to understand where they are now and to project where they will go in the future.

A significant feature of narrative inquiry is that it enables the researcher – and the reader – to get closer to the experience of those whose lives are ordinary, marginalised and silenced (Riessman, 2008). School counselling has been labelled as a kind of auxiliary or marginal service in the Hong Kong educational setting (Shek, 2013). School counsellors' experiences are largely unspoken. Using narrative inquiry to study school counselling in Hong Kong is rare. In addition, no research has been conducted previously on school counsellors' experiences and professional identities in that context. If we consider that they are change agents and key players in educational reform, their experiences can significantly influence the implementation of school counselling. It is valuable to hear this silenced but critically important voice of the practitioner in a changing educational context. The school counsellors' stories can help all of us to comprehend the assumptions, difficulties and goals that are embedded in their practice. Their stories will also shed light on their professional practice, policy formulation and advancement of research.

Good narratives typically approach the 'complexities and contradictions of real life' (Flyvbjerg, 2006, p. 237). The school counsellor must work closely with the stakeholders in the school system, which is situated in a larger social and cultural context. The personal-social dimension is emphasised because the inquiry not only focuses on individual experience but also on the social, cultural and institutional narratives within which it is constituted, shaped, expressed and enacted (Clandinin & Rosiek, 2007). Using narrative inquiry provides a new lens for me and for other researchers to understand the complexities of the local education context and to explore the real-life situation of the school counsellors. This can lead to insightful revelations about the interaction between personal beliefs and values and about the influence of the school system, policy ideology and other contextual factors on their perceptions, decision-making and professional practice.

Complexities of applying narrative inquiry in the Hong Kong context

Narrative inquiry is an unfamiliar term and not a prevalent research methodology in Hong Kong. It was introduced into the context by a small group of academics about 15 years ago (Yu & Lau, 2011). I therefore had to explain it to potential participants when I invited them to be involved in this study. The school counsellors asked me to give them a list of interview questions, as they had received in other studies, so that they could prepare. For the pilot interviews, I did so, but after listening to the audio recording I realised that my guiding questions had framed the interview. As a result, I could only collect episodes of stories rather than a coherent and connected story. After reviewing the pilot interviews, I recognised that the participants and I had been constrained by the traditional structure of the semi-structured interview. I had felt that, without some guiding questions, both researcher and participants might feel insecure and uncertain. On reflection, I found that the major problem was my unfamiliarity with narrative interviewing and my discomfort about abandoning my previous interview practice. As a narrative inquirer, I wanted to capture the wholeness of the story. I therefore decided to only tell the participants in advance about the interview's focus, instead of having a list of questions, in order to collect long accounts of stories. In addition, I also had to exercise my attentiveness in a different way to follow the flow of the narrator's stories. This is a shift from interviewer-directed to narrator-centred interaction.

Self-disclosure is risky for some people. When I invited the school counsellors to participate in both the individual interview and the RTP, they asked me the same question: 'Who will be invited to be in the reflecting team?' Two of them told me that they were worried that there would be someone in the team that they did not like. Their relationships with the others were important for them in deciding whether or not they would participate in the RTP. I had not confirmed all the participants at the time of the initial contact, so could not tell them the names of the others. I deliberated whether it was appropriate to let the participants know each other's names before the RTP took place. For Confucius, the self is related to others in one's personal development and human relationships are of great concern in Chinese culture (Luk-Fong, 2006). To self-disclose in a reflecting team is a risk-taking process and resonance occurs through trusting dialogue with others. I therefore concluded that participants had the right to know in advance who else would be in the team. After obtaining their consent to disclose their names to other participants, I passed this information to all of them. Finally, they all felt comfortable joining the RTP even though they did not know each other.

Like other narrative inquirers working in Hong Kong, I had to deal with the complexity in language representation in composing the research text (Yip, 2013; Yu & Lau, 2011). All individual interviews and the RTP were conducted in Cantonese, a spoken language that allowed the school counsellors to recount their stories freely and comfortably. The conversations were audio recorded for detailed transcription as field text in Chinese (the written form of the language) for subsequent analysis. I analysed the field text in Chinese and then translated the excerpt into English to represent the stories in the research text. I am aware that there might be discrepancies in the back translation. In the process of struggling with translating word for word or meaning for meaning, I had to listen to some phrases from the audio recording again in order to understand the meaning of the expressions used. In my representation, after I had deliberated on the words used by the school counsellors and their meanings, I decided to change some words, especially slang terms, to represent their original meaning more clearly in English. All the research texts and my interpretations were sent to the school counsellors for comment to ensure I had represented their meaning accurately. They were able to understand both languages and to verify whether the research text was an accurate representation of their stories. This member checking is one of the criteria for the establishment of trustworthiness and credibility (Niekerk & Savin-Baden, 2010). After receiving feedback from the school counsellors, I clarified the meanings with them and made revisions if necessary.

The reflecting team process as a collaborative research method

The (RTP was developed by Tom Andersen (1987). It emerged in the context of family therapy and has been diffused to counselling training (Cox *et al.*, 2003; Fine, 2003; Shurts *et al.*, 2006; Stinchfield *et al.*, 2007) and education (Frake & Dogra, 2006; Trahar, 2011). In family therapy, the RTP involves an interview between therapist and client occurring in front of a silent and observing team who are sitting apart or in an adjacent room with a one-way screen. In a midsession break, the team members turn to one another for feedback on the issues explored during the interview, whilst the interviewee and therapist listen to their reflections. Once the team has finished its conversation, the therapist resumes the interview to explore the interviewee's responses to the feedback. The RTP consists of a shift between being a talking participant and a listening participant around the same issue and is a powerful method of creating new descriptions and explanations within the mind of a participant (Andersen, 1991). As a research method, the RTP offers a way of creating dialogic contexts that share the core elements of narrative inquiry, namely collaboration and participation, to encourage dialogue among members (Trahar, 2011). It emphasises reflection as a means to understand one's lived experience, and provides multiple perspectives on both personal and social experience in context (Brownlee *et al.*, 2009).

Apart from having intrinsic merit, the RTP is a useful method to apply in the Hong Kong context. First, the pace of life in Hong Kong is fast and school counsellors lack the time to listen deeply to their inner voice and reflect on their different experiences. In the RTP, the school counsellors passed through various internal and external dialogues and came to understand their professional identity and the context differently. This sense-making process inspired the reconstruction of both professional identity and practice in different ways. Second, as the only counselling specialist in a school, counsellors seldom engage in constructive dialogue with other professionals to reflect critically on their practice in relation to the school context. In a trusting environment without judgmental interference, meaningful narratives can emerge and genuine responses given. Through their resonances, the school counsellors can see one experience in terms of another (Conle, 1996). They experienced similar struggles and triumphs as a professional, including the feeling of 'I am not alone.' The RTP provides multiple perspectives to help participants become aware of and challenge their own dominant beliefs, values and knowledge. Third, in a Chinese society where the embedded ideology of collectivism and harmony is still emphasised, it is a kind of relief to listen to the resonances of other professionals talking about the challenges they have encountered. The school counsellors may perceive their problems as a collective feature of the Hong Kong context instead of ascribing them uniquely to themselves. No story is a single story but is mediated by social, historical and cultural influences. In comparison with other methods of data collection, the RTP creates a supportive atmosphere which facilitates participants to disclose their internal thought processes through which to tell the stories that they live by both naturally and comfortably (Hawley, 2006).

Negotiating space for school counselling in the educational reform process

Fanny was the first person interviewed in the RTP to express her sense of the challenges presented by the education reform.

Fanny: I did not have time to work on school counselling. . . . I had to deal with a lot of administrative work but school counselling had to be left to last. I feel guilty putting the thing which I 'should' do last.

I: Why have such changes?

Fanny: Starting from the implementation of the New Funding Mode, I was given a new and important role to take care of the students with Special Educational Needs (SEN). I had to establish the SEN support group and shoulder all the coordination work whilst taking the leading role in the school counselling group. Once the SEN group had been developed, it became the major part of my work.

I: Leading the SEN programme seems to be your key role in school. Is there any other administration work you have to be responsible for?

Fanny: I was assigned to coordinate the school anniversary event last year and spent much time on it. Then, school counselling had to be put aside again.

I: How do you feel when you put the counselling work aside?

Fanny: Of course, I will meet the students who are in crisis but other cases which are not urgent may be put aside. This seems to stray from school counselling. Counselling is relationship building but not so task oriented. . . . . Surely, it would be better to meet the students frequently if I have time and space.

Lack of space seems a prime difficulty for Fanny. She is juggling multiple roles, priorities, and tasks within a limited amount of time. After the first interview with Fanny, the three other counsellors turned to each other to share their resonances while Fanny and I listened to their dialogue.

Man: I echo Fanny's view on lack of time for school counselling. It was a change . . . this change started in 2002, the implementation of the CSGS, I was fully involved in a school because the mode changed.

I became an administrator. So, I always attend the administrative meetings which are irrelevant to school counselling. The principal treats me as an administrator but it totally wastes my time. In my school, I have to teach the whole curriculum of Personal Growth Education (PGE) to all students. . . . . Sometimes, I have to substitute for other teachers on duty at recess, and supervise students at lunchtime. There is not much to distinguish my role from other teachers.

Marie: I always think that my job is so hard. After I listened to Man's sharing, I realise that I am in sheer bliss. I resonated with Fanny's experience in that I also lack the time to do counselling work due to administrative duties. While I am listening, I am reflecting on myself. I have time to handle the students' cases. It is not necessary for me to teach the PGE but to supervise other teachers to implement it. To compare with Fanny's situation, I am only responsible for part of the SEN support. Why do I always consider quitting my job? I think I have unrealistic expectations of myself. My stress mainly comes from my colleagues but I do not think my stress is so high in comparison with you. I need to do some self-evaluation about whether I have to quit or decide to enjoy my work.

Yan: I have to design, evaluate and supervise teachers to implement the PGE. I understand there are difficulties for different parties. If I were Man, I would quit my job due to feelings of phobia *[laughter]*! Supporting SEN students is one of the major responsibilities of the school counsellor in my school. The vice-principal is the SEN coordinator but my workload is heavier than hers. Nevertheless, our teamwork is good and we will support each other . . . . I was given enough space to work in my school and have good communication with my principal.

Role confusion associated with new reform policies

Role confusion was the major difficulty encountered by the school counsellors in their workplaces. The mixed roles of school counsellors, teachers and administrators caused confusion about their professional identities. Such a shift emerged from the implementation of the CSGS policy in 2002 and the New Funding Mode in 2004 to support SEN students, both of which were borrowed from the US (Gysbers & Henderson, 2012; Lee & Wong, 2008) and the UK (Crowther *et al.*, 2001; Mackenzie, 2007), respectively. In the school counsellors' stories, their level of involvement in SEN support and the implementation of PGE were quite different depending on the school management and division of labour. Borrowing policy from foreign countries is a customary practice in Hong Kong. However, in this case, the government has merely implemented a policy and provided additional financial support for its operation, while neglecting the importance of leadership to effect change.

In Fanny and Man's dialogue, it can be seen that they were driven by the external demands of the school and social context that had converted their roles and made them confused about their sense of self. As Fanny said, she felt guilty when she left the counselling work aside which was the thing she felt she 'should do' within her self-conceptualised professional identity. Under the competing priorities, the space for the counselling service has diminished.

Professional space: given or negotiated

What one should do as a professional is developed at the early stages of the career, and allows school counsellors to identify, clarify and re-clarify their self-concepts (Auxier *et al.*, 2003; Luke & Goodrich, 2010; Nelson & Jackson, 2003). I wondered, however, if these school counsellors could simply decide what they should do in the school context. In a tidal wave of reform initiatives, policymakers, principals and other teachers also act as a force to influence counselling practice in a chaotic school context. These counsellors employed different approaches in responding to the problem of a lack of space for their work within the education reform process. Fanny and Man were driven by external changes to assume new roles, Yan was given her professional role by collaborating with other staff, and Marie's reflexivity directed her to create an internal space by adjusting herself after she had compared her own situation with those of the others. Through a process of interacting with the social context, they negotiated their space and restored congruence with the internal meaning of their professional identities.

After she had listened to the reflecting team's resonances, Fanny expressed her reflections:

Fanny: I resonate with your experience. Teachers' workload has increased enormously because of education reform. We, school counsellors, need to share the teachers' workload but it is difficult to share our counselling work with them.

Reorientation of the school counselling profession within education reform

In the second round of the RTP, I invited Marie to share the challenges she had encountered in implementing the CSGS. Marie loved the CSGS model but had had difficulties involving her colleagues in school counselling due to their heavy workloads.

Marie: Not having a direction is the major problem of our education reform. Every Division of the Government regards their programme as important but there is no connection among those initiatives. Today, we are talking about education reform. Then I am thinking about what should we do? Could we stand firm to seek for our own direction?

I: What are those initiatives?

Marie: For instance, the 'Read and Write: Programme of Learning Support' in Chinese, 'Fun Reading' in English, 'Cooperative Learning' in Curriculum Development, and the Maths Division is conducting a research project in my school. If we only respond to external demands, we will lose our direction . . . . We decided not to fulfil all the tasks but select only those that responded to our school's direction.

I: How did you select?

Marie: If we're unable to do something, we have to abandon it. We need to grasp our own direction but not be so ambitious . . . only select one to two key items to work on. I think this would be better. For example, we cut some content of the PGE to reduce teachers' workload and offered time for students to practise what they learned.

Fanny initiated the dialogue in the reflecting team and other school counsellors shared their resonances in relation to the factors influencing a school's direction and their profession as a whole.

Fanny: I wrote down the word – direction. The school leader is influential over the school direction. Coordination and cutting down the duplication of tasks is crucial. After changing to a new principal, over these three years, our colleagues are getting lost. I think my new principal is an ambitious person who likes to implement new initiatives but without considering the actual operation. . . . So, I am reflecting at the moment. Loss of direction is the critical problem of my school.

Man: I consider that we have to be assertive to uphold our own direction. Despite the Guidance Section asking me to implement different programmes, I insisted on rejecting those programmes which are irrelevant to our school's direction. . . . To receive a few thousand dollars of support, I have to account for its use and report to many people. If I can serve all students and provide them with a good service, I do not think that I must add new programmes to my service.

Fanny: The important point is that we know what we are doing.

Yan: Direction is influenced by personal style. In my experience, it is important to develop the direction with school personnel. Of course, the school principal has to discern to what extent we are responding to the government's requirements. Our colleagues will analyse the school's strengths, weaknesses, risks, and opportunities in order to select the suitable way for development. I think the leader has an important role and is a gatekeeper.

Marie responded to the reflecting team after listening to their resonances.

Marie: Through your sharing, I realise that direction is very important. You have given me different perspectives to review what my school and I possessed. Every school has unique conditions.

Who is leading the direction of school counselling?

In Marie's story, her agenda had been derailed by new initiatives in educational reform, but she then renegotiated her professional space with other staff by enabling them to revisit their own direction. For Fanny and Yan, the school's direction was closely related to the principal's leadership style. Fanny portrayed the principal as an authoritative figure, with staff having limited power to negotiate their practices in the school context. Controlling practices is a common feature in the Chinese educational context (Zhou *et al.*, 2012) as the cardinal human relationship of superior–subordinate (Luk-Fong, 2006) is emphasised. Yan depicted her principal as a gatekeeper who controlled access to external demands for reorientation. The principal has a significant role in terms of interacting with the school counsellor, and inevitably influences professional practice and decision-making. Man used assertiveness to resist external influences on her internally constructed guidelines for the school counselling profession. Who will be the final decision maker about the direction of school counselling? Is it the policymaker, principal or school counsellor?

To cope with external challenges in a chaotic context, all these counsellors engaged in a process of re-examining the internal, self-conceptualised meaning of their profession, and reconsidered what they valued in it, in order to reorient their trajectories. When I listened to Man's story, her assertive behaviour towards authority seemed alien. Like many Chinese in Hong Kong, I was socialised in a traditional Chinese family and encouraged to be compliant rather than assertive. To maintain harmonious relationships, it seems obvious to Chinese people that we must adjust ourselves and learn to adapt to the world (Luk-Fong & Brennan, 2004). Cultural differences or conflicts may emerge not just from the external context, but also be embedded in our personal values that influence the development of our professional identity (Hue, 2008). Man's assertiveness enabled her to defend her internal professional direction and practice. I became aware that these school counsellors had equal power to educate their principals about their role and, in turn to shape the principals' perceptions (Jonson et al., 2008).

Creating a space for methodological development

The relationship between culture and counselling is a critical area for further exploration in Hong Kong and elsewhere in the Asian region, as it can inform both research and practice in the educational landscape. Narrative inquiry has created a space for school counsellors to tell their diverse stories, which differ from those narrowly shaped by policymakers. Through listening to the stories of these insiders in the educational reform process, we can grasp a deeper understanding of the complexities of the contemporary education landscape. We can also understand that there is a gap between policy statements and implementation. Our government cannot merely transfer a theoretical framework or use funding to implement a new policy, but also needs to consider the leadership of change agents and critically examine the barriers in the school context. Context is important. These school counsellors' narratives provide rich and critical material for policymakers to reconsider the personal, social and cultural factors that may bridge the gap between policy formulation and implementation in future.

Narrative is a way of promoting reflective practice through engaging participants to review their experience and its relationship to the social context. These school counsellors recognised that the narrative interviews and RTP were valuable spaces for them to review their professional practice. The ways in which they resonated with each other provided different perspectives on improving their professional practice and shed light on their future planning. As a teacher educator, the school counsellors' experiences facilitated me to reflect on the complexities of the personal, social and cultural influences on the implementation of school counselling in the local context. My reflections can inform appropriate curriculum design of school counselling programmes for prospective and in-service teachers. The knowledge gained from the reflecting team allows me, the school counsellors, and readers to critically review key concepts and practices of school counselling in a context of education reform.

Nowadays, more Asian countries transfer Western policies to their local context. Cultural difference is one of the decisive factors in successful policy implementation. Through the narratives of the school counsellors in this study, their relationships with authoritarian leaders, tendency for compliance in the interests of respect for authority, and maintenance of a harmonious group environment in a Chinese society were revealed. A strength of narrative inquiry is that it can enable understanding of personal and social aspects. This, it is an essential way for a researcher to examine closely the cultural influences on a person's experience in relation to their context.

Formation of professional identity is an ongoing process

From the school counsellors' stories, I could also reflect on my assumptions about the leading role of the school counsellor and the complexities of implementing the CSGS. Although the participants had constructed a self-conceptualised meaning of their profession, their professional decisions and practices were constrained by the problems of unconnected reform initiatives or borrowed policies in the social context, and their embedded Chinese culture of cardinal human relationships and harmony. Narrative inquiry is a way to engage professionals with an ongoing process of making sense of their professional identity and reflecting on their lived stories in historical, social and cultural contexts. As such, it is an eminently suitable methodological approach for Hong Kong.

References

Adelman, H. S., & Taylor, L. (2002). School counselors and school reform: New directions. *Professional School Counseling, 5(4)*, 235–248.

Andersen, T. (1987). The reflecting team: Dialogue and meta-dialogue in clinical work. *Family Process, 26*, 415–428.

Andersen, T. (1991). *The reflecting team: Dialogues and dialogues about the dialogues*. New York, NY: W.W. Norton.

Appiah, K. A. (2005). *The ethics of identity*. Princeton, NJ: Princeton University Press.

Auxier, C. R., Hughes, F. R. & Kline, W. B. (2003). Identity development in counselors-in-training. *Counselor Education and Supervision*, *43*, 25–38.

Baker, S. B. (2000). *School counseling for the twenty-first century*. Upper Saddle River, NJ: Prentice-Hall.

Bemak, F. (2000). Transforming the role of the counselor to provide leadership in educational reform through collaboration. *Professional School Counseling*, *3*, 323–331.

Brownlee, K., Vis, J.-A. & McKenna, A. (2009). Review of the reflecting team process: Strengths, challenges, and clinical implications. *The Family Journal*, *17*(2), 139–145.

Cheng, K. M. & Wong, K. C. (1996). School effectiveness in East Asia: Concepts, origins and implications. *Journal of Educational Administration*, *34*(5), 32–49.

Chong, S., Low, E. L. & Goh, K. C. (2011). Emerging professional teacher identity of pre-service teachers. *Australian Journal of Teacher Education*, *36*(8), 50–64.

Clandinin, D. J. & Rosiek, J. (2007). Mapping a landscape of narrative inquiry. In D. J. Clandinin (Ed.), *Handbook of narrative inquiry: Mapping a methodology*. Thousand Oaks, California: Sage Publications, pp. 35–76.

Conle, C. (1996). Resonance in preservice teacher inquiry. *American Educational Research Journal*, *33*(2), 297–325.

Connelly, F. M. & Clandinin, D. J. (2006). Narrative inquiry. In J. L. Green, G. Camilli & P. B. Elmore (Eds), *Handbook of complementary methods in education research*. Washington, D.C.: American Educational Research Association, pp. 477–487.

Conyne, R. K. & Cook, E. P. (Eds) (2004). *Ecological counseling: an innovative approach to conceptualizing person-environment interaction*. Alexandria, VA: American Counseling Association.

Cox, J. A., Bañez, L. & Hawley, L. D. (2003). Use of the reflecting team process in the training of group workers. *Journal for Specialists in Group Work*, *28*(2), 89–105.

Crowther, D., Dyson, A. & Millward, A. (2001). Supporting pupils with special educational needs: issues and dilemmas for special needs coordinators in English primary schools. *European Journal of Special Needs Education*, *16*(2), 85–97.

Day, C., Kington, A., Stobart, G. & Sammons, P. (2006). The personal and professional selves of teachers: Stable and unstable identities. *British Educational Research Journal*, *32*(4), 601–616.

Dobrow, S. R. & Higgins, M. C. (2005). Developmental networks and professional identity: a longitudinal study. *Career Development International*, *10*(6/7), 567–583.

Education and Manpower Bureau (2003). *Implementation of comprehensive student guidance service*. Education and Manpower Bureau Circular No. 19/2003, pp. 72–80.

Education Commission (1990). *Education Commission report No. 4*. Hong Kong: Hong Kong Government.

Fine, M. (2003). Reflections on the intersection of power and competition in reflecting teams as applied to academic settings. *Journal of Marital and Family Therapy*, *29*(3), 339–351.

Flyvbjerg, B. (2006). Five misunderstandings about case-study research. *Qualitative Inquiry*, *12*(2), 219–245.

Frake, C. & Dogra, N. (2006). The use of reflecting teams in educational contexts. *Reflective Practice*, 7(2), 143–149.

Gibson, D. M., Dollarhide, C. T. & Moss, J. M. (2010). Professional identity development: A ground theory of transformational tasks of new counselors. *Counselor Education and Supervision*, 50(1), 21–37.

Gysbers, N. C. & Henderson, P. (2012). *Developing & managing your school guidance & counseling program* (5th ed.). Alexandria, VA: American Counseling Association.

Hawley, L. D. (2006). Reflecting teams and microcounseling in beginning counselor training: practice in collaboration. *The Journal of Humanistic Education and Development*, 45(2), 198–207.

Herr, E. L. (2002). School reform and perspectives on the role of school counselors: a century of proposals for change. *Professional School Counseling*, 5(4), 220–234.

Howard, E. E., Inman, A. G. & Altman, A. N. (2006). Critical incidents among novice counselor trainees. *Counselor Education and Supervision*, 46(2), 88–102.

Hue, M. T. (2007). The influence of classic Chinese philosophy of Confucianism, Taoism and legalism on classroom discipline in Hong Kong junior secondary schools. *Pastoral Care in Education*, 25(2), 38–45.

Hue, M. T. (2008). The influence of Confucianism: A narrative study of Hong Kong teachers' understanding and practices of school guidance and counseling. *British Journal of Guidance & Counselling*, 36(3), 303–316.

Jonson, C., Milltello, M. & Kosine, N. (2008). Four views of the professional school counselor-principal relationship: A Q-methodology study. *Professional School Counseling*, 11(6), 353–361.

Lee, B. S. F. & Wong, C. K. F. (2008). Transition to comprehensive student guidance service in Hong Kong. *Counselling, Psychotherapy, and Health*, 4(1), Counselling in the Asia Pacific Rim: A coming together of neighbours special issue, 17–23.

Lewis, R. E. & Hatch, T. (2008). Cultivating strengths-based professional identities. *Professional School Counseling*, 12(2), 115–118.

Luk-Fong, P. Y. Y. (2006). Hybridity in a guidance curriculum in Hong Kong. *International Journal for the Advancement of Counseling*, 28(4), 331–342.

Luk-Fong, P. Y. Y. (2010). Towards a hybrid conceptualization of Chinese women primary school teachers' changing femininities: A case study of Hong Kong. *Gender and Education*, 22(1), 73–86.

Luk-Fong, Y. Y. P. & Brennan, M. (2004). In search of a guidance curriculum for Hong Kong schools. *Journal of Educational Enquiry*, 5(1), 55–84.

Luke, M. & Goodrich, K. M. (2010). Chi Sigma Iota chapter leadership and professional identity development in early career counselors. *Counselor Education & Supervision*, 50(1), 56–78.

Mackenzie, S. (2007). A review of recent developments in the role of the SENCo in the UK. *British Journal of Special Education*, 34(4), 212–218.

Miller, J. & Garran, A. M. (2008). *Racism in the United States: Implications for the helping professions*. Belmont, CA: Thomson Brooks/Cole.

Nelson, K. W. & Jackson, S. A. (2003). Professional counselor identity development: A qualitative study of Hispanic student interns. *Counselor Education & Supervision*, 43(1), 2–13.

Niekerk, L. V. & Savin-Baden, M. (2010). Relocating truths in the qualitative research paradigm. In M. Savin-Baden & C. H. Major (Eds), *New approaches to qualitative research: Wisdom and uncertainty*. New York, NY: Routledge, pp. 28–36.

Pratt, M. G., Rockmann, K. W. & Kaufmann, J. B. (2006). Constructing professional identity: the role of work and identity learning cycles in the customization of identity among medical residents. *The Academy of Management Journal, 49*(2), 235–262.

Reisetter, M., Korcuska, J. S., Yextey, M., Bonds, D., Nikel, H. & McHenry, W. (2004). Counselor educators and qualitative research: Affirming a research identity. *Counselor Education and Supervision, 44*(1), 2–16.

Riessman, C. K. (2008). *Narrative methods for the human sciences.* Thousand Oaks, CA: Sage Publications.

Romano, J. L., Goh, M. & Wahl, K. H. (2005). School counseling in the United States: Implications for the Asia-Pacific region. *Asia Pacific Education Review, 6*(2), 113–123.

Shek, M. M. P. (2013). Hong Kong school guidance and counselling service: Development and approach. In P. Y. Y. Luk-Fong & Y. C. Lee-Man (Eds), *School guidance and counselling: Trends and practices.* Hong Kong: Hong Kong University Press, pp. 1–26.

Shurts, M., Cashwell, C. S., Spurgeon, S. L., Degges-White, S., Barrio, C. & Kardatzke, K. (2006). Preparing counselors-in-training to work with couples: Using role-plays and reflecting teams. *The Family Journal, 14*(2), 151–157.

Stinchfield, T. A., Hill, N. R. & Kleist, D. M. (2007). The reflective model of triadic supervision: Defining an emerging modality. *Counselor Education and Supervision, 46*(3), 172–183.

Studer, J. (2007). Erik Erikson's psychosocial stages applied to supervision. *Guidance and Counseling, 21*(3), 168–173.

Trahar, S. (2011). 'Burt's story reminded me of my grandmother': using a reflecting team to facilitate learning about narrative data analysis. In S. Trahar (Ed.), *Learning and teaching narrative inquiry: Travelling in the borderlands.* Amsterdam: John Benjamins Pub. Co, pp. 141–156.

Watkins, C. (2001). Comprehensive guidance programme in an international context. *Professional School Counsellor, 4*(4), 262–271.

Watkins, C. & Wagner, P. (2000). *Improving school behaviour.* London: Paul Chapman/Sage.

Webster, L. & Mertova, P. (2007). *Using narrative inquiry as a research method: An introduction to using critical event narrative analysis in research on learning and teaching.* London: Routledge.

Yip, C. P. L. (2013). A conversation with Ah Leung. In S. Trahar (Ed.), *Contextualising narrative inquiry: Developing methodological approaches for local contexts.* New York: Routledge, pp. 122–139.

Yu, W. M. & Lau, C. K. (2011). Teaching narrative inquiry in the Chinese community: A Hong Kong perspective. In S. Trahar (Ed.), *Learning and teaching narrative inquiry: Travelling in the borderlands.* Amsterdam: John Benjamins Publishing, pp. 71–86.

Zaffuto, S. R. (2005). Integration of traditional Japanese educational guidance with school counseling: A collaborative approach for the challenges of program implementation. *Asian Journal of Counselling, 12*(1), 17–45.

Zhou, N., Lam, S. F. & Chan, K. C. (2012). The Chinese classroom paradox: A cross-cultural comparison of teacher controlling behaviors. *Journal of Educational Psychology, 104*(4), 1162–1174.

7 Enhancing understanding across generations through sharing personal narratives

Yu Wai Ming

> We are born into a world of stories. Our births mark the beginning of a distinctive story in which each of us assumes a leading part. Our deaths end our unique stories, which live on in the minds and hearts of our survivors.
>
> Bochner *et al.*, 2000, p. 11

Introduction

My passion for narrative inquiry drives me to move forward in the academic work I pursue. Besides using narrative inquiry in designing research, I also use it in my teaching. In this chapter I share the experience of using narratives to create a common learning platform for people from different generations to understand each other. In 2010 I developed and taught a course called 'Narrative Perspective of Stories in Life' to undergraduate students. I have continued to develop this course and, in recent years, it was opened to students from the Elder Academy in the Hong Kong Institute of Education (HKIEd). The elderly students are all aged over 60 and retired. This is one of the courses that allows young people and the elderly to learn together in the same class.

The establishment of the Elder Academy in HKIEd is a response to the expanding aging population in Hong Kong, as in many other developed countries, with an aim to encourage lifelong learning and promote active and healthy life styles for the elderly. The elderly can choose to attend courses that are of interest to them. The courses are not tailor made for the elderly but are regular courses for the young undergraduates. 'Narrative Perspective of Stories in Life' is one of these courses. It transpired that in this particular course, the elderly did not only learn passively together with younger people but a special chemistry, between students of different ages, backgrounds and life experiences was sparked in the class.

The design of this course was inspired by fundamental ideas in narrative inquiry emphasising making meaning of one's own life experience and those of others. In this course, students are introduced to some basic concepts in narrative inquiry, and are given opportunities to tell their personal stories and listen to other people's stories. Participants use storytelling intensively within and beyond the classroom. Storytelling becomes a relational activity that allows participants to listen to and understand each other more deeply. My role is as the teacher and facilitator in class. As a teacher, I am also a practitioner researcher, always reflecting on my practice. The course adopts an experiential approach. There are two major assignments: (a) writing and presenting students' own chronicles and (b) conducting a narrative inquiry, mainly through in-depth interviews, on a significant person in the student's life. Thus, through a safe community we build together, students tell their own stories.

You are about to join my journey into exploring how storytelling is used to cross different generations. In this chapter, I share with you some positive effects that narratives can bring in improving the understanding between the elderly and young people. I choose some of the stories individuals shared in the mixed group of elderly and young adults to show their struggles and everyday life experiences. These stories are in the form of autobiographies. The sharing of these stories shows the potential of using narratives to increase understanding across generations in Hong Kong.

Cross generations . . . sometimes filled with misunderstandings

Earlier research showed that older adults' perceptions of children's attitudes toward them were more negative than the children's actual attitudes (Nishi-Strattner & Myers, 1983, p. 389). Most early research about intergenerational communication between young people and those aged 65 years and over generally reported their communication as negative because young people felt they had to handle painful self-disclosures from the elderly.

In Williams' and Giles' study (1996), conversations between college students and non-family elders aged 65–85 years, were dissatisfying when respondents perceived older people as being under-accommodative, complaining about their ill-health and difficult life-circumstances (Coupland *et al.*, 1988), and when they were overly self-disclosive (Coupland *et al.*, 1991). Research results seemed to have supported the phenomenon that older people might be stereotyped as complaining and moaning about their lives and their aches and pains and they were criticised as more narrow-minded than the young (Williams and Garrett, 2011, p. 273).

In Hong Kong, the misunderstandings and conflicts between generations have become a very concrete and continued focus of investigation by different social organisations, for example, The Hong Kong Federation of Youth Groups (2008) and Hong Kong Young Women's Christian Association (2009). Similar conflicts between generations were reported. Older generations seem to have stereotyped younger people as less hard working, ambitious but less realistic and taking advantage of living with their parents for longer periods than previous generations. They are sometimes labelled as 'post 80s', and in English as Generation Y. In the study Wu (2010, p. ii) carried out on the post 80s in Hong Kong, he found that they are in a disadvantaged position of 'higher unemployment rates, lower starting salaries, and insecure jobs . . . protracting [their] transition from school to work and from childhood to adulthood [difficult]'. This is the result of growing up in the context of rapid social changes, in particular, the economic restructuring and educational expansions in the 1990s.

Despite constant research findings pointing to generation gaps, other intergenerational studies suggest 'more positive relations with others are associated with better psychological well-being' (Xu, 2012, p. 44). It is important to note that people's personal evaluation of their own life – whether they perceive many pleasant things, engage in interesting activities and are satisfied with their life in general – may contribute to joy and happiness (Ryan & Deci, 2001). Particularly for the elderly, the more emotional support they receive from their adult children, the more likely they are to be satisfied with their own lives (Xu, 2012, p. 44).

To conclude, research findings may not offer concrete evidence for the existence of a real generation gap. Yet, there is a continual intergenerational debate on the lack of communication between generations. Research findings also suggest that positive communication could possibly bring better psychological well-being for different generations.

Narrative inquiry as a research methodology in a Chinese community

My curiosity in using stories in academic research started in 1998 from the first course I did as part of my doctoral journey. To me, narrative inquiry was a new approach to research with which I did not feel comfortable. Instead, in my first encounters with narratives, I was often torn between the research concepts I had learned from my previous academic training in Hong Kong and Britain in the 80s and 90s and the new narrative concepts I was exposed to in my doctoral courses at the Ontario Institute for Studies in Education of the University of Toronto (OISE/UT). From the narrative theses I read, the new understanding of teacher education I obtained undoubtedly gave me different perspectives on human experiences but also caused tensions at work. Those colleagues who shared my excitement in the new understanding of educational research also questioned the significance of telling stories in an academic world. I have shared these tensions in other writing (Yu, 2005; Yu and Lau, 2011).

Since I started my doctoral thesis journey with my supervisor, Professor Michael Connelly, I have been cautious about the possible tensions in using narrative inquiry in the local context of Hong Kong. I completed my thesis in 2005, and in the past ten years or so, from time to time, a small group of colleagues, also Professor Connelly's students, work together collaboratively on research projects. In collaborating outside this small circle, however, I find it hard to adopt narrative inquiry in research design, as the majority of colleagues in my workplace do not use it – and moreover are sceptical about its value. Narrative inquiry is still new to the educational field in Hong Kong no matter how established a methodology it has become in other contexts.

Human beings have been filling the world with stories for as long as we have been able to talk, but still, narrative inquiry appears new, in particular in its relatively recent emergence as a methodology in the field of social science research (Clandinin and Rosiek, 2007). This marks a shift of inquiry focus from objects to meanings, following the interpretive turn (Rainbow and Sullivan, 1987). Bochner *et al.* (2000) recognise a new generation of social scientists who are beginning to appreciate the profound significance of narrative in the lived experience of personal relationships. Over the past 30 years, interest in narrative among social scientists has mushroomed in the European and North American contexts.

In the Chinese communities of Mainland China, Taiwan and Hong Kong, narrative inquiry has started to gain attention in the recent decade even though the pace of its development in these places differs (Yu and Lau, 2011). In Hong Kong, more people have become interested in narrative inquiry but the number is still in the minority. The number of educational research projects funded by the Research Grants Council (RGC)[1] under the University Grants Committee (UGC) gives an idea of the distribution of funding for educational research in Hong Kong higher education. A great majority of the 108 projects funded in the education field in the past five years, between 2009 and 2013, follow the quantitative orientation.

The meanings of stories are interpreted and analysed (Chase, 2003) following the narrative way of thinking – a unique way of understanding experience in the narrative approach. In Clandinin and Huber's view (2010), narrative inquiry is a way of thinking about and studying experience, a specific feature that other qualitative methods may not have. Narrative inquiry allows us to understand the world at a micro-level, which is much needed in any study of experience. As Freeman (2006) argues, there is an increasing emphasis in narrative inquiry on 'small' stories rather than 'big' stories. These stories are those that human beings have lived out and told about living for as long as we have been able to talk and are ways we fill our world with meaning.

I adopt the frame developed for narrative inquiry by Clandinin and Connelly (2000), later modified by Clandinin and Huber (2010), created by the commonplaces of temporality, sociality and place. Narrative inquiry, in this frame, highlights ethical matters and shapes new theoretical understandings of people's experiences. Attending to experience through inquiry into all three commonplaces distinguishes it from other methodologies. To think narratively is to understand that our world is shifting, changing and personal. It is distinguished from the dominant views of seeing the story of a phenomenon as fixed and unchanging. This distinction was named by Clandinin and Huber (2010, p. 438) as the 'ongoing temporality of experience'. In the course, I attempt to promote this particular way of thinking by helping students see our experience as developing along with temporality. I also use the metaphor of parade (Geertz, 1996) to capture the change of experience over time. In a parade, it is impossible to look at only one event without seeing the event nested within the wholeness of the parade. It is this way of thinking that I consider to be typical of a narrative inquiry.

Narrative inquiry as a tool for enhancing cross generational understanding

It is generally agreed by narrative inquirers that

> people shape their daily lives by stories of who they and others are and as they interpret their past in terms of their stories. Story somehow, becomes a portal through which a person enters the world and by which their experience of the world is interpreted and made personally meaningful.
>
> Connelly & Clandinin, 2006, p. 375

Storytelling is used as a tool for intergenerational communication as it plays an important and powerful role in understanding and organising human experience. It is used in a course offered to a mixed age group to facilitate students in organising and reflecting their own experiences. 'Storytelling is a direct and obvious form of recollecting memories, because the modalities of experience are temporal and the images preserved in memory are cinematic, transient episodes that gain significance and continuity by being situated in a story' (Crites, 1971, p. 291). Students were encouraged to complete a chronicle and present it in class. They also used narrative interviews to complete a mini narrative inquiry project.

My role is therefore as a researcher studying my own experience in using narratives to create a platform for communication across generations and a facilitator building a zone of comfort for students to share their personal stories. As a practitioner researcher, all relevant qualitative methods like journalling, participant observation and unstructured interviews are used. As a facilitator, I promote the importance of confidentiality, respect and trust to be built among participants. In every chronicle presentation, I repeatedly remind participants to respect each other's privacy, to keep what they hear in strict confidence, in order to build a trustworthy and safe space for sharing personal stories.

How older and younger adults come to learn together

It was an opportunity created in the winter of 2013. In one of the courses I teach, I started to recruit elderly students so that young university students will learn together with them. This is a general education course on narrative inquiry offered to both undergraduates and elderly students coming from the Elder Academy in the HKIEd. Among the 45 students enrolled in this cohort, five are elderly students. Students are encouraged to tell personal stories by means of chronicling and to collect stories from someone they choose, probably outside the group, by means of carrying out a narrative inquiry, as explained earlier.

Besides lectures, students gain knowledge by applying narrative inquiry in the course of learning. In other words, the course employs experiential learning (Kolb, 1984; Moon, 2004) in order to enable students to gain a first-hand experience of narrative by making meaning from their own life experience and that of other people. Such design is also based on a strong belief that the best way to learn narrative is by experiencing it. Narrative learning happens naturally from the stories people tell about their lives. It becomes both a means of 'knowing' and a way of 'telling' about the social world (Bochner *et al.*, 2000, p. 16; Brody, 1987; Richardson, 1990).

Two assignments including the construction of a personal chronicle and conducting of narrative interviews are required. The first assignment of a chronicle is used based on the belief that 'our births mark the beginning of a distinctive story in which each of us assumes a leading part' (Bochner *et al.*, 2000, p. 13) and that narrative is a way people express a continuity of experience over time (Crites, 1986). Reflecting on what one has lived thus far is a valuable learning process. Students are required to plan for a 15-minute presentation of their own chronicles in class around the main theme of 'How I became who I am'.

In the second assignment, students are asked to interview someone they want to know more deeply and then write a report on the interviewee's life stories. Based on the belief that narrative inquiry often begins in the midst of ongoing experiences and concludes still in the midst, no strict interview direction is given to the students to begin the inquiry journey. Instead, I emphasise to them that narrative inquiry is composed around strong curiosity in other people's life experience rather than thinking about framing a research question with a precise definition or expectation of an answer. Narrative inquirers carry 'a sense of a search . . . a sense of continual reformulation' in the process of inquiry (Clandinin & Connelly, 2000, p. 124).

Changing the stereotype of seeing young adults

During the presentation of chronicles, one elderly student started to share the experience of young students. After listening to the students' chronicle presentations, an elderly student who used to have negative impressions of young people, came to me and shared her different understanding:

> We start to see our younger generation differently now. Before hearing their stories, I always stereotype them as simple minded, reliant, less responsible and less mature than we were in our younger days, as we usually see from the media's criticisms of today's young people. By hearing the stories they told of themselves in their presentations, I have a very different view about them. Before coming to class, we heard and were inclined to agree that our younger generation becomes more and more dependent on their parents. It is a different picture we see after hearing them tell their stories.

This comment was made with reference to stories the young adults told in class about their 20 years of life. In this section, the excerpts from two stories are reported as examples that have contributed to a different understanding of the younger generation for the elderly students. Stories in this chapter are used with the consent of students and pseudonyms are used. I will now present the stories verbatim to preserve their raw form, while further analysis is made in the latter part of this chapter.

Jonathan's story

I used to be an introvert, very timid, pessimistic and have low self-esteem. I come from a single-parent family. We used to live in the poor rural outskirts of Hong Kong in my childhood because we were extremely poor at that time and could not afford high rent in urban areas.

I was told that my mother had been forced to marry my father by my grandfather. She was then forced to live in deep agony and pessimism. Later in her life, she got an unknown disease and became very ill. My father, unfortunately, died when I was very small. My mother's experience has had some negative effect on my character. I grew up with my mum and also with very low self-esteem.

I studied in a shabby village school with a small number of students. Throughout my school years, I was always among the bottom students in class.

My childhood was full of bitter memories. I was quite attached to a very naughty boy during my primary school years. One day when I was wandering with him in the village after school, I hurt myself badly after imitating him jump over a wide ditch. He landed on the other side safely, but unluckily, I fell into the ditch and landed on a wooden log hammered with sharp rusty nails. Both my classmate and I did not know what to do about the bleeding from my arm and leg. A villager passed by and helped cover my wounds with some smashed weed taken from the nearby slope to stop me bleeding. As a result, my wounds were infected and I got a fever and was sent to the hospital a few days later.

Another incident was even more miserable. During my stay in mainland visiting my grandmother, I went to play around in nearby villages with some kids there. The hygiene then in the village area was extremely poor. I remembered seeing used medical equipment like needles and bandages lying around uncovered. That day, I walked past a narrow pathway while a small boy was swinging a needle-sharp object, which hit me in my right eye. This accident brought irreparable damage to my eye, and till now, even with lens changed, I still need to have regular checkups and cannot read without my thick glasses.

Jessica's story

I was brought up in a single-child family in Beijing. I used to live with my parents and grandparents, who treated me like a princess. I did well in my study and was luckily admitted to a popular high school where I made good friends with whom I established some long lasting relationships. I concluded my chapter of secondary school life as *simple* and *happy*.

In 2009, I left my family and a familiar place to pursue university study in Hong Kong. The first difficulty I encountered was the communication problem. Till then, I spoke only Putonghua and had no experience in communicating with people who did not know my mother tongue. However, in Hong Kong, the major medium of instruction in university is Cantonese and English. It took me a long time to get accustomed to learning in a foreign language, besides learning to be independent and living far away from home.

When I started to gain some confidence in studying in Hong Kong, an exchange opportunity in Germany came to me. I spent half a year there as an exchange student in the first semester of my Year 2. I made many friends coming from elsewhere around the world, and we learnt from each other's culture and stories we shared. I concluded my first two years in university as *curious, humble, treasured* and *grateful.*

In the summer of Year 2, I gained a working holiday trip to Korea. I did not speak any Korean at that time. I went there to work as a full-time clerk for two months in an international business firm. It is a part of an overall programme extending student teachers' learning experiences in other contexts. That summer became the busiest summer I have ever had. In this working trip, I learnt to be patient and strong. I also realised that to respect and being respected is a two-way interactive process. I concluded my current chapter of life as *rich, satisfied* and *lucky.*

Widening perspectives of young adults on the elderly

The fisherman's story reported here is taken from a student's second assignment – the mini narrative inquiry. The majority of the younger students chose to interview their parents and some even managed to interview their grandparents. In the reflections they appended to their reports, students wrote about the lessons they learnt. Many of them wrote in their conclusions that they understood their interviewees – mostly their parents – in a different way after hearing them tell stories. The story a fisherman father told is selected to give readers some sense of the stories students wrote. What follows is the reflection the student made after interviewing his father. Again, further analysis is made in the latter part of this chapter.

A fisherman father's story

I was born into a fisherman's family in mainland in the late 1950s. Life at that time was miserable. The whole family worked extremely hard on a fishing boat to make ends meet for the nine members of my family. The catch fluctuated. Even with a high catch, we were unable to make good money. The merchants always cheated us in trading, as my parents were illiterates. The social welfare systems then were less established. Only rich people could afford to go to school.

My parents heard people say that Hong Kong was a land of gold. Many people were attracted to Hong Kong because almost all those who had emigrated illegally had returned with riches, at least by appearance. Subsequently, a large number of mainlanders risked their lives to migrate to Hong Kong.

Somehow, my father managed to find a way to trade his fishing licence for a legal identity for one family member – their eldest son – me. I moved unwillingly to Hong Kong, alone, when I was just a teenager. I sought shelter at my uncle's house in Hong Kong, far away from home.

Later, I found out the main reasons why my parents sent me to Hong Kong. One was to study; the other was to create access to Hong Kong for other family members. Apart from studying, my greatest pastime was listening to the radio.

Whenever I heard Danny Chan's song, I would be deeply touched and closely linked to my family members who were fishing far away. My tears would run naturally down my cheeks. The faces of family members came to my mind always when there were boats passing by on the sea where I was living. The reflection of the moon on the sea always reminded me of the time I spent with my family.

Jack's reflection

In the reflection, Student Jack wrote the following:

The song about remembering the love of parents sung by a local pop singer, Danny Chan who passed away at a young age, has become my father's favourite. The extract of the lyrics ran like this:

> *Lonely long night accompanying it is an empty pillow by my side*
> *Miles and miles away*
> *Crystal green sea represents my heart*
> *Love from my dear mom and dad*
> *Is as kind as the clear moon*
> *Lingering in my mind*
> *How can I not feel sad*

I understand why the lyrics of Danny Chan's song touched my father's heart so dearly. As the eldest son of the family, he needed to accomplish his father's wish of migrating the whole family to a brighter future in Hong Kong. He needed to help the other siblings to move to gain opportunities to study. Yet, he himself was just a teenager at that time. From my father's story, I can see the extremely heavy load on his shoulders.

This explains why he has become so tough in his later days. He never fears anything, not even death. He recalled the historical background during his boat life – in the mid-60s, people in mainland China were faced with great political turbulence and suffered from civic wars and the Cultural Revolution. Many mainlanders started to emigrate to Hong Kong illegally. Frequently when my father's boat sailed near the border of Hong Kong and Macau, they would see people swimming in the hostile sea to their dreamland – Hong Kong.

Sometimes in the fisherman's catch, they did not only get fresh seafood but also 'salted fish' (slang for dead people). These people died of exhaustion or from being attacked by sharks. The dead bodies might not be whole pieces. This scenario was very frightening to a kid of eight or nine but my father told me that he eventually got used to it. From these experiences, he realised how fragile and shaky life is.

My father told me that his life experiences had made him grow much more mature than his age and he learnt to treasure life and his family members much more. In his childhood, wealth was never his concern. He could easily feel satisfied if his family could stay together. He enjoyed his time with his brothers and sisters. Though their life was poor, their hearts were full of love and joy.

Meanings of narrative for cross generational understanding

Narrative inquiry is used as an umbrella term that captures personal and human dimensions of experience over time and takes into account the relationship between individual experience and the cultural context (Clandinin & Connelly, 2000). From my observation, the elderly and the younger generation start to move towards each other in some very subtle ways. This is seen as the effect brought about by storytelling. In Weinstein's view (1988), storytelling is not only the way we understand our relationships; it is also the means by which our relationships are fashioned. A personal relationship, in this sense, is a work of art, something we make rather than give.

Narrative thinking happening at different layers

In completing two assignments, students have to first of all, tell their own life stories in the form of a chronicle; second try out narrative inquiry by interviewing and writing a report on a targeted person. In the ways they make meaning from their stories, narrative thinking is observed. Students did not perceive the stories as static facts but started to appreciate the rich and fluid meanings in their social and historical contexts. In the process of telling, the stories become something more than a chronological series of events. 'It is a gathering together of events into a meaningful story' (Polkinghorne, 1988, p. 131). In the construction of their own chronicles, students make sense of their own experiences in different times and places. Both Jonathan and Jessica were given a safe environment in which to tell their stories. I shared my own stories that further resonated by hearing their stories. After hearing each chronicle presentation, students were required to write their feedback to the presenter on a small piece of paper. All feedback was collected and distributed to the presenter near the end of the course.

Through telling and listening to other people's life stories, students found that everyone's life stories are socially and historically situated in their lives. By telling their life stories, the students do not only recall their life experiences, they also have to frame their experiences in the form of stories and explore what their stories mean to them. Jonathan and Jessica also made meaning of what they understood about their own experiences accessible to others by telling classmates their stories. Baddeley and Singer (2007, pp. 177–178) review its significance by confirming that a life story is 'not simply an expression of the underlying construct of identity, but it is the fundamental way in which we know ourselves and to a large extent are known by others'.

In addition, in doing the mini narrative inquiries, when students began to use narrative interviews with other people, they also made use of storytelling to delve into other people's experiences. By reconstructing the stories of the fisherman parent, experiences between birth and death were revisited. We rely on

> stories circulating through our culture to make sense of our everyday lives and guide our actions. Much of who we are and what we do originates in the tales passed down to us and the stories we take on as our own.
>
> Bochner *et al.*, 2000, p. 13

The students reflected that they had a good opportunity to exercise narrative at different stages, both in reviewing their own life experiences and those of other people. Also, they saw that their 'relationships are not objective or static' in Dindia and Duck's words (2000, p. xi). Students reflected that they understood their experiences as framed by stories in a different perspective – one which they might not be able to name – but which we know potentially as a narrative way of thinking. This new perspective has somehow helped people cross generations. They agreed that they know each other not only from a single perspective but from each other's viewpoint.

Gaining a new understanding of each other from storytelling

By creating a platform for telling stories, the elderly students gained a chance to enter into the young people's world. They heard stories even young people themselves might not tell at home. Two of the elderly students who had children of a similar age told me that they could not afford to miss the chronicle presentations and thus ended up achieving a full attendance record. Both of them were mothers and they treasured the chance to reach the hearts of the younger generation. In their presentations, young people told us how they had made meaning from their life experiences.

Narrative is the means through which we integrate experience to explain how we have remained the same or changed (Bruner, 1986; McLean, 2008; Pasupathi & Mansour, 2006). In Jonathan's story, the elderly students learned that some less fortunate students had led a poor life in a developed city like Hong Kong. This understanding contradicted the stereotype of young people created by the media as immature and irresponsible. Moreover, Jessica's story represents another version of a young person, of one who has not been spoilt as a single child but who has lived to be independent, open-minded and adventurous. She has strived hard to learn and explore the unknown world with her young mind. 'The reflective process of autobiographical reasoning takes time: that is, developing an understanding of links between the past and the self takes distance and perspective' (Xu, 2008, p. 254).

The elderly and young students might not have miraculously become close friends after storytelling. However, it is seen that both of them began to navigate into each other's world with a more open mind. Storied lives often possess a relational focus, first, because the story defines who an individual is in relation to others, and second because self-accounts attempt to achieve harmony with the significant others of the narrator and of themselves (Rosenwald & Ochberg, 1992).

Co-construction of new meaning in lives

As demonstrated earlier, narratives somehow enable the elderly to understand the young adults from a different perspective. In this section, narrative is seen to have allowed young adults to understand the elderly, mainly their parents, with a closer relationship being established. Younger students have not yet had a chance to understand the elderly in class as the elderly students can choose not to do homework and those in this class chose not to do any.

In the second assignment, in which interviews were conducted with their family members, new relational understandings emerged. The reflective reports students wrote about their parents have suggested new insights gained of their elderly family members at home. Their stories reflected one way they came to understand how their parents had become who they were. The relationship between them seemed to have been linked more closely. Some students even revealed that they heard some family stories that they had never had a chance to hear before. This construction of personal relationships is seen as the conversational work through which 'two people negotiate, co-construct, and story the meanings and values of essentially incomplete experiences' (Bochner *et al.*, 2000, p. 17). The focus here is the process of co-constructing meaning with others (Bochner, 1994; Duck & Pittman, 1994).

In the fisherman's story, Jack happened to realise how tough his father had become because of the poverty he suffered in his childhood. He understood that successful coping with stressful turning points in life is dependent on one's ability to construct meanings (Bochner *et al.*, 2000; Harvey *et al.*, 1992; Weber & Harvey, 1994). From what his father told him, Jack started to learn why he had not feared death. Jack also learnt the deep meaning of family to his father. 'Some narrative inquirers see themselves and their participants as co-composing each aspect of the inquiry as well as their lives as they live out the inquiry' (Clandinin & Huber, 2010, p. 437). This part of the assignment is co-created by the joint actions of two people. A personal relationship lives as a contingent sequence of intertwined experiences, given shape and meaning by the stories that form and inform its enactments. To have or be in a relationship is to have or be in a story and, usually, to want to tell about it. When we tell others about our relationships, we portray events in the form and language of stories: who did what to whom, where, when and why (Bochner *et al.*, 2000, p. 17). Through engaging with participants, narrative inquirers see themselves and participants as each retelling their own stories, and as coming to changed identities and practices through the inquiry process.

Conclusion

In this chapter, I have focussed on storytelling used as a relational activity that gathers people to listen to and understand one another. The generation gap is not understood simply as being narrowed by elderly and young students moving toward each other. From the feedback of both elderly and young students, some positive effect was seen in cross generational relationships. On the one hand, elderly students found a new understanding of today's young people through the chronicles they presented. On the other hand, young students who have listened to their parents' stories found that they had begun to know older family members differently. Some of the stories they shared were never told before.

Narrative inquiry may not be a solution in bridging the generation gap, but it is clearly a possible platform for enhancing understanding between generations in Hong Kong.

Note

1 Research Grants Council (RGC) operates under the University Grants Committee (UGC) and is responsible for allocating research grant funding from the Government to the public funded universities in Hong Kong. The number of successful grants gained by an individual university are considered reflective of the higher status of its research capacity.

References

Baddeley J. & Singer, J. A. (2007). Charting the life story's path: narrative identity across the life span. In D. J. Clandinin (Ed.), *Handbook of narrative inquiry: mapping a methodology*. Thousand Oaks, CA: SAGE Publications, pp. 177–201.

Bochner, A. P. (1994). Perspectives on inquiry II: theories and stories. In M. Knapp & G. Miller (Eds), *Handbook of interpersonal communication*, 2nd ed. Newbury park, CA: Sage, pp. 21–41.

Bochner, A. P., Ellis, C. & Tillmann-Healy, L. M. (2000). Relationships as stories: Accounts, storied lives, evocative narratives. In K. Dindia & S. Duck (Eds), *Communication and personal relationships*. Chichester: John Wiley and Sons, Ltd, pp. 13–29.

Brody, H. (1987). *Stories of sickness*. New Haven, CT: Yale University Press.

Bruner, J. (1986). *Actual minds, possible worlds*. Cambridge, MA: Harvard University Press.

Chase, S. E. (2003). Learning to listen: narrative principles in a qualitative research methods course. In R. Josselson, A. Liebich & D. P. Mc-Adams, (Eds). *Up close and personal: The teaching and learning of narrative research*, Washington, DC: American Psychological Association, pp. 79–100.

Clandinin, D. J. & Connelly, F. M. (2000). *Narrative inquiry: Experience and story in qualitative research*. San Francisco: Jossey-Bass.

Clandinin, D. J. & Rosiek, J. (2007). Mapping a landscape of narrative inquiry. *Journal of Teacher Education*, 58:1, 21–35.

Clandinin, D. J. & Huber, J. (2010). Narrative inquiry. In B. McGaw, E. Baker & P. P. Peterson (Eds), *International encyclopedia of education* (3rd ed.). New York, NY: Elsevier.

Connelly, F. M. and Clandinin, D. J. (2006). Narrative inquiry. In Green, J., Camilli, G. and Elmore, P. (Eds), *Handbook of complementary methods in education research*. Mahwah, NJ: Lawrence Erlbaum, pp. 375–385.

Coupland, N., Coupland, J. & Giles, H. (1991). *Language, society, and the elderly: discourse, identity and aging*. Oxford: Blackwell.

Coupland, N., Coupland, J., Giles, H. & Henwood, K. (1988). Accommodating the elderly: Invoking and extending a theory. *Language in Society*, 17:1, 1–41.

Crites, S. (1971). The narrative quality of experience. *Journal of the American Academy of Religion*, 39:3, 291–311.

Crites, S. (1986). Storytime: recollecting the past and projecting the future. In T. Sarbin (Ed.), *Narrative psychology: the storied nature of human conduct.* New York: Praeger, pp. 152–173.

Dindia, K. & Duck, S. (Eds) (2000). *Communication and personal relationships.* Chichester: John Wiley and Sons, Ltd.

Duck, S. W. & Pittman, G. (1994). Social and personal relationships. In M. Knapp & G. Miller (Eds), *Handbook of interpersonal communication,* 2nd ed. Newbury Park, CA: Sage, pp. 676–695.

Freeman, M. (2006). Life 'on holiday'?: In defense of big stories. *Narrative Inquiry,* 16:1, 131–138.

Geertz, C. (1996). *After the fact: Two countries, four decades, one anthropologist.* USA: Harvard University Press.

Harvey, J. H., Orbuch, T., Weber, A. L., Merbach, N. & Alt, R. (1992). House of pain and hope: Accounts of loss. *Death Studies,* 16:2, 99–124.

Hong Kong Young Women's Christian Association. (2009). *Research report on the situation of conflicts between youth and parents.* Hong Kong: Youth and Community Service Survey and Research Group, Hong Kong Young Women's Christian Association. In Chinese.

Kolb, D. (1984). *Experiential learning: Experience as the source of learning and development.* Englewood Cliffs, NJ: Prentice Hall.

McLean, K. C. (2008). Stories of the young and the old: Personal continuity and narrative identity. *Developmental Psychology,* 44:1, 254–264.

Moon, J. (2004). *A handbook of reflective and experiential learning: Theory and practice.* London: Routledge Falmer.

Nishi-Strattner, M. and Myers, J. E. (1983). Attitudes toward the elderly: An intergenerational examination. *Educational Gerontology,* 9:5/6, 389–397.

Pasupathi, K. & Mansour, E. (2006). Adult age differences in autobiographical reasoning in narratives. *Developmental Psychology,* 42:5, 798–808.

Polkinghorne, D. E. (1988). *Narrative knowing and the human sciences.* Albany: State University of New York Press.

Rainbow, P. & Sullivan, W. (1987). *Interpretive social science: A second look.* Berkeley, CA: University of California Press.

Richardson, L. (1990). Narrative and sociology. *Journal of Contemporary Ethnography,* 19:1, 116–135.

Rosenwald, G. C. & Ochberg, R. L. (Eds) (1992). *Storied lives: The cultural politics of self-understanding.* New Haven, CT: Yale University Press.

Ryan, R. & Deci, E. (2001). Self-determination theory and the facilitation of intrinsic motivation, social development, and well-being. *American Psychologist,* 55:1, 68–78.

The Hong Kong Federation of Youth Groups (2008). Youth Poll Series Nos. 154 & 155: *The views of parents and youth on parent-child conflicts.* Hong Kong: The Hong Kong Federation of Youth Groups. In Chinese.

Weber, A. L. & Harvey, J. H. (1994). Accounts in coping with relationship loss. In A. L. Weber & J. H. Harvey (Eds), *Perspectives on close relationships.* Needham Heights, MA: Allyn & Bacon.

Weinstein, A. (1988). *The fiction of relationship.* Princeton, NJ: Princeton University Press.

Williams, A. & Giles, H. (1996). Retrospecting intergenerational conversations: The perspective of young adults. *Human Communication Research,* 23:2, 220–250.

Williams, A. & Garrett, P. (2011). Teenagers' perceptions of communication and 'good communication' with peers, young adults, and older adults. *Language Awareness*, 21: 3, 267–278.

Wu, X. (2010). *A central policy unit commissioned report: Hong Kong's post-80s generation: profiles and predicaments*. Hong Kong: Hong Kong University of Science and Technology.

Xu, J. (2012). Filial piety and intergenerational communication in China: A nationwide study. *The Journal of International Communication*, 18: 1, 33–48.

Yu, W. M. (2005). *An experiential study on the application of narrative inquiry in teacher development in Hong Kong*. Unpublished doctoral thesis.

Yu, W. M. & Lau, C. K. (2011). Teaching narrative inquiry in the Chinese community: A Hong Kong perspective. In S. Trahar (Ed.). *Learning and teaching narrative inquiry: travelling in the borderlands*. Amsterdam: John Benjamins Publishing Company, pp. 69–84.

8 Is the silent mode on?

Researching teachers' voices in Macao through narrative research

Sou Kuan Vong and Matilda Wong

Sou Kuan: Matilda, so as far as I remember this is our *first* time to sit down and talk about this [narrative research] so seriously.

Matilda: It's true, Sou Kuan, despite the fact that we have had some collaborations since 2006. We had some discussions on 'narrative inquiry' and then we had some interviews to collect 'life stories' and 'critical incidents' from teachers but we have never focussed our discussion on 'narrative research'.

Sou Kuan: Exactly! It seems that we were on the same ground. But, are we?

Matilda: Maybe not! My understanding of narrative research is mainly based on the perspective of Connelly and Clandinin. Yours is perhaps more from a sociological or critical perspective!

Sou Kuan: However, we do share the same ground because we are interested in exploring teachers' narratives, life and career and, furthermore, we are more concerned about teachers' empowerment.

A conversation in April, 2013

Matilda: We need to speed up a bit to meet the deadline [of this book chapter]!

Sou Kuan: Deadline again! Are we going to live with all these never-ending deadlines? Sigh!

Matilda: True! We have been so busy with our teaching work, administrative meetings, student recruitment and entry admission examination, and public services requested by the local government and many others. I just feel I'm living in a pressure cooker.

Sou Kuan: Yes! Just feel so vulnerable! And yet, doing all this has nothing to do with our career progression and promotion! The system relies on *visible outcomes,* that is, publications!

Matilda: This, in fact, makes me feel uncomfortable, particularly when we are working in the field of education. We always say in Chinese, 'It takes ten years to grow trees, but 100 to nurture people', so we may not even see the outcomes in our lifetime!

Sou Kuan: This is the exact feeling that I have! The current system purports to measure things and a person with some visible criteria, but those values which are significant [to education and teacher education] and that cannot be measured are all considered unimportant! It seems to me that it is not only a local issue in Macao, but a global issue!

Matilda: Yup! It is a bit ironic, isn't it? While we are concerned about the teachers' empowerment in Macao, we as teacher educators are disempowered in some way.

Sou Kuan: Very good observation! Well, wouldn't it be possible for us to incorporate this idea in our work [this book chapter] to develop a parallel public narrative to exhibit our counter-motion/emotion to this hegemony?

A conversation in January, 2014

Overture

The two conversations just given attempt to demonstrate parts of the original idea and evolution of this book chapter. We have been working on teachers' narratives for almost ten years, although we have different backgrounds and fields of specialisation. What, then, brings us together? In a broad sense, we have been working together in the field of teacher education in the same place for more than a decade; we are immersed in the same historical, social and cultural context and we witness and feel the pressing changes in Macao. Perhaps, this is not the sufficient condition for our collaboration. We believe that our shared interest in teachers' lives, life stories and their voices contributes to and, to a great extent, 'converges', despite not sharing the same training in narrative research. We use 'narrative research' in this chapter instead of 'narrative inquiry' because the latter is a specific conceptual framework, initiated by Connelly and Clandinin (1990), referring to a way of understanding and inquiring into experience through 'collaboration between researcher and participants, over time, in place or series of places, and in social interaction with milieus' (Clandinin & Connelly, 2000, p. 20). The three commonplaces of narrative inquiry, namely temporality, sociality and place, specify the dimensions of an inquirer and are the constructs of the whole conceptual framework. Owing to the fact that the story we discuss in this chapter does not strictly follow the complex research process of narrative inquiry as developed by Clandinin and Connelly, we do not use the exact term 'inquiry', but we refer to our work loosely as 'narrative research'. However, we acknowledge and consider our work as taking the same important stance of narrative inquiry in giving a voice to teachers through their own stories. We believe that narrative research, as Casey (1995) states, is an overarching category for a variety of contemporary research practices, including the collection and analysis of autobiographies, biographies, life writing and personal narratives, among many others. As such, some discussions on the use of narrative research in this chapter will be explained in later sections.

The theme of this chapter is the use of narrative research to enable voices to be heard. It builds on various narratives: the researchers' narratives, institutional narratives (interchangeable with public narratives) and teacher narratives. The researchers' narratives provide a background concerning the birth of this piece of work. The institutional narratives afford a comprehensive contextual background that crystallises the necessity of hearing Macao teachers' voices. We attempt two major objectives; namely, to tell the story and to tell it in such a way as to make the voices more accessible to a wider audience. Regarding the latter, we use a lively presentation, an attempt to 'break through' the traditional format of narration in a scholarly book. For instance, we incorporate our conversations at the beginning of the chapter in order to engage our readers with the central aspect of our context and actions. We also employ musical concepts to illustrate both the cultural aspect and the rhythm of this narrative. In effect, we are inspired by a notion from Dewey (1934) in his book entitled *Art as Experience*; thus we adopt a different form to narrate a story, as we believe that form is informed by experiences as well as being an expression of experiences. We want to show that there are many forms or ways to recover our voices (teachers' voices) and make them heard. And, narrative research is one of the ways of reviving and appreciating teachers' voices in Macao in the midst of the dominant quantitative research paradigms.

Regarding the 'form' that we mentioned earlier, we employ a set of musical concepts as signposts to relate our story. Why musical concepts? We have a story to tell. Last year, we visited Portugal. Sou Kuan had studied there many years ago but it was Matilda's first visit. Upon arrival, Matilda repeatedly mentioned the similarities between Macao and Lisbon, particularly the 'calçada', the Portuguese pavement. This reflects the colonial relationship of the two places. During the trip we intended to go to a 'Casa do Fado' (Fado Restaurant) but the restaurant was full. 'Fado' is a typical Portuguese music genre. It is a form of music infused with a sentiment of resignation, fatefulness, sadness and *saudade* (a Portuguese word which means 'longing' or 'missing a person') relating to nostalgia arising from sea navigation in the fifteenth and sixteenth centuries. *Fado*, in itself, narrates the encounter of Macao and Portugal in this specific historical context. After more than 450 years, when we relate the stories of teachers in Macao it is, in fact, a dialogue between the present and the past, between the Portuguese and Cantonese cultures. We use 'Overture' to introduce the objectives and overall structure of this chapter. The section entitled 'Composers' describes our backgrounds and epistemological beliefs. The section on 'Developing variation' outlines the literature review in respect of narrative research and our position with regard to this in the context of this chapter. The section on 'Fado and Cantopop' provides a dense contextual backdrop to elucidate the ways in which teachers' voices are monitored. The notions of 'Fado' and 'Cantopop' here convey a message concerning the interaction between the Portuguese heritage from the previous administration of Macao and the local Cantonese heritage. This section presents three narratives, namely 'A world of difference, the difference is Macao', 'Can you hear me?' and, 'Is narrative research travelling on a long and broken road in Macao?' The final section, 'Finale', concludes the chapter.

Composers

We use 'Composers' as a subtitle to define our narratives. This section explains who we are and why we want to tell our stories. We begin our story with a collective 'we'. The use of 'we' is perhaps provocative in narrative research, particularly in personal narratives because it may tend to render the story as less personal and more institutional (public). Therefore, it is necessary to explain this before we go further. The notion of 'we' in this context not only implies that our beliefs are in common but also embraces our differences originating from our subjectivities and positions. Middleton (1992) states that writing one's autobiography is in itself a process of disclosing the constitution of one's subjectivity. As such, the telling and retelling of a story is all about selection. In other words, what we *select* to narrate is related closely to our subjectivities and, possibly, our positions. As mentioned earlier, we have different educational and social backgrounds. For instance, the first author, Sou Kuan, obtained her doctoral degree in the UK in the area of the sociology of education and is very committed to social justice and teacher empowerment from a critical perspective. The second author, Matilda, holds a doctoral degree in teacher development from the Ontario Institute for Studies in Education, University of Toronto. She specialises in English language teaching and focusses her work on second language teacher development, particularly on teachers as reflective practitioners. Although we have differences, we are both enthusiastic about teacher education and teacher development. This is how our personal interests intersect with each other and connect to teacher narrative research in the context of Macao. MacIntyre (1981, p. 206) states that 'a story of a life is embedded in the story of communities where identity is formed'. Hence, when we talk about the personal narrative in a specific context, we are turning our narrative into one that is more institutionally based; that is, more socially situated and becoming more *public*. Stemming from this epistemological perspective, we argue that personal and institutional narratives are two sides of the same coin, each of which informs the other.

Although we have different learning experiences, we share some common beliefs about educational research. In one of the conversations during our initial collaboration, we both expressed our dissatisfaction with regard to the inadequacy of the dominant quantitative research paradigm in representing and generalising teachers' voices. Taking the perspective of a teacher educator in academia, we noticed that teachers' voices were 'present in aggregate through imprecise statistics' (Goodson, 2008, p. 1) under the current educational research practice in Macao. This type of research practice, i.e. quantitative research informed by positivism, continues to remain the dominant paradigm in the territory and, instead of giving voice to teachers, it keeps them silent. Furthermore, most teachers involved as participants in large-scale, quantitative surveys are not aware of how their opinions are being used or represented in statistical terms. It is perhaps morally 'incorrect' to produce a kind of research knowledge which is 'alien' to the researched community. As such, we attempt to make use of narrative research to disclose, recover and revive teachers' voices. To some extent, the use of narrative research in this context serves as a counter discourse to that of the hegemonic research paradigm. Each individual has, at least, a voice in the narrative; some voices are loud and powerful while others are silent and unheard. Regarding the latter, it is the objective of this chapter to reveal in what ways and why these others are silent and unheard and to create possible means to facilitate the re-emergence of their voices. In this chapter, we make use of various kinds of narrative approaches, such as autobiographical accounts of the authors and collaborative biographical studies with teachers to reveal teachers' voices (including ourselves). Furthermore, our attempt to incorporate narrative research practice in our teacher education programme is designed to assist student-teachers in developing their professional identities.

Throughout the last decade, we have also witnessed frontline teachers becoming more and more vulnerable during the recent process of educational and school reforms. Paradoxically, as 'frontline' academics in teacher education, we have a feeling that the situation is now similar to that of the frontline teachers; that is, academics' vulnerability has increased in the 'new regime of excellence' in higher education. Under the *new regime*, the mission and vision of an academic are based on visible and measurable evidence, such as the number of publications, frequency of citations and impact factors that are driven by commercial marketing companies. This is particularly challenging for us as teacher educators who still believe that the vocation of a teacher is more than merely publications. This kind of shared professional experience, perhaps not only a regional issue, brings us to reflect deeply upon how narrative research can enable academics' voices to be heard. Therefore, together with telling the stories of narrative research development in Macao in general, this chapter also gives voice to two teacher educators in order to express their own professional and institutional narratives and to contemplate in greater depth the development of higher education in Macao and, specifically, teacher education. In short, we see narrative research as both a possibility and a counter-discourse to achieve and revive teachers' 'authentic' voices. It is this shared epistemology that informs the narrative research discussed in this chapter.

Developing variation

'Developing variation' is a technique in music composition for developing and producing a piece of music from one basic theme accompanied by harmony through transformation of the same elements in the basic theme. This section comprises a brief discussion of narrative research together with our epistemological stance in this chapter.

Narrative stems from a long history of literary tradition and has been increasingly expanded for various usages and interpretations. Silverman (2006) describes the narrative approach as pertaining to form, structure and the discovery of social information, and it is employed within the qualitative paradigm. The term 'narrative' relates to both the research method and the phenomenon (Pinnegar and Daynes 2006), the phenomenon and the process (Connelly and Clandinin 1990), as a method of inquiry, research methodology, the means of data collection and the data itself (Goodson & Gill, 2011; Webster & Mertova, 2007). Spector-Mersel (2010, p. 220) further considers that narrative research should be recognised as an interpretive-qualitative paradigm that closely binds 'the "hows" of investigation (methodology) to the "whats" and "whys" (ontology and epistemology)'. It allows for many more expansive entry points into educational research than a traditional technical approach does (Huber *et al.*, 2013).

Although there is a lot of discussion concerning the definition and delineation of narrative research, it remains a many-sided concept. Casey (1995, p. 211), in her article entitled *The New Narrative Research in Education*, points out that 'narrative research, in all of its various manifestations, is deeply implicated in contemporary conflicts over theory, methodology, and politics in scholarly investigation'. It is now widely employed in various disciplines, such as historical, sociological, psychological, cultural and anthropological studies among many others, each with different underlying ontological commitments. In effect, narrative research develops almost in parallel to the social sciences movement. Bruner (1986) mentions that the growing popularity of narrative research in the 1980s may be due to the fact that there was a move in the social sciences from a traditional positivist stance towards a more interpretative posture. MacIntyre (1981) and Ricoeur (1988, 1992), from a hermeneutic perspective, argue that life and narratives are internally informed, one and the other. They consider that people make sense of their life in/by narratives and through narration. Ricoeur (1992, p. 114) further states that 'self understanding is an interpretation, the self, in turn, finds in the narrative'. Similarly, Atkinson (1998, p. 1) points out that through telling the story of our own life, we are increasing our 'working knowledge' of ourselves through self-reflection.

As stated previously, narrative research in this chapter refers to a broad sense of research with its focus of/on/with/for/through narratives. In other words, narrative research represents story-based approaches in research (Webster & Mertova, 2007) where narrative is a method of inquiry, research methodology, the means of data collection and the data itself. In the field of education, Connelly and Clandinin (1990) first coined the term 'narrative inquiry' as an approach to teacher education, in addition to other fields and disciplines that focus on personal storytelling. From their point of view, narrative inquiry is a way of studying and understanding experience (Clandinin & Caine, 2013; Clandinin & Connelly, 2000; Connelly and Clandinin, 1990, 2006). It is deeply shaped by Dewey's theory of experience (1938) which sees education, life and experience as one and the same; to study life and to study education is to study experience. Conle (2001, p. 30) explains that narrative inquiry refers to

> a practice where researchers, teacher educators, in-service or student teachers study their own experience or that of other people, explore institutions and places with the understanding that action and beliefs are grounded in personal, cultural histories and should not be inquired without accounting for these.

The process of narrative inquiry includes engaging with participants in the field, creating and writing field texts, interim texts and final research texts (Clandinin & Connelly, 2000).

Rather than strictly following the process of narrative inquiry in our data collection for our study of teachers' lives and their stories, our stance in respect of narrative research in this chapter is much influenced by the work of Ivor Goodson, such as *Teachers' Lives and Careers* (Goodson & Ball, 1985), *Studying Teachers' Lives* (Goodson, 1992), Investigating *the Teacher's Life and Work* (Goodson, 2008) and *Developing Narrative Theory – Life Histories and Personal Representation* (Goodson, 2013). As Goodson (2008) points out, the new turn of narrative research seeks to broaden the focus of work with teachers ranging from life history and biographical studies, to collaborative biography, to teachers' professional, micro-political knowledge and many others. The analysis of a teacher's life and work, in Goodson's words, is a 'counter culture to resist the tendency common in research studies to leave teachers "in the shadows"', which will place 'teachers' voices' at the centre of the research action (Goodson, 2008, p. 6). Therefore, the employment of narrative research in this chapter hopes to act as a counter discourse to the dominant quantitative research paradigm on the one hand; and to revive teacher's voices on the other. We have collected a series of life stories and life histories of teachers in Macao for the project entitled *A Study of Teachers' Voices and Stories: Researching on the Many Facets of Macau Teachers' Professional Lives* and some from this project are used in this chapter for illustrative purposes.

Goodson and Sikes (2001) see life history research in educational settings as a related approach to narrative research, as narratives in life history essentially involve a collaborative and reciprocal process of developing understanding of the participants. Goodson (2013, p. 6) distinguishes life story and life history as follows: 'Life story work concentrates, then, on personal stories, but life histories try to understand stories alongside their historical and cultural backgrounds.' He further explains that 'life histories focus not just on the narrative of action but also on the historical background' that he calls 'the genealogy of context', which refers to a way of studying 'embracing stories of action within theories of context' (Goodson, 2013, p. 5). In this regard, stories are seen as social constructions as they can be located in time, space and historical context.

Informed by the narrative theory of Goodson (2013), in particular the notion of life histories, this chapter seeks to differentiate forms of narrativity and demonstrates how one's life history is socially and historically positioned and interconnected. There are four types of narratives interwoven in this chapter. The first is a short biographical account of ourselves, the two authors, to demonstrate the interconnectedness between our epistemological belief of this research and our life histories. The second is an institutional narrative. It outlines the Macao context in general and education in particular to illustrate in the ways in which the Macao teachers are shaped and positioned by the discursive social institutions. Furthermore, in the field of education or teacher education, the dominant quantitative research practice in Macao also contributes to harmonise teachers' voices by means of numbers and is thus unable to make their voices heard. The third is the teachers' narratives. Through interviews, specifically collaborative biography, we co-construct meaning with teachers and, through this constructed meaning, open up an opportunity for making their voices heard. The fourth is the narrative of certain 'counter actions' to be taken by us in order to make teachers' voices heard.

Fado and Cantopop

This section, entitled 'Fado and Cantopop, aims to give a sense of how the past Portuguese heritage and culture interact with the present. It presents some historical, political and social features as well as the educational research practices in the present context of Macao and, in particular, the educational landscape in which teachers are now positioned.

'A world of difference, the difference is Macao'

'A world of difference, the difference is Macao' is a slogan that the Macao Tourist Office employs to promote tourism around the world. In the domain of social development, Macao is also considered 'different' in several aspects when compared to other places in the world. The following presents a brief social and educational development of the territory.

Macao is located at the southern tip of Mainland China with a population of more than half a million, over 95 per cent of which is of Chinese origin. It is an area of 29.9 square kilometres and was a Portuguese colony for four centuries until the rule ended on 19 December 1999. This background shows how the Portuguese 'fado' encounters the 'Cantopop'! In effect, Macao is 'different' in many aspects when compared to other places in the world. For instance, Macao was a very special category of 'colonisation', when compared to that of Timor, Goa and Brazil, where Portuguese is still an official and daily language. This is not the case in Macao. In Macao, Portuguese is only a symbolic official language; only around 2.4 per cent of the population can speak Portuguese (Statistics and Census Service, 2012). The pre-colonial Macao-Portuguese administration had little participation in the everyday life of the Chinese community and this resulted in a relatively weak governance. Interestingly, this did not cause any disruption in the local society; on the contrary, one Macao historian commented that the Portuguese and Chinese lived side-by-side in harmony for over 400 years (Zepp, 1991). The positive side of this scenario is that people in Macao are peaceful. However, it also demonstrates that people are passive recipients, even of unfavourable and unjust situations. De facto, the city is significantly influenced by Confucian beliefs such as ordering relationships, tolerance, persistence, patience, respect and kindness among others. As a result, from the outsider's point of view, people in Macao are often considered well disciplined.

Macao was left unattended by China and Portugal long before 1974, as both countries underwent internal political reforms themselves. The Sino-Portuguese

Joint Declaration in 1987 was a turning point for Macao in that it recaptured the extensive attention of both countries. The pattern of discontinuity in overall policies and practices was a prominent feature before the political handover and the field of education was no exception. According to the information provided by the Education and Youth Bureau, the government body in charge of the non-tertiary education sector (Direcção dos Serviços de Educação e Juventude, also known as the DSEJ), in the academic year 2012/2013, there was a total of 75 schools registered under the DSEJ (Direcção dos Serviços de Educação e Juventude, 2013). Among these schools, 11 were government schools; 53 were private schools that had joined the free education system and 11 were private schools that did not belong to this system (ibid.). The feature of education provision in the non-tertiary education sector demonstrates the imbalance of power between the government and the market (private). Furthermore, according to the Macao Special Administrative Region Law, the so-called mini constitution of the territory, these private schools are entitled to great autonomy, as stated in Article 122, Chapter VI Culture and Social Affairs (People's Republic of China, 1993):

> [T]he existing educational institutions of all kinds in Macao may continue to operate. All educational institutions in the Macao Special Administrative Region shall enjoy their autonomy and teaching and academic freedom in accordance with law. Educational institutions of all kinds may continue to recruit staff and use teaching materials from outside the Macao Special Administrative Region. Students shall enjoy freedom of choice of educational institutions and freedom to pursue their education outside the Macao Special Administrative Region.

On the surface, this Article safeguards a smooth transition in the field of education. In effect, it pinpoints the phenomenon of diversity in the schooling system prior to the political transition and that private schools have a relatively great amount of power in negotiation. So, in this educational landscape, what are teachers in Macao like? Owing to the historical constraints, the existing diversity between schools and non-centralised practice and, specifically, the lack of a centralised curriculum, may be interpreted as a 'weak regime' in terms of governance. In other words, every school has its own management system and a diversified teacher pay scale. Teachers who work in government schools have a standard pay scale as they belong to the civil service system. In contrast, the pay scale for teachers who work in private schools varies from school to school. This demonstrates the large discrepancy between government and private schools.

Can you hear me?

For years, teachers have become used to grumbling among themselves about the injustice they face but they rarely take any further actions. We can summarise a few reasons for this from our various interviews with local teachers, for the project mentioned earlier. First, Macao is a very small and conservative Chinese society. Teachers are expected to be the role model for integrity and discipline. Very often, teachers are not expected to participate in any open or social actions; for instance, any protests to defend their own rights are considered as radical and disruptive. Teachers receive pressure from both parents and the school management for not setting a *good* example for students. Second, teachers have little negotiating power as there are no teachers' associations to defend their rights. The Macao Chinese Educators' Association and the Joint Association of Catholic Schools are the largest education associations in Macao; in particular, the former has a majority of frontline teachers registered as members. However, both associations share one characteristic, which is they are chaired by school principals or senior school management staff. In this regard, the managerial perspective is more prominent than the frontline opinions of the teachers. On 1st May 2011, International Labour Day, a few hundred young frontline private teachers joined in a protest to demand a fair salary between government and private schools. The teachers wore masks, dressed in white shirts and walked in silence with eight demands: 'no more delay of the *System Framework for Private School Teaching Staff of Non-tertiary Education*[1](Framework); establishment of a fair communication mechanism; effective supervision of public money; fair adjustment of educational funds; enhancement of teachers' professional status; attention to the stability of the professional development; assistance to enhance professional training and perfection of the ten-year education plan'. The Framework was finally approved on 29th February 2012. In the same year, the Chinese Educators' Association of Macau initiated the 'Teachers' Convention' (The Chinese Educators' Association of Macau, 2012). The 'Convention' places great emphasis on the responsibilities of teachers but there is no discussion or elaboration of their rights. The imbalance between responsibilities and rights in the teaching profession seems to be a common discourse in Macao. To a great extent, teachers ultimately are hypnotised into accepting this as *truth*. Third, after the political handover, 'harmony' has become a major discourse of the local government in order to maintain social stability. At the same time, the discourse of harmony is always reinforced with money-driven measures to reduce noise and, possibly, to harmonise voices. The following are extracts from our project which allow some voices to be heard. The story is not representational but gives a rather individual distinctive voice.

Elsa (pseudonym) is an experienced primary school teacher. She has been teaching for 26 years. She said:

> [A]t that time [before 1995], there was no specific qualification requirement to be a teacher. However, I thought that if I learned something about teaching, it would be helpful for my work. So, when I finished my senior secondary school, I enrolled in a one-year daytime teacher education programme affiliated to a secondary school before I joined teaching. After teaching for some years, there was an evening in-service teacher education programme launched in Macao. I enrolled in the programme. It took me five years to get the bachelor degree; that is, three years for a bacherelato degree

(no equivalent term, it is more than a higher diploma) and two more years for a bachelor's degree. During the five years, my life was occupied by work and study. There were no such words called 'personal life' in my dictionary. [3-P-el–120706_12–30]

Elsa's life story, to a great extent, reflects the historical development of education as well as teacher education. Teaching was not regarded as an important profession in Macao, particularly before the Sino-Portuguese Joint Declaration in 1987. This echoes the late government intervention in the field of education mentioned earlier. Furthermore, Elsa outlined some of the difficult moments in her career:

[W]ell, difficult moments in my career . . . I was scolded by the parents of my students. I was very upset. They used all kinds of language, including foul language. I remember there was a very naughty boy in my class some years ago. He was very disruptive and had difficulties with paying attention in class. One day, he was punished by staying behind in school. His mother came to pick him at school and scolded him in front of me: 'Son, please behave better. Your teacher receives a very low salary. If you continue like this, your teacher will suffer more. . . . ' Some parents are supportive; they trust teachers and the school, but some are very barbaric! They consider that teachers are their servants and maids. I remember some parents used to say, 'Who pays you? Remember I am the one who pays you. . . . ' Some of them do not trust teachers. They are always standing in an opposite stance. Sometimes I feel very disappointed particularly because the school management does not give us any moral support when we confront these parents. Sometimes, I think . . . as a teacher, we don't have as many rights or as job security as we deserve![3-P-el–120706_80]

From Elsa's sharing of her experiences, we can see that teaching in Macao was highly demanding but not respected work. As stated, the private school is the major component of the schooling system in Macao. Based on the market-driven principle, the parental choice has a great impact on school development. Quite often, when 'conflict' arises between teacher and parent, the school will take the parent's side. This is why for Elsa there is a lack of job security. She then continued her story:

[I] am now recovering from my cancerous disease. Three years ago, when I was identified as having the disease, I was laid off by the school. It is very disappointing, isn't it? I had been working there for more than 20 years. . . . [*sigh!*] I think there is no such thing as job security and protection. I was ill and lost a job at the same time. Later, someone told me, the principal had said, 'That teacher can't do anything! Even if she recovers from the disease, she can't work for longer hours, nor assume big responsibilities. This teacher does not have any value . . . ' [*sigh, with tears*] I think as teachers we don't have any job security! [3-P-el–120706_88]

From Elsa's case, we can see that there was no minimum job security for teachers. Under the principle of marketisation, schools, like any other business, aim to maximise their efficiency and 'profits'. Teachers are regarded as instruments. Of course, Elsa's disappointment did not merely come from the lack of job security from her teaching career as a whole. Her disappointment also came from the leadership. In effect, the government had approved the *System Framework for Private School Teaching Staff of Non-tertiary Education* in order to enhance teachers' job security, but Elsa has her own views:

> [T]he biggest advantage for me is that I have become a first grade teacher [there are six grades in the Framework, the lowest is the sixth grade] and receive my professional subsidies from the government. However, the bad news is, most schools are reluctant to employ senior grade teachers because it means that they need to pay higher salary according to their seniority [the salary of Macao teachers is composed of two parts, one from the school and one from the government, in the name of professional development subsidies]. I heard that there is a tendency to lay off more senior grade teachers in order to save money. Nowadays, there are a lot of young teachers with higher qualifications and we, in the category of mid-life teachers, are less competitive in the job market. [3-P-e1-120706_92]

The positive side of the Framework is that it standardises and reduces the diversified pay scale among private schools. Furthermore, teachers are more motivated as they now have a professional ladder. However, the negative aspect, as Elsa mentioned, is that those teachers in the higher grades will have a greater likelihood of being laid off by schools. Job security in Elsa's narrative is the dominant discourse throughout her teaching career. In reading her story, we are engaging in the social and historical development of the teaching profession in Macao and also have come to understand how teachers are discursively shaped and positioned in this institution. It is similar to what Goodson (2013, p. 5) says, 'life histories focus not just on the narrative of action but also on the historical background' that he calls 'the genealogy of context'. Through Elsa's story, we can see how personal and institutional narratives form the two sides of the coin. In retelling Elsa's story, we are well aware that Elsa is silenced by the present institution and we do not attempt to generalise, but rather Elsa's experience is illustrative of the narration of collaborative life history in order to make the teacher's voice distinctive and heard. Let us imagine, if we had not interviewed Elsa, her stories would have been buried – and buried forever.

Is narrative research travelling a long way on a broken road in Macao?

In view of the discursive settings in which teachers are situated, we teacher educators are very concerned about the ways in which educational research can assist in enabling teachers' voices to be heard. The Faculty of Education at the University of Macau is the major provider of teacher education. When we survey the master's theses in order to examine the kind of research knowledge that has been produced and reproduced, we find that there are a total of 318 theses from 1998 to 2012. Amongst these, there are 13 research methods that master's graduates claimed to have employed in their studies and this includes questionnaire survey (165)[2], telephone survey (77), experimental method (49), quantitative method (28), observation (77), interviews (77), documentary analysis (43), action research (14), historiography (1), case study (19), statistical comparative study (10), qualitative method (19) and content analysis (22). These numbers cannot be read as an absolute value because in some cases action research and observation are more based in quantitative research. Nevertheless, if we use the 'quantitative' and 'qualitative' divide, the ratio is about 7:3. In other words, qualitative research is not popular in Macao. Furthermore, there are fewer than ten theses that employ narrative methods to explore teachers' lives and work.

The misconception of students (postgraduates or undergraduates) regarding undertaking research remains an obstacle to the advancement of qualitative research and, more specifically, narrative research. We recalled a seminar session some years ago on the use of action research in education and its relationship with teacher development. At the end of the seminar, time was left for discussion. Instead of raising questions, students started complaining that they did not know anything about statistics, that they could not believe that research could be done without any numerical data and that they were weak in mathematics. In effect, this perception or distortion is quite popular among the frontline practitioners. We do not know where this idea comes from but, certainly, we teacher educators can provide more options and alternative ways to understand our practices and ourselves and, to us, the option is, for instance, engaging in narrative research.

We speculate that quantitative research will possibly remain the dominant research paradigm in the field of education, particularly in view of the emergence of a global education governance through certain worldwide educational standardisation tests, for instance, Programme for International Student Assessment (PISA), in which schooling is tightly tied to economic efficiency (Meyer & Benavot, 2013). In effect, the rise of these massive datasets shapes educational practices and successfully *mobilises* more academic effort in dealing with these global data and performing international comparisons. This tendency does not simply generalise the education picture of each region and country but also *harmonises* diversified educational research practices. To date, the effects of 'global development' led by international organisations (IOs) are almost irreversible. However, we would argue that the educational development of each region is deeply rooted in its social context and history and that we should not lose sight of the 'local' discourses, that is, teachers' voices in this regard. Upholding this belief, we consider that narrative research is one of the counter-discourses to this hegemonic educational practice and can facilitate local teachers' voices to be heard. In the past decade, we have used narrative research to effect changes in research practice and teacher professional development in Macao. Long before the introduction of narrative research to the field of education, there were already some people carrying out oral history in other fields. We acknowledge their effort and contribution to building the body of knowledge about both narrative research and the place of Macao. However, in this chapter we confine our focus on narrative research of, and for, teachers.

The following section presents a chronological development of narrative research in the field of education in Macao. We relate some of the efforts that have been made to advance narrative research in Macao from three aspects: research practice, dissemination and teacher preparation.

The first glimpse of some initial attempt to offer a different perspective from the dominant quantitative research paradigm was seen in 1996 at the Faculty of Education of the University of Macau. In that year, 'Qualitative Research Method' ('Investigação Qualitativa') was first introduced as a compulsory course in the bachelor of education programme, with Portuguese as the medium of instruction. Parallel to this, 'Action Research' also became part of the graduation requirement in the bacharelato programme[3] for teachers. With these courses, local pre-service teachers were made aware of the possibility of conducting studies for an in-depth understanding of a phenomenon or a situation in a specific context and they were encouraged to critically reflect on their own practice in order to enable possible improvement.

In the years following 1996, other attempts were made to enhance the development of qualitative research on teachers. In 2000, the manuscript entitled 'Story-Telling as a Research Methodology: snapshot of Teachers in Macao' (Vong, 2000) first appeared in a local conference proceedings and this provoked some discussions among postgraduates regarding the form of presentation and research methodology. The first master's dissertation using narrative research entitled 'An Educational Career Journey: an Inquiry into the Professional Development of Two Primary School Teachers' was a significant breakthrough in 2004 (Kuok, 2004). In 2010 and 2011, a few more dissertations taking the qualitative stance and/or narrative perspective to disclose teachers' practical knowledge came into view. Some examples are 'New Stories of the Educational Veteran's Career – a Self-narrative Enquiry on Teachers' Personal Practical Knowledge' (Chen, 2010), 'A Tale of Two Preschool Teachers: a Narrative Study of the Professional Development of Two Kindergarten Teachers in Macao' (Chan, 2011) and 'A Qualitative Study of Knowledge Base Construction in Pre-service Teacher Education: the Case of Two English Student Teachers in Macao' (Ye, 2011). Though small in number compared with the other studies, mainly quantitative, conducted in other master's theses, these qualitative studies are an important effort to raise both pre-service and in-service teachers' awareness of the tacit knowledge and lived experiences that they possess and how these represent their voice in the teaching profession.

Apart from research practice, efforts have also been made to disseminate narrative research in Macao through workshops and conferences. On 5th October 2008, a workshop entitled 'Stories from Teachers, Stories about Teachers' was held for local teachers who were encouraged to actively participate and share their practical wisdom in order to achieve self-empowerment (Vong, 2013).

On 23rd–25th October 2009, a conference with the same title of 'Stories from Teachers, Stories about Teachers' was organised by the Faculty of Education of the University of Macau and co-organised by the Macao Chinese Educators' Association and the Joint Association of Catholic Schools. The conference managed to attract around 300 participants from the four Chinese regions, namely Mainland China, Taiwan, Hong Kong and Macao. On 26th February 2011, a workshop entitled 'Teachers' Life Stories and Professional Dialogue' was organised for nursing educators to consider using life story as both a research methodology and a means of professional empowerment.

Throughout this chapter, it is not difficult to see our prominent concerns regarding the voices of teachers. Situated in the context of Macao, we are particularly anxious about the ways in which teachers can speak up and give voice. We believe that pre-service teacher preparation is a significant stage in building up one's professional identity and reflective power. In the past few years, curriculum reform was conducted at the University of Macau. A new 'four-in-one' pedagogical model, which consists of discipline-specific education, general education, research and internship education and community and peer education, is being implemented (University of Macau, 2014a). On the surface, this has been well-received, but in reality, the research component is only offered on an optional basis (University of Macau, 2014b). In view of this limitation, in the last few years, we started to incorporate the 'narrative' and 'research' components into some of our courses, for instance, 'Sociology of Education'. The objectives of inserting some 'narrative' and 'research' components in the course aim to create an opportunity for the pre-service teachers to think/re-think about their learning experiences, to share their stories with their peers, to apply their listening and questioning techniques in interviews and to analyse the stories collected from in-service teachers. This is planned as a semester project and students enrolled on the course pair up to do the project. In order to be more operational for the students, the following steps have been designed:

- Every student is required to write his/her own story about learning or school experiences.
- After writing, each group member is required to organise a formal meeting to tell his/her story to the other members. After listening to each, there is time for questions and clarifications. All the procedures should be recorded.
- Each member is required to compare or relate the story to see if there are any commonalities or differences.
- The groups are required to compare and analyse their stories in a written form.
- Having understood their own lived experiences in their stories, the groups are required to seek understanding of in-service teachers and their work in the profession.
- Interview techniques are introduced during class to facilitate interviews with in-service teachers.
- A brainstorming session for interview design, analysis framework and research ethics is offered.

- The groups are advised to recruit interviewees in their own specialisation levels such as teachers from kindergarten, primary or secondary schools. The basic purpose is to serve as a kind of professional socialisation.
- All the interviews should be recorded.
- The groups are required to undertake interview transcription and analyse the data according to the interview and analysis framework.
- After the interview analysis, the groups are required to relate their own stories to the stories of the interviewees to see if there are any commonalities or differences.
- Each group member is required to write a reflection for the whole project and compile a final report.

This example demonstrates the possibility of disseminating the idea of narrative research among the pre-service teachers. Our hope is to create an awareness in pre-service teachers that they are capable of articulating their voice and this can be achieved through narrative work. Students find the project interesting and easy to handle and it enables them to understand more about the teaching profession through interviews with teachers. From the students' report and presentation, we also find that this project has an impact on informants and in-service teachers too, as some of them expressed the view that they had been given a chance to refresh their teaching beliefs during their interviews. Indeed, it is our additional objective that we want to disseminate narrative research to in-service teachers through action i.e. interview. So, returning to the subtitle of this section: Is narrative research travelling a long way on a broken road in Macao? Considering the historical and institutional constraints, global dominant quantitative research discourse, we believe that narrative research in Macao still has a long way to go. This project has been running for three years. Teachers are enthusiastic in telling and sharing their professional and life stories to their juniors. We believe that, in a way, we have built up a narrative culture, practice and bond between in-service and pre-service teachers.

Finale

A finale is the ending of a piece of music and, in this section, it signifies the ending of our narrative (for now). This chapter itself is a narrative of narrative research in and of Macao. It builds upon various but interconnected narratives, namely our biographical and professional narratives, institutional narratives and collaborative teacher life stories and life history. Drawing upon the specific social, cultural and historical context and our concern about teachers' voices from the perspective of teacher educators, this conclusion reflects on the negotiations and the interplay between the global educational research practice and the local institutional practice in monitoring the voices of frontline teachers of all levels, including those in the higher education sector, in Macao.

This chapter has sought to reveal the complexities of realising teachers' voices in view of the reproduction of hegemonic educational research practice in the field of teacher education and the localised, small Chinese community where the responsibilities of teachers override their own rights. We argue that, to a great extent, the voices of teachers in Macao are monitored and harmonised by the social, historical conditions as well as the dominant educational research culture. In relating the story of teachers' voices in the context of Macao, we understand that we are not, as researchers, external to the researched, but simultaneously, we are participants, bearing witness to, and reflecting on, our own stories and those of frontline teachers. We feel and share a similar kind of vulnerability and are in fact being marginalised by the dominant research practice. In particular, as teacher educators working in higher education, we find it even more challenging. The current institutional practice puts more weight on measurable outcomes such as the number of publications and the frequency of citations. Success in the career path is mostly, if not solely, determined by publications and, in this sense, quality teaching is only paid lip-service. The saying 'publish or perish' is cruel in the field of teacher education because teaching is subjugated to publications. This reminds us of a saying originally from George Bernard Shaw but later elaborated on by others, 'Those who can, do; those who can't, teach; and those who can't teach, teach teachers'. We do not intend to demean the value of research and publications but we realise that the powerful Social Sciences Citation Index that incenses most academics is in fact operated by Thomson Reuters, which is a multinational media and information corporation. So, when we talk about the professional empowerment of frontline teachers, have we ever thought that our own professional autonomy is being shaped by an external discourse and the game of academic promotion? In this regard, in the chapter we, as teacher educators, also make use of narrative to speak up for academic freedom and to call attention to this 'epidemic' spreading in higher education, in particular, in the field of teacher education.

In writing this chapter, we adopt a lively writing style, such as using musical concepts as metaphors to bring the essence of cultures, conversations and direct quotes in the engagement of a wider audience. Our adoption of this, to a great extent, reveals our dissatisfaction with academic conventions:

> [W]hile I personally find scholarly writing boring and prefer to spend my time reading novels, academic elitism is a part of every graduate student's socialisation. I mean that academic writing is not English but is written in a shorthand that only members of the profession can decipher . . . I think it is a way to maintain group boundaries of elitism. . . . Ideas are supposed to be written in such a fashion that they are difficult for untrained people to understand.
>
> Becker, 1986; cited in Ely *et al.*, 1991, p. 168

In effect, our engagement in undertaking narrative research is an attempt to reveal teachers' voices and disseminate their voices in order to inform practice and educational reforms. Therefore, we believe that a language without 'boundaries of elitism' can grant access to a wider audience and effect greater changes.

Upholding this belief, we incorporate narrative research as a component in teacher education programmes, much in line with Thomas's (1995, p. xiv) belief that,

> [T]he encouragement of the entry of the personal into training and subsequent professional development, and the admission of the individual teacher's voice into educational monologue, is a powerful and necessary counterpoise to the discourse of teaching and training dominated for too long by those with claims to ownership of that discourse with its remote language of theoretical and prepositional knowledge.

All we can try to do is to attempt to introduce narrative research to pre-service teachers in their degree programmes and to in-service teachers through workshops, so that we can disseminate teachers' stories. Is the *silent* mode on? Yes, quite obviously. However, we believe that narrative research is one of the possible alternatives to effect changes, create noise and facilitate voices. Adopting a famous quote from Heraclitus of Ephesus, we agree that 'You can never step into the same river, for new waters are always flowing on to you'. Similarly, we do not know how long it will take to effect real changes – and how much we can change – but we believe that once the story is told, things will be different!

Notes

1 The Law No. 3/2012 is also known as 'System Framework for Private School Teaching Staff of Non-tertiary Education'. It is the first ever legal system for private teachers to enhance the remuneration and welfare of teaching staff, as well as to promote their professional development. It also delineates the criteria for admission and promotion of teachers.
2 Numbers in the brackets refer to the frequency count.
3 Bacharelato programme is a Portuguese higher education system referring to a non-degree three-year programme with specialised training.

References

Atkinson, R. (1998) *Life Story Interview*. London: Sage publications.
Bruner, J. (1986) *Actual Minds, Possible Worlds*. Cambridge, MA: Harvard University Press.
Casey, K. (1995) The New Narrative Research in Education. *Review of Research in Education*, 21, pp. 211–253.
Chan, H. S. (2011) *A Tale of Two Preschool Teachers: A Narrative Study of the Professional Development of Two Kindergarten Teachers in Macao*. Macao: UM. Unpublished thesis.
Chen, X. S. (2010) *New Stories of the Educational Veteran's Career – A Self-Narrative Enquiry on Teachers' Personal Practical Knowledge*. Macao: UM. Unpublished thesis.
Clandinin, D. J. & Connelly, F. M. (2000) *Narrative Inquiry: Experience and Story in Qualitative Research*. San Francisco, CA: Jossey-Bass.
Clandinin, D. J. & Caine, V. (2013) Narrative Inquiry. In A. A. Trainor & V. Caine (eds) *Reviewing Qualitative Research in the Social Sciences*. New York: Routledge.

Conle, C. (2001) The Rationality of Narrative Inquiry in Research and Professional Development. *European Journal of Teacher Education*, 24(1), 21–33.

Connelly, F. M. & Clandinin, J. D. (1990) Stories of Experience and Narrative Inquiry. *Educational Researcher*, 19(5), 2–14.

Connelly, F. M. & Clandinin, J. D. (2006) Narrative Inquiry. In J. Green, G. Camili & P. Elmore (eds) *Handbook of Complementary Methods in Education Research*. Mahwah, NJ: Lawrence Erlbaum.

Dewey, J. (1934) *Art as Experience*. New York: Capricorn.

Dewey, J. (1938) *Experience and Education*. New York: Collier Books.

Direcção dos Serviços de Educação e Juventude (2013). *2012/2013 School basic information*. Available online at http://202.175.82.54/dsej/stati/2012/c/edu_num12_part4.pdf. (accessed 21 December 2014).

Ely, M., Anzul, M., Friedman, T., Garner, D.& Steinmetz, A. M. (1991) *Doing Qualitative Research: Circles within Circles*. London: Falmer Press.

Goodson, I. F. (ed.) (1992) *Studying Teachers' Lives*. London: Routledge.

Goodson, I. F. (2008) *Investigating the Teacher's Life and Work*. Rotterdam: Sense Publishers.

Goodson, I. F. (2013) *Developing Narrative Theory: Life Histories and Personal Representation*. London: Routledge.

Goodson, I. F. & Ball, S. (1985) *Teachers' Lives and Careers*. London: Falmer Press.

Goodson, I. F. & Sikes, P. (2001) *Doing Life History in Educational Settings: Learning from Lives*. Buckingham: Open University Press.

Goodson, I. F. & Gill, S. R. (2011) *Narrative Pedagogy*. New York: Peter Lang.

Huber, J., Caine, V., Huber, M. & Steeves, P. (2013) Narrative Inquiry as Pedagogy in Education: The Extraordinary Potential of Living, Telling, Retelling and Reliving Stories of Experience. *Review of Research in Education*, 37(1), 212–242.

Kuok, W. I. (2004) *An Educational Career Journey: An Inquiry into the Professional Development of Two Primary School Teachers*. Macao: UM. Unpublished thesis.

MacIntyre, A. (1981) Ideology, Social Science and Revolution. *Comparative Politics*, 5(3), 321–341.

Meyer, H-D. & Benavot, A. (2013) (eds) *Pisa, Power, and Policy: The Emergence of Global Educational Governance*. Oxford: Symposium Books.

Middleton, S. (1992) Developing a Radical Pedagogy: Autobiography of a New Zealand Sociologist of Women's Education. In I. Goodson (ed.)*Studying Teacher's Lives*. London: Routledge, pp. 18–50.

People's Republic of China (1993) *Basic Law of the Macao Special Administrative Region of the People's Republic of China*. Available online at http://bo.io.gov.mo/bo/i/1999/leibasica/index_uk.asp (accessed: 18 December 2013).

Pinnegar, S. & Daynes, J. G. (2006) Locating Narrative Inquiry Historically: Thematics in the Turn to Narrative. In Clandinin D. J. (ed.) *Handbook of Narrative Inquiry*. Thousand Oaks, CA: Sage.

Ricoeur, P. (1988) *Time and Narrative*. K. McLaughlin & D. Pellauer (Trans.). Chicago: University of Chicago Press.

Ricoeur, P. (1992) *Oneself as Another*. K. Blamey (Trans.). Chicago: University of Chicago Press.

Silverman, D. (2006) (3rd ed.) *Interpreting Qualitative Data*. London: Sage

Statistics and Census Service (2012) *Results of 2011 Census*. Macao: Statistics and Census Service.

Spector-Mersel, G. (2010) Narrative research: Time for a paradigm. *Narrative Inquiry*, 20(1), 204–224.

The Chinese Educators' Association of Macau (2012). *The Teachers' Convention*. Available online at www.tpdmacao.org/plus/list.php?tid=2. (accessed 20 January 2014).

Thomas, D. (1995) (ed.) *Teachers' Stories*. Buckingham: Open University Press.

University of Macau (2014a). *Homepage of University of Macau*. Available online at www.umac.mo/about_UM.html. (accessed 20 January 2014).

University of Macau (2014b). *Homepage of Faculty of Education*. Available online at www.umac.mo/fed/program_bachelor.html. (accessed 20 January 2014).

Vong, S. K. (2000) Story-Telling as a Research Methodology: Snapshot of Teachers in Macao. In S. O. Leung (ed.) *How Macao Education Advance in the New Era*. Macao: University of Macau.

Vong, S. K. (2013) Re-Thinking the Possibility of Educational Research from an Oral History Perspective. In H. Y. Li (ed.) *Stories by Ordinary People: Theory and Practice of Oral History in Chinese Societies*. Macao: Macao Polytechnic.

Webster, L. & Mertova, P. (2007) *Using Narrative Inquiry as a Research Method*. Oxon: Routledge.

Ye, Y. (2011). *A Qualitative Study of Knowledge Base Construction in Pre-Service Teacher Education: The Case of Two English Student Teachers in Macao*. Macao: UM. Unpublished thesis.

Zepp, R. A. (1991). Interface of Chinese and Portuguese Cultures. In R. D. Cremer (ed.) *Macau: City of Commerce and Culture, Continuity and Change*. Hong Kong: API Press, pp. 153–164.

9 Narrative inquiry and the exploration of culture for improving teacher education

Esther Y. M. Chan

Introduction

In the Chinese communities such as Mainland China and Hong Kong, teachers have traditionally been symbols of authority and generators of expert knowledge requiring their students to memorise (Ho, 1994; Rao & Chan, 2009). Under a long term didactic mode of teaching, Hong Kong Chinese students have become passive, uncritical and prone to rote learning (Biggs, 1996; Chan, 2012; Mok, 2005). This learning style is generally perceived to be shaped by the Confucian heritage culture (CHC) but Tran (2013) challenged this conception with an argument that teaching methodologies affect the learning of Chinese learners. As a teacher educator, I face a challenge of promoting active learning, while sustaining the strengths of the 'traditional' CHC approaches. Watkins and Biggs (2001) stressed that Chinese people value both memorisation and understanding, which are regarded as important in achieving high-quality learning outcomes. A set of learning virtues including resolve, diligence, endurance of hardship, perseverance and concentration is found to be developed among CHC learners (Li, 2009). According to Clandinin and Connelly's (2000, p. 26) view, 'context makes all the difference' in terms of narrative notions and narrative inquiry is considered as an effective way of knowing because of its relevance to recognise the context in learning and teaching. The teacher education institution in which I work has the goal of shaping the future, and our stated aim is to prepare our students to become effective teachers who will be agents of change in the communities that they serve (Hong Kong Institute of Education, 2013). However, from my own working experience, teachers as curriculum planners are always blamed for the lack of creativity and flexibility that hinders change and innovations. An attempt to foster teachers' awareness to change and innovate is therefore critical to the work of teacher training. Chan and Elliot (2004) stress an importance of encouraging student teachers to participate more actively in reflective thinking to reduce their excessive dependence on authoritarian knowledge in their learning and to be reflective practitioners in the classroom. Agreeing with Connelly and Clandinin (2000a) that teaching is an act of inquiry and reflection, I decided to make my teaching a site for inquiry and learning because I considered ongoing exploration and educational inquiry were necessary aspects to improve teacher education.

In this chapter, I begin with an inquiry into what I can do to transform students into active learners. I trace my past experiences of learning in order to understand how student teachers have been nurtured through a traditional curriculum with rote learning and memorisation as the primary learning approaches. I believe that an innovative approach is needed for bringing changes to the learning habits of student teachers and it is wise if we can strengthen its connection to the Confucian heritage culture. Since this inquiry is positioned in the context of Hong Kong, where Eastern and Western cultures meet, the blending of these two cultures remains a significant resource for the future, and therefore my attention is drawn to acquire an understanding of the relationship between culture and various contexts of development (e.g. family and education) in which a child's development is affected. According to Connelly and Clandinin (1990), Van Manen (1990) and Eisner (1993), narrative is a way to study experience through attending to the lives of people who live in their embedded stories. I adopt narrative as a means to recollect the essence of lived experiences to understand the impact of culture on learning. In this perspective, storytelling is an educational activity because it gives rise to a reflection about how cultural values became embedded in people's mind and subsequently affect learning preferences.

In this chapter, I begin by presenting the context of how I developed my interest in adopting narrative inquiry in my approach to educating teachers. I then inquire into the Hong Kong culture that opens up understanding about how it shapes Hong Kong Chinese learners into bicultural individuals. In the eyes of Hong *et al.* (2000, p. 710), bicultural individuals are 'people who have internalized two cultures to the extent that both cultures are alive inside of them'.

From there, I focus on why narrative inquiry can be a valuable methodological approach in my context. First, I discuss the use of storytelling as a means of understanding personal experience and improving teacher education practices. Then I illustrate how I explore personal narratives collaboratively with two student teachers, to exemplify how narrative inquiry is adopted as a pragmatic approach to help teachers learn from their own narrative knowledge. I argue that narrative inquiry offers opportunities for both teachers and learners to make sense from their lived experiences to facilitate reflection that gives rise to changes in learning.

The context

The ability to design developmentally appropriate practices is considered a basic element of an effective teacher, and the acquisition of child developmental theories is essential in helping them to stimulate children's learning interest that gives rise to changes in many aspects. It is the reason why child development has become a core module of our teacher education programmes. As a teacher educator involved in conducting the child development course, I pondered on the kind of approaches that should be adopted to develop students' awareness of active learning. Then I recalled the time when I was a student teacher attending the child development course in a lecture theatre. It was funny that the students called the theatre a 'fishing terrace' because they would always fall asleep there like people who fall asleep when fishing. I remember a lecturer standing in the centre of the room, presenting various developmental theories that I found difficult to understand. Those theories were contradictory in some ways, and the arguments about the basic themes and issues in child development further confused me. Furthermore, the content was presented in English and originated from the West, thereby making it even more difficult to comprehend. In order to prepare for the examination, I made an effort to memorise all the theories, which were alien to the local context. However, no sooner did I memorise them than I forgot about them.

The memory of the learning episode in the lecture theatre reminded me of the hard time that I had in the study of child development. Now, as a teacher educator teaching child development to student teachers, I am aware of the importance of the teaching approaches as well as the learning materials that I should adopt and utilise in order to achieve course effectiveness. In my view, the knowledge of child development needs to be based on one's cultural beliefs about children, personal history, the observation of children and the developmental theories constructed by child psychologists. Hinde (1989, p. 273) highlighted that a 'full understanding of development requires an integration of many approaches and many types of knowledge'. The contributions of developmental theories to the study of child development and the importance of child observation have been reviewed recently and have become major forces in modern child development research (Astington, 1993; Daniels *et al.*, 2002; Ginsburg, 1997). However, scant attention has focussed on the relationship between teachers' personal history and their shaping of cultural values about children. In my work, the emphasis is placed on exemplifying how inquiry into narratives and personal experiences can be adopted in understanding child development. I call this a narrative approach. As explained in the works of Connelly and Clandinin (1988, 1990, 2000a), teachers' lived experiences can be a source of knowledge for classroom practices. Through reflecting upon our own autobiographies, embedded stories and personal histories, we can understand how our underlying principles and philosophies are formed. These reflections offer opportunities for both teachers and learners to make sense from their lived experiences to facilitate change and transformation in learning. Rogoff (2003) stressed that human development is a cultural process in which children's cultural backgrounds and social dispositions often intertwine as key factors shaping their learning and living experiences. In this perspective, the study of child development cannot be separated from the context in which it takes place. The Hong Kong culture was basically a Chinese one and was gradually transformed into the intermingling of Eastern and Western cultures under the British rule. To what extent the cultural values and beliefs affect students' learning is my puzzle, as exemplified by the view that 'all human conduct is culturally mediated' (Rosaldo, 1993, p. 26). This is the reason why I turn now to inquire into the impact of culture on students' learning. Such an inquiry gives rise to an understanding about the development of our culture which affects the lives of students with whom we work.

A mixed culture of East and West

Hong Kong was ceded to the United Kingdom as a colony in 1842 and reunited with her motherland, China in 1997. For the past 170 years, it has experienced rapid political, economic, social and cultural changes that have eventually made up a community characterised by the intermingling of Eastern and Western cultures. In the following sections, the relationships between culture and various contexts, like family and education, are addressed because they embody particular cultural norms and social values that affect learning.

Chinese family and culture

The population of Hong Kong is approximately 7 million; 93.6 per cent of the population is Chinese and 86.1 per cent of them are Cantonese speaking (Census and Statistics Department, 2011). Geographically, Hong Kong lies close to Guangdong Province, mainland China, where Cantonese is used as a dialect. Since the early inhabitants of Hong Kong were mainly migrants from mainland China, they brought along with them great Chinese traditions which have been significant in shaping individuals' identities. According to the memory of my mother, the *Three Character Classic* (三字經 Sanzi Jing) is the first book she studied at home. It is the ancient Chinese primer and has undergone constant updating since the original edition was compiled during the Southern Sung Dynasty (AD 1127–1279). It is a book that embodies Chinese history, culture, philosophies and the Chinese world-view. Based on Xu's (1994) edition, it is composed of 376 sentences in groups of three words or characters. Very often, four sentences are joined together to form a story or a metaphor that conveys meaning. When I asked my mother about the content of the book, she recited this passage:

> [M]an (sic), by nature is good. People's inborn character is similar, but learning makes them different . . . . When a person is young, he (sic) should study; when he (sic) grows up, he (sic) should practice what he has learnt. One should devote oneself to the monarch, and bring benefits to the people. When one becomes famous, one brings honour to one's parents. He (sic) who brings honour to his ancestors and leaves his (sic) estate to his (sic) offsprings will have a joyous life; and the offsprings will be able to lead a well-off life.
>
> Xu, 1994, p. 2; pp. 182–184

This passage highlights human nature as fundamentally good and stresses the importance of learning. A metaphor is used to describe that a young man (sic) will not know righteousness if he (sic) does not want to study, just like a piece of jade cannot be turned into an ornament until it is polished (Xu, 1994). The message is rather clear that a child should study diligently to achieve success. However, what it means, by success, is not talking about the fortune for oneself but the honour brought to the ancestors and the whole family (Lin & Fu, 1990).

It is the reason why Chinese parents always put high expectation on their children's academic success. I wonder if children could memorise the passage and make sense of it later in their lives, what effects it would bring to their growth and development, particularly the shaping of moral disposition and personal philosophies. Fung (1976, p.1) stressed that 'the life of the Chinese people is permeated with Confucianism', and researchers have used the shared CHC, a philosophy that has evolved over time, as a context to understand Chinese students as learners (Ebrey, 1993; Higgins & Zheng, 2002; Lau & Yeung, 1996). However, Hong Kong has experienced rapid social and cultural changes in the past decades. These changes result in affecting our cultural values and philosophical thinking about children in many aspects. The extent to which the CHC is being sustained in Hong Kong is a puzzle in my mind. Hayhoe (2011) acknowledged that Hong Kong has a set of educational resources arising from the British heritage and its synergies with Confucian values which could be extremely valuable in the implementation of future reforms. The cultural integration reflected in past studies identifies Hong Kong Chinese students as bicultural individuals who have incorporated the cultural systems of both the East and West (Hong *et al.*, 2000). Although the *Three Character Classic* is no longer a major source of family education, the deeply rooted cultural beliefs have already passed down through parenting, modelling and reinforcement. For example, children are requested to pick up a great many morally relevant behaviours like respect for and deference to adult authority. It is apparent that the family education has played an important role in transmitting CHC to the next generation.

Language, education and culture

Hong Kong implemented nine years of free and compulsory education in 1978, providing six years of primary schooling and three years of junior secondary schooling. Due to her historical and cultural backgrounds, the medium of instruction (MOI) has been shaped in different ways at the different levels of schooling. Almost all Hong Kong primary schools have used Chinese (Cantonese) as their MOI, whereas the MOI is reversed to English in secondary schools. Despite the strong objection from society, the Hong Kong Special Administrative Region (HKSAR) government implemented the 'mother tongue education' policy in September 1998, consisting of streaming primary-school leavers to EMI and CMI secondary schools depending on their relative academic performance in Chinese and English. To lessen the conflict between CMI and EMI schools, the 'fine-tuning policy' was adopted in September 2010, which gave secondary schools more flexibility to decide which language to select as the MOI for a particular class or subject. However, parents generally favour English because knowledge of English is found to be correlated with high social and cultural status (Lee, 1997; Lee & Tseng, 2013). To maximise the chance of their children being allocated to an EMI secondary school, some parents moved into neighbourhoods with a marked concentration of EMI schools or arranged their children with private tutorial classes that further aggravate the predominant tuition culture.

It is common that children are drilled by teachers and private tutors for English proficiency starting from early childhood. From my own teaching experience, students in EMI contexts are used to learning by rote because they need to memorise the English vocabulary words in the textbook prior to the mastery of the content knowledge. Language policy is therefore more than an educational issue, since it influenced the cultural development in Hong Kong and thus affected the learning of Hong Kong Chinese.

Hong Kong currently provides 15 years of free education in which secondary schools are ranked and identified by a 'banding' rating system from bands 1 to 3. Chan (2012) revealed in her study that the school banding system further encourages elitism and the exam-oriented culture in Hong Kong. Hong Kong students have long been regarded as examination robots who lack critical thinking and self-reflection in learning. In this connection, what can one expect of a student teacher nurtured in this tradition? What can I do to transform students into active learners? I reflected upon my past experiences of learning in order to understand how student teachers have been nurtured through a traditional curriculum with rote learning and memorisation as the primary learning approaches. Since 'the teacher's narrative of experience would shape the curriculum' (Clandinin & Connelly, 2000, p. 30). I became aware that a teacher's lived experience has a significant role to play in the formulation of practical knowledge since it guides their future practices. This, in turn, led me to explore the Hong Kong culture, and through this inquiry I came to understand Hong Kong Chinese students as bicultural individuals who are still sticking to a traditional mode of learning. With a commitment to develop a more effective pedagogy for teacher education, I adopted narrative inquiry not only as a teaching approach but also a tool for research into teaching. In the following sections, I illustrate how narrative inquiry is used in my approach to educate teachers and to explore how teacher education can be improved.

Narrative inquiry

Narrative inquiry is a methodology that can be valuable in understanding the personal dimension of teaching. I draw on a wide-range of personal reflections and narratives to consider how narrative knowing has improved my professional practices. I have learned that one of the key elements to success in teacher education is to make teaching a site for inquiry. Narrative inquiry with its emphasis on creating space for critical thinking and self-reflection is therefore my choice for both teaching and research. Connelly and Clandinin (1988) advocate narrative inquiry in which storytelling is acknowledged as a powerful tool for reflection on the personal practical knowledge that teachers hold and how such knowledge is formulated. They further point out that teacher narratives are both personal and social, since they reflect a person's life history and the professional contexts in which teachers live (Connelly and Clandinin, 2000b). When teachers share experiential stories, reflection and resonance can be fostered. As Schon puts it, the aim of reflection is to 'lead the person to think differently in such a way that she might inquire differently or better on the next round of experience' (cited in Connelly & Clandinin, 1992, p. 5). Carter (1993) also supports the use of stories with teachers because these stories are closely linked to teachers' reflections in and on action. In this chapter, I explore the place of narrative in teacher education through the case of Sandy and Kate (pseudonyms) who are student teachers. I met them in the autumn of 2009 when they enrolled in the 'Human Development' course. I became their mentor and invited them to participate in my research in 2012. I did this following the submission of grades in order to meet the requirement of the ethical review committee because in our institution, a researcher is not allowed to do this kind of research while students are still being taught and graded by the teacher researcher. The rationale behind this requirement is to ensure that the selection process is not only ethical but also fair to all students in the class. But still, there are ethical complexities in involving students as participants in my research due to its emphasis on sharing of lived experiences. I need to accept a certain loss of personal privacy but what we have gained is the closer teacher-student relationship as well as the long-term friendship creating among us. In our inquiry process, we each developed our family stories, tracing our past experiences with our family members and our memories of specific childhood episodes. We wrote our stories and invited each other to reflect on the meaning of the stories. The stories they wrote became the major sources of their autobiography. The questions that helped to stimulate our thinking were: Who were you as a child? How do you describe your childhood experience and was it a happy one? What can you remember in terms of parent – child, sibling or neighbourhood relationships? Did your childhood experiences affect the knowledge construction of child development? If yes, how do they differ when compared with the normative theories that guide your future practices? Although I do not teach child development primarily through grand theories, I agree with Bronfenbrenner (1986) and Vygotsky (1962), who maintained that the earliest influences on a child usually come from the socialisation provided by the parents and family. Inquiries into stories help us understand who we are and show us what legacies to transmit to future generations. For Clandinin and Connelly (1995, p. 12), 'teachers know their lives in terms of stories. They live stories, tell stories of those lives, retell stories with changed possibilities, and relive the changed stories'. In this connection, storytelling is a reflective act during which further inquiry takes place through the telling and response to the stories.

In the previous sections, I have shared my own experience in adopting narrative inquiry as a reflective tool to acquire an understanding about the impact of culture on learning. Such an inquiry is meaningful and worthwhile because it enables us to experience how we are shaping into bicultural individuals yet continuing to adhere to a traditional mode of learning. In the following sections, I illustrate how I work as a co-participant to examine how student teachers conceptualise knowledge from their lived experiences that give insight into how teacher education practices can be improved.

Making meaning through inquiries into narratives

Sandy and Kate (aged 21–25) are labelled as the post 80s generation. They were born in Hong Kong and brought up in a family of four children. Sandy has an elder sister whereas Kate has an elder brother. They completed Form 7 in the Hong Kong schooling system and became classmates when studying in a teacher education programme. Since the family is the child's first and longest-lasting context for development, it is natural that Sandy, Kate and I begin our conversation about the family. We inquired into the role of parents and then the social setting that affects our growth and development.

Sandy's story

Sandy described how scared she was when her father lost his temper. She became quiet at home because any disobedience and misbehaviour would lead to a punishment. For example, she was requested to follow the Chinese tradition 'keep a distance of three feet from the table when dining', otherwise she would be beaten up. She shared with me one incident that highlighted the importance of interaction.

> [A]t the age of ten, I quarrelled with my parents because of my insistence on keeping my hair long. My father then beat me up with a cane. I felt deeply wounded not only on my hands but also in my self-esteem. I'd never requested permission to have long hair and gradually became non-expressive because I was afraid of the punishment.

Sandy was upset when telling her family stories. Her reflections of her own patterns of learning in the family context were often critical reflections in that she developed an awareness of how her self-esteem was hindered, and, following on from her own painful experiences, of the importance of enhancing children's self-expression.

> [I] regret my lack of opportunities to learn how to interact with my parents when I was young. Low self-esteem was developed because my parents seldom showed their love, concern and appreciation for me. Early childhood should be a critical period to learn self- expression . . . . Instead of solely insisting on obedience, I think nowadays parents are able to accept new ideas when teaching children, such as respecting children as unique beings and respecting their ways of thinking. We should encourage children to express their views.

Esther's story

> [I] feel the resonance when listening to Sandy's childhood stories.
>
> 　I was scared to communicate with my father because of his authoritarian image. 'Do as I say!' was his attitude. He would resort to force and punishment if I did not comply with his ideas. In contrast, my mother's image as

kind, caring and responsive was deeply rooted in my mind and became a model of affection for me. I recall one incident that led me to rethink what factors affected the shaping of her character and led me to wonder about the impact of Chinese culture on a woman's life in the last century.

My mother took me to visit my maternal grandma once a month. We were dressed up beautifully every time before we went out. When my grandma asked about my mother's situation at home, she merely shared with her the happiness but not the sorrow. I was curious and asked her why she didn't make complaints about the grievances at home. She said, 'A good woman should hide bad things from both sides of the family'.

I admire her great virtue of being a good daughter, wife and mother in her oral narrative that fits into the image of a traditional Chinese woman. She taught me what the 'three aspects of compliance' are: at home, you should comply with your father; after marriage, you should follow your husband; when you are old, you should depend on your son. I do not know how such a theory and the belief 'one life, one husband' was formulated in my mother's mind but it has definitely guided her practices in the past 80 years. I remember she made every effort to play all her roles and positions well, and it is no wonder that she has suffered much in her life. As a Chinese woman living in the twenty-first century, who stresses equality with men, I do not think I will imitate all of my mother's behaviours and adopt all her values. However, I will model her parenting style that highlights warmth, responsiveness and control when working with children.

Kate's story

Kate described her childhood memory as a happy one and how she benefited from warm, supportive parent–child ties.

[I] studied at a whole-day primary school and therefore my mother brought me food during lunch time. She was expected to come every single afternoon. At home, she was requested to be my playmate. Whenever I had difficulties in doing homework, I'd ask her for help. If I was unhappy, I'd talk to her.

Kate was excited when telling her childhood stories in which her mother's expression of caring and affection was a source of security that has supported many aspects of her social development. The reflective writing that follows may exemplify how Kate constructed knowledge on child development.

[P]sychologists like Ainsworth pointed out that children who had been secure infants had more favourable relationships with peers, closer friendships and better social skills. Perhaps the attachment security served to build up a good foundation for my growth and development, and I am glad to find that many people loved me. I believe that infants can't develop healthily if they lack caregivers' warm support.

Berk (1997) pointed out that harmony between parents could serve as effective support for children's development because when parents were warm and considerate toward each other, they tended to stimulate their children more and scold them less. Kate showed an appreciation towards her parents for their warm and responsive involvement with their children. In the Chinese culture, it has long been accepted that harmony is crucial for prosperity. I remember my parents always said, 'Harmony at home makes everything prosperous, whereas endless quarrel leads to the failure'. Whenever there was sibling rivalry, they would use this Chinese idiom to remind us of the importance of harmony. My puzzles are how and why our Chinese culture places great emphasis on 'home' and 'harmony', and how we can achieve harmony at home and then extend it to the of whole society. Due to the fact that culture makes all the difference in a child's development, our Chinese thinking would affect us when considering theories of child development that are all adopted from the West. According to Berndt *et al.* (1993), Chinese adults describe their own parenting techniques and those they experienced when they were children as demanding. This seems to reflect deeply ingrained Confucian values that continue to exist in Chinese parents' minds. It is evident that Chinese parents like Sandy's and my father tend to impose stricter disciplines on children who are requested to comply with cultural norms. However, I wonder whether these kinds of cultural values still continue to survive in twenty-first century Hong Kong and, if they do, to what extent they exist. Hong Kong people are seen as more Westernised than their mainland counterparts due to the 'East meets West' image. There is no uneasiness about this image which is further reinforced by the language policy 'biliteracy and trilingualism', which means mastering written Chinese and English and speaking fluent Cantonese, Putonghua and English (Tung, 2001, p. 13). To achieve the 'biliterate and trilingual' educational goal established by the HKSAR government, it is natural that the young parents put multi-literacies and multi-languages in the early years as typical cultural and educational expectations for young children (Lee & Tseng, 2013). In this connection, the 'East meets West' culture makes the Hong Kong identity something more than just a Chinese identity. Moreover, the widespread use of the English language in society has an implication for the shaping of language policy that affects students' learning. Sandy, when she was at school in Hong Kong, experienced great tension. In the following excerpt from her autobiographical writing, Sandy describes her learning experience in English as very stressful, and the poor academic performance that led her to doubt her ability. It reflects the demerits of the examination culture.

[M]y academic performance was not good in my elementary school years. I always failed in English subject which made me feel I was extremely weak in English proficiency. I thought there's no room for improvement even though I kept trying. I felt helpless and blamed my ability for poor performance. This negative evaluation lowered my learning effectiveness and affected my ways of thinking as well as emotions.

In CHC contexts, parents and teachers believe that success depends much more on effort than on ability, therefore trying hard is a moral responsibility. It seems that Sandy was overwhelmed by negative thoughts and anxiety leading her to develop learned helplessness. Participating in this narrative inquiry, Sandy chronicled those critical events and reflected in writing to help her understand the impact of early experiences on later growth and development. In the following excerpt, she continues to explain how she has recovered from failure.

> [S]econdary 2 and 3 signified my best performance in sports and arts. I won overall champions continuously in two athletic meets, and was rewarded for the outstanding performance in art and design, and also home economics. In addition, I received a merit of Outstanding Talent in Cultural Activities Scholarship in Secondary 3. These achievements helped me to rebuild the self-confidence. I came to realise that when working with students who lacked competence or interest in academic subjects, one should try to develop their potential in other areas like arts and sports. It is important to let them know they have talents in some areas as compared with their peers, and their self-confidence can then be strengthened through achievements in those areas.

Sandy's reflections of her school performances created a space for knowledge construction. It is critical that she developed an awareness of respecting individual differences in style of learning. In this connection, the writing of stories of experience was a cognitive process through which Sandy tried 'to make sense of life as lived' by untangling the complex narrative threads that had contributed to her knowledge and practices (Clandinin & Connelly, 2000, p. 77). Kate's stories of her own schooling were resonated after listening to the stories that Sandy has told in the meeting. Her narratives reflect the complexity of the struggles and hardships when studying in the CHC context. She realised that peer support was vital for her development. In the following excerpt from her autobiographical writing, Kate articulates an awareness of how she has gone through those hardships:

> [M]y best friend gained admission to a top banding EMI secondary school but mine was a band 2 rating. We still met frequently when attending private tutorial lessons. In Secondary 4, she began to get worried about the public examination because she wanted to achieve well in every subject. I didn't want to lag behind and therefore I studied diligently. The outcome was rewarding since I received a school prize of 'good improvement in learning'. Luckily, we were promoted to Secondary 6, and still kept seeing each other once every week when attending private English lessons. She said that we should aim to become university students to achieve our own goals and dreams. Although we failed for the first entry, we didn't give up and always sent support and encouragement to each other. Eventually we made it! . . . . In the past ten years, I have really appreciated having her as a working

partner. We studied in different secondary schools but it enabled me to learn independently instead of relying on her . . . . I see my life as different dots; when connecting them together, it becomes one or another line that is shaping who I am today.

Through the telling and retelling of autobiographical stories, Sandy and Kate have opportunities to reflect on what they have experienced in their lives and tell the meaning that lived experience has for them. Instead of playing a passive role of listen, accept and learn, they have demonstrated active roles by providing feedback as well as making sense from their past experiences through inquiries. In this way, they become active learners who construct what is to be learned according to their own experience and existing understandings.

A teacher educator reflects

In my recent teaching and research work, the purpose of adopting narrative inquiry is to improve teacher education practices. I have used narrative inquiry as a strategy of teaching, and continue to use it in my approach to educate teachers and inquire how learning can be improved in the context of Hong Kong. It has been argued that teachers, as cultural workers (Freire, 1998; Giroux, 1998), embedded with cultural beliefs and values, play a significant role in shaping children's learning and living experiences culturally. To develop an increased awareness about the impact of culture on learning, it is imperative to draw teachers' attention to the idea of human development as a cultural process in which children's cultural background is a key factor shaping their lived experiences. To echo Ladson-Billings' (1995) notion of culturally relevant pedagogy, I adopt narrative inquiry as a pedagogical strategy in teacher education because storytelling can function as a mediation tool that helps teachers understand the impact of CHC on children's learning. In the contemporary educational landscape in Hong Kong, teachers are still overwhelmingly Chinese and bilingual whereas children are increasingly diverse in cultural backgrounds and mother tongue. However, students are expected to become biliterate and fluent in three languages due to the 'biliteracy and trilingualism' policy to enhance global competitiveness as the former British colony gradually evolves into a knowledge-based economy (Tung, 2001, p. 13). As I have discussed in the previous section, this policy reflects the 'East meets West' culture which affects children's ways of thinking and behaving. It is critical that teachers working in such a bi-cultural context as Hong Kong increase their awareness of the role that culture plays in shaping beliefs about children and their learning behaviours. Narrative inquiry as a means of learning is found to be different from the traditional CHC approaches which consider teachers as generators of expert knowledge. The teacher's knowledge and wisdom are often taken for granted and not to be questioned leading to the passiveness of CHC learners. Narrative inquiry is the study of experiences as story. Telling or collecting stories is the beginning of the process, but it is through the exploring of these stories to construct knowledge that practices are informed.

In this perspective, narrative inquiry is a methodology that can enhance our understanding of ourselves as learners, our contexts and our practices. In my teaching context, narrative inquiry is what I refer to as a culturally relevant pedagogy in which the written and oral texts that teachers create are windows to understand cultures. Most importantly, it can stimulate reflection and inform practices (Phillion, 2005).

Widespread change and reform in education has occurred throughout the world in the last decade (Fullan, 2007), and the success of such change and reform is reliant on teachers' efforts. Teachers as agents of change are often asked to reflect on their practices but, without being taught effective methods for personal and professional inquiry, it is difficult for them to succeed. The narrative inquiry method presented in this chapter is what I perceive as an innovative approach to help teachers examine their practices so as to foster reflection and, given the pace of educational change in Hong Kong, is a very appropriate and powerful way to enable them to do so. Educational changes take time. Teachers who engage in meaning making through narrative inquiry can facilitate change since 'autobiographical reasoning' creates the conditions for personal transformation that makes learning more effective and more likely to be sustained (Baddeley & Singer, 2007, p. 178). In Carter and Doyle's (1996) view, teaching is deeply personal, learning to teach is a negotiated process and mastery in teaching takes a long time. The use of narrative inquiry as a pedagogical strategy is to encourage continual reflection to enable teachers to become lifelong self-directed learners. Storytelling and autobiography are particularly helpful to equip them to record, interrogate and interpret experience in an intentional and deliberate manner. To promote storytelling as a reflective tool for teacher development, I have made my teaching practices more authentic and relational. Retelling my story to student teachers resonated with their stories as learners to create experiential and contextualised learning in teacher education programmes. This allowed them a new way to tell their stories as part of the process of acquiring knowledge for professional practices. In creating such a space for student teachers to narrate and inquire, I hoped they would participate more actively in reflective thinking so that they would be more open to growth and change as they examined their past experiences as teachers in their own classrooms. To conclude, I emphasise that the application of narrative inquiry does not imply the exclusion of other approaches or knowledge. Hinde (1989) stressed that no one approach will provide us with all the answers to the problems of learning. The narrative inquiry method presented and illustrated in this chapter is particularly helpful in exploring and critically examining the impact of culture on learning.

References

Astington, J. W. (1993). *The child's discovery of mind.* Massachusetts: Cambridge, Havard University Press.

Baddeley, J. & Singer, J. A. (2007). Charting the life story's path: Narrative identity across the life span. In J. Clandinin (Ed.), *Handbook of narrative inquiry: Mapping a methodology.* California: Sage, pp. 177–202.

Berk, L. E. (1997). *Child development*. Boston: Allyn and Bacon.

Berndt, T. J., Cheung, P. C., Lau, S., Hau, K. T. & Lew, W. J. F. (1993). Perceptions of parenting in mainland China, Taiwan, and Hong Kong: Sex differences and societal differences. *Developmental Psychology* 29(1), 156–164.

Biggs, J. B. (1996). Learning, schooling, and socialization: A Chinese solution to a Western problem. In S. Lau (Ed.), *Growing up the Chinese way: Chinese child and adolescent development*. Hong Kong: The Chinese University Press, pp. 147–167.

Bronfenbrenner, U. (1986). Ecology of the family as a context for human development: Research perspectives. *Developmental Psychology* 22(6), 723–742.

Carter, K. (1993). The place of story in the study of teaching and teacher education. *Educational Researcher,* 22(1), 5–12.

Carter, K., & Doyle, W. (1996). Personal narrative and life history in learning to teach. In J. Sikula, T. J. Buttery, & E. Guyton (Eds), *Handbook of research on teacher education: A project of the Association of Teacher Educators* (2nd ed.). New York: Macmillan Library Reference, pp. 120–142.

Census and Statistics Department (2011). *Hong Kong 2011 population census summary results*. Hong Kong: Government Printer.

Chan, K. W. & Elliot, R. G. (2004). Relational analysis of personal epistemology and conceptions about teaching and learning. *Teaching and Teacher Education*, 20(8), 817–831.

Chan, Y. M. E. (2012). The transforming power of narrative in teacher education. *Australian Journal of Teacher Education*, 37(3), Article 9, 111–127.

Clandinin, D. J. & Connelly, F. M. (1995). *Teachers' professional knowledge landscapes*. New York: Teacher's College Press.

Clandinin, D. J. & Connelly, F. M. (2000). *Narrative inquiry: Experience and story in qualitative research*. San Francisco: Jossey-Bass.

Connelly, F. M. & Clandinin, D. J. (1988). *Teachers as curriculum planners: Narratives of experience*. New York: Teachers College Press.

Connelly, F. M. & Clandinin, D. J. (1990). Stories of experience and narrative inquiry. *Educational Researcher*, 19(4), 2–14.

Connelly, F. M. & Clandinin, D. J. (1992). An interview with Donald Schon. *Orbit:Story Matters*, 23(4), 2–5.

Connelly, F. M. & Clandinin, D. J. (2000a). Teacher education: A question of teacher knowledge. In J. Freeman-Moir & A. Scott (Eds), *International and critical perspectives on teacher education*. Christchurch, New Zealand: Canterbury University Press in association with Christchurch College of Education, pp. 89–105.

Connelly, F. M. & Clandinin, D. J. (2000b). Narrative understandings of teacher knowledge. *Journal of Curriculum and Supervision, 15(4)*, 315–331.

Daniels, D. H., Beaumont, L. J. & Doolin, C. (2002). *Understanding children: An interview and observation guide for educators*. New York: McGraw-Hill.

Ebrey, P. B. (Ed.) (1993). *Chinese civilization: A sourcebook*. (2nd ed.). New York: The Free Press.

Eisner, E. W. (1993). Forms of understanding and the future of educational research. *Educational Researcher*, 22(7), 5–11.

Freire, P. (1998). *Teachers as cultural workers: Letters to those who dare teach*. Oxford: Westview.

Fullan, M. (2007). *The new meaning of educational change* (4th ed.). New York: Teachers College Press.

Fung, Y. L. (1976). *A short history of Chinese philosophy*. New York: The Free Press.

Ginsburg, H. (1997). *Entering the child's mind: The clinical interview in psychological research and practice.* New York: Cambridge University Press.

Giroux, H. A. (1998). *Teachers as intellectuals: Toward a critical pedagogy of learning.* New York: Bergin & Garvey.

Hayhoe, R. E. (2011). *Education reform and human resource development: A perspective on Hong Kong.* A keynote speech presented at the Internal Educational Forum and Expo. Available online at https://cd.edb.gov.hk/IEFE/doc/Keynote1_Paper_Draft_RH_110718.pdf (accessed May 16 2014).

Higgins, L. T. & Zheng, M. (2002). An introduction to Chinese psychology – its historical roots until the present day. *The Journal of Psychology,* 136(2), 225–239.

Hinde, R. A. (1989). Ethological and relationships approaches. In R. Vasta (Ed.), *Annals of Child Development, vol. 6.* Greenwich, CT: JAI press, pp. 251–285.

Ho, D. Y. F. (1994). Cognitive socialization in Confucian heritage cultures. In P. Greenfield & R. Cocking (Eds), *Cross-cultural roots of minority child development.* Hillsdale, NJ: Erlbaum, pp. 285–313.

Hong, Y. Y., Morris, M. W., Chiu, C. Y. & Benet-Martinez, V. (2000). Multicultural minds: A dynamic constructivist approach to culture and cognition. *American Psychologist,* 55(7), 709–720.

Hong Kong Institute of Education (2013). *Strategic plan 2013–2016.* Hong Kong: Author.

Ladson-Billings, G. J. (1995). Toward a theory of culturally relevant pedagogy. *American Education Research Journal,* 35(3), 465–491.

Lau, S. & Yeung, P. P. W. (1996). Understanding Chinese child development: The role of culture in socialization. In S. Lau (Ed.), *Growing up the Chinese way: Chinese child and adolescent development.* Hong Kong: The Chinese University Press, pp. 29–44.

Lee, I. F. & Tseng, C. L. (2013). Young children's living and learning experiences under the biliterate and trilingual education policy in Hong Kong. *Global Studies of Childhood,* 3(1), 26–39.

Lee, W. O. (1997). Social class, language and achievement. In G. A. Postiglione & W. O. Lee (Eds), *Schooling in Hong Kong: Organization, teaching and social context.* Hong Kong: Hong Kong University Press.

Li, J. (2009). Learning to self-perfect: Chinese beliefs about learning. In C. K. K. Chan & N. Rao (Eds), *Revisiting the Chinese learner: Changing contexts, changing education.* Hong Kong: The University of Hong Kong: Comparative Education Research Centre/Springer Academic Publishers, pp. 35–69.

Lin, C. C., & Fu, V. R. (1990). A comparison of child-rearing practices among Chinese, immigrant Chinese, and Caucasian-American parents. *Child Development* 61(2), 429–433.

Mok, M. M. C. (2005). Assessment for learning: Its effect on the classroom and curriculum. In P. C. Miller (Ed.), *Narratives from the classroom: An introduction to teaching.* Thousand Oaks, CA: Sage Publications, pp. 183–201.

Phillion, J. (2005). Narrative in teacher education. In P. C. Miller (Ed.), *Narratives from the classroom: An introduction to teaching.* California: Sage, pp. 1–12.

Rao, N. & Chan, C. K. K. (2009). Moving beyond paradoxes: Understanding Chinese learners and their teachers. In C. K. K. Chan & N. Rao (Eds), *Revisiting the Chinese learner: Changing contexts, changing education.* Hong Kong: The University of Hong Kong: Comparative Education Research Centre, Springer Academic Publishers, pp. 3–32.

Rogoff, B. (2003). *The cultural nature of human development.* Oxford: Oxford University Press.

Rosaldo, R. (1993). Culture and truth. Boston, MA: Beacon Press.

Tran, T. T. (2013). Is the learning approach of students from the Confucian heritage culture problematic? *Educational Research for Policy and Practice,* 12(1), 57–65.

Tung, C. H. (2001). *The 2001 policy address: Building on our strengths. Investing in our future.* Hong Kong: Hong Kong Government Printer.

Van Manen, M. (1990). *Researching lived experience: Human science for an action sensitive pedagogy.* Albany, NY: SUNY Press/Althouse Press.

Vygotsky, L. S. (1962). *Thought and language.* Cambridge, MA: Massachusetts Institute of Technology Press.

Watkins, D. A., & Biggs, J. B. (Eds). (2001). *Teaching the Chinese learner: Psychological and pedagogical perspectives.* Hong Kong: Comparative Education Research Centre: The University of Hong Kong.

Xu, C. (Ed.) (1994). *Three Character Classic in Pictures.* Singapore: EPB.

10 Ethical boundaries and considerations in cross-cultural narrative inquiry

Shijing Xu

Introduction

In narrative inquiry, there have been discussions about the tension between the need to be fully involved in the experience studied while still keeping relational distance in the study. Clandinin and Connelly (2000) point out how novice narrative inquirers find themselves at the boundary between narrative inquiry and formalistic inquiry. On the one hand, researchers cannot truly understand the lives explored unless they become fully involved in the experience studied; on the other hand, to become fully involved may imply a risk of losing objectivity from a formalistic point of view. In this chapter, in addition to the issues related to the institutional research ethics in narrative research, practical and relational issues and ethics of care in relational, fluid inquiry will be addressed. In particular, I will share my own lived experience of narrative inquiry into Chinese newcomer family narratives of schooling in Canada and how the ethical tensions generated in this work shed light on how to define our research role and how to live in roles beyond that of researcher. I discuss a range of ethical issues and tensions in the study of education at the intersection of cultural boundaries.

The topic in question

In narrative studies, as Clandinin and Connelly (2000) point out, the researchers cannot truly understand the lives explored unless they become fully involved in the experience studied; on the other hand, to become fully involved may imply a risk of losing objectivity from a formalistic point of view. As narrative inquiry is a way of understanding people's lived experience and hence is always relational – the tensions around relational distance are always present (Clandinin & Connelly, 2000; Huber & Clandinin, 2002). Clandinin and Connelly (2000, pp. 81–83) wrote about the need for, and the risks of, researchers 'falling in love' with their participants – the idea that researchers need to, and often find themselves, wrapped up in participants' lives and concerned about the particular outcomes. But they have not written about the other side to this phenomenon, which might be labelled participants 'falling in love' with the researcher.

This metaphor is used in the sense of a close and trusting friendship in which the research and its purposes fade into the background and a participant comes to see the researcher in intimate interpersonal terms. In my narrative inquiry into Chinese immigrant families' cross-cultural schooling experience, I encountered such ethical boundary issues as the inquiry progressed. This was a boundary issue in which I became privy to more detailed, intimate and potentially risky information provided by participants. I found myself crossing boundaries by being expected to assume roles that would be defined in the Canadian school system as jobs for social workers, counsellors, teachers, translators and other professional resource persons and that would be considered far more beyond my role as a researcher.

The study and the fieldwork

My narrative inquiry into newcomer families in search of home in Canada on[1] landscapes in transition is a three-year intensive study at Bay Street Community School (pseudonym), an inner-city school in Toronto. Bay Street Community School is typically one of the 'settling schools' (Gagne, 2004) in downtown Toronto because of the fluidity of the immigration and settlement patterns. At the 'settling' school, people constantly move in and out of the school community. Many Chinese newcomer families locate their temporary home upon arrival, but they move out of the neighbourhood when they find a job or as soon as they are able to afford a better home out of the downtown neighbourhood.

When I first started my negotiation of entry into Bay Street Community School, I was located at the Parent Centre as a research assistant of the larger school-based project funded by the Social Sciences and Humanities Research Council of Canada (SSHRC) and conducted by Connelly and Clandinin. I began my work in the Parent Centre where I made the following friends: Carmen, the staff member at the Parent Centre; Freeman, a Chinese grandpa who had been a volunteer at the school for a dozen years and also served as a school council member, and acted as a liaison between the Chinese community and the Black community. With the narrative approach taken in my study, narrative thinking and understanding of fieldwork was key to my inquiry. With the Parent Centre as my "home base" at the school, along with the support and help of Freeman and Carmen, my inquiry path diverged from the Parent Centre into several classrooms, extra-curricular programmes, school events, school council meetings, parent-teacher interviews, newcomer students' homes, and the local community centres. My fieldwork consisted of 3–5 days a week of school visits and ongoing follow-up visits and continuous participation in school events. These visits involved observing and volunteering in the school's Parent Centre, English as a Second Language (ESL) programmes, international languages programme (such as Mandarin classes) and extra-curricular programmes. Fieldwork also included home visits, participant observation of teacher-parent interviews, fieldtrips and school council meetings. In addition, I interviewed parents, grandparents, children, the school principal, teachers and community workers.

Ethical issues

Following the university's ethics review protocol form and guidelines, I had my invitation letter and consent forms carefully drafted and officially approved. To help my potential Chinese participants understand the purpose and the nature of the study, I translated my invitation letter and consent form into Chinese. I asked Freeman, a highly respected grandparent and volunteer in the school and in the neighbourhood of diverse ethnic communities, who was fluent in Cantonese, Mandarin and several dialects, to review the Chinese version of my letter to make it sound appropriately colloquial and accessible to Chinese people from all walks of life in the community. I also took time to explain my study when I gave potential participants the invitation letter and consent form.

Several interesting questions emerged during the participant recruitment process. These questions reflected the cultural characteristics of the research and provided further insight into my quest of newcomers' search for home. First, I needed to explain why I had to keep everything and everyone anonymous if there was to be no risk or harm in the nature of the study. Another question was that since I promised to keep them unidentified, why I asked them to sign a letter to have their names printed on a written document. During the fieldwork, some families were willing to tell me fascinating intriguing stories about their lives but they were unwilling to sign the letter, in which case, I could not include their stories due to the university ethical restrictions that I had to follow. Some participants like Freeman preferred me to use their real names as they saw their participation as an honorable contribution to the research and to education in general. They did not understand why I had to give them pseudonyms and keep them anonymous. As Freeman put it, 'It seems to suggest that you do not trust me. It seems that you do not believe what I will tell you is true.' A similar question was encountered by Tse (2002) in a study of education in one of the Hong Kong island communities in which his participant felt as if he were not trusted when he was asked to sign a consent form.

In some cases I obtained the consent from the teacher and initial oral consent from a student and his or her mother, but eventually could not take some families as my participants, due to the objection of the boy's or the girl's father. In a somewhat analogous situation, Bariana (1997) faced similar difficulties in her study of a Sikh community when she required permissions of married women. Several of her participants agreed on the condition that the husband, who they judged would not permit them to participate, would not be informed.

Being Chinese, I understood why some families were concerned and reluctant to make their family stories public. Words like 'research' or 'study' in Chinese tend to be used together or interchangeably with the word 'investigation', and hence carry a connotation of investigation by officials to some Chinese families, especially those who are in Canada on refugee status. As a result, I was not able to include several intriguing family stories in my study as the parents were not willing to sign the consent forms although I explained the different connotations of the word 'study' in English and the non-risk nature of my school-based study.

Ethical boundaries

Somewhat to my surprise, I encountered yet another ethical issue as the inquiry progressed. This was a boundary issue in which I became privy to more detailed, intimate and potentially risky information provided by participants and where I was expected to take on roles that were more than, or beyond, that of a researcher. Clandinin and Connelly (2000, p. 81) write about the tensions between the need for researchers to become fully involved in their participants' lives; or to 'fall in love' with their participants, and the need to step back and see their own stories in the inquiry, the stories of the participants, and the larger landscape on which they all live. With the progress of the inquiry I became fully involved in the school community; yet, I found I was faced with the other side of the phenomenon that Clandinin and Connelly have not written about, which might be labelled participants 'falling in love' with the researcher. This metaphor is used in the sense of a close and trusting friendship in which the research and its purposes fade into the background and a participant comes to see the researcher in intimate interpersonal terms.

More than a researcher: participating in the lives under study

Intellectually, it had been my intention to present a picture of the diversity and the dynamics of the linguistically and culturally diverse school life in which Chinese families were not homogeneous but diverse from family to family. So in my early fieldwork, I had girls and their families as my potential participants and also paid attention to diversity in terms of the social, economic and educational background of the family. However, as I situated myself in all aspects of the school life and worked more intensively at the school with the children and the families, teachers, other school staff members and the community people, the path of my fieldwork in the school was shaped and reshaped by the lives under study rather than being guided by my research agenda. The boys got into the minds of the grandparents and parents, of the teachers, the principal, social worker and the community workers because the boys tended to turn everything upside down at the Parent Centre, in the classroom and on the street during school fieldtrips. My attention and energy went particularly to newcomer boys such as Zhi Gao, Zhi Hui and Yang Yang, when they seemed to be at risk of failing the school system in their transition from China to Canada and from childhood to adolescence. From initially being an observing researcher, I became a participant in the lives of those under study.

The boys shaped and reshaped my inquiry path and hence the study. Just as Clandinin and Connelly (2000) illustrate, I 'fell in love' with my participants and became fully wrapped in the lives studied.

Being bilingual in Chinese and English, I found myself constantly negotiating and adjusting my roles across and in between many boundaries, both ethically and culturally. I helped the principal to contact the Chinese families and served as interpreter and culture broker between home and school at parent–teacher interviews, parent school council meetings and other school events and activities; as well, I was a teacher and friend to the families and the children. The newcomer boys and girls from two classes would often fight for me to join their class every time I visited the school. The boys' mothers sometimes called me at home late in the evening after work to discuss issues about their boys. They often asked me to talk with their boys, as several mothers told me, 'My boy listens to you. One word said by you is worth ten words said by me to my son'. Some mothers, whose boys were not in the classes I worked with and who heard about me from other Chinese parents and students, asked Freeman if he could ask me to talk with their boys. It was during the intensive work of helping the Chinese newcomer families of boys, as well as my work at different settings in the school, that I realised how the issues of boys' education stood out. At the same time, I realised that I was taking and expected to take roles which were more than those of a mere researcher. Throughout my three-year intensive study, I had to remind my participants of my role as a researcher, especially through the university required annual ethical review process. However, I had become so much a part of the school life, they almost saw me as everything but a researcher.

I will now tell the story about newcomer boy Zhi Gao to illustrate the point and discuss the topic in question.

Life in transition: newcomer boy Zhi Gao

Zhi Gao 志高 was a newcomer boy from Guangdong 广东, China. I initially hesitated to perceive him and other newcomer boys of his class as potential participants for my study when I was still very much guided by my research agenda. My attitude towards Zhi Gao changed from my early hesitance to full support of him and his family through working closely with the school, the teachers and staff members and community people to prevent him from dropping out of the school. This change reveals the nature of narrative inquiry being relational as well as being fluid. I experienced a process of an evolving sense of inquiry as I 'lived' in the stories that these people under study lived by in between landscapes of schools in transition.

Zhi Hui 智辉, a newcomer boy from Fujian 福建, China, is also an important character in this story. Zhi Gao 志高 and Zhi Hui 智辉 were like two inseparable twin brothers, for when one was in trouble, the other was surely involved.

Zhi Hui 智辉 and other newcomer boys 'jumped' into my attention and everyone else's at the Parent Centre when the Newcomer Support Class came there for a buddy reading programme and the newcomer boys turned the Parent Centre upside down. Partly because of these boys, my narrative path at the school was expanded beyond my early expectations to other classrooms, fieldtrips, parent-teacher interviews, school council meetings, school events – Multicultural Night, Curriculum Night, Transition Night, spring musical, winter concert, TRIBES Day – and home visits.

Zhi Gao 志高 arrived in the Newcomer Support Class from Guangdong, China. The first time he came to the Parent Centre with his class, he 'flew' into everyone's attention as he threw a book at Zhi Hui before he walked into the room. Lin Lin 琳琳, a girl in the class, told me that on the first day of his arrival, Zhi Gao had a fight with another boy in class; Zhi Gao often swore in Chinese with a word that insulted one's mother. Zhi Hui cautioned other boys and girls that they had better not talk with Zhi Gao if they did not want their mothers to be insulted. Unlike Zhi Hui, who was cheerful and fun-making, Zhi Gao appeared solemn and angry, wearing a look that even made me uneasy. I wondered what made a boy of his age carry such anger in his eyes.

Because of his behaviour and my concern that he would not be cooperative, I did not, initially, think of Zhi Gao as a potential participant. To my surprise, he was more willing to participate than was Zhi Hui, when I asked him to take home my invitation letters and consent forms. Over time, he seemed to listen when I stopped him from swearing and misbehaving. Later, during a home visit, Zhi Gao's mother urged me to talk with him as she believed that,

> [O]ne word said by you is worth ten words said by me. Zhi Gao listens to you. He often comes home and tells me about you. He said, 'We have a teacher in our class who speaks Chinese. She is a woman, but she is a doctoral student!'

I observed and talked with Zhi Gao in class, at maths tutorials, on fieldtrips, in the library, at the Parent Centre and even as I escorted him to the main office. I wondered what accounted for his behaviour. I discussed this question with his English teachers, Chinese language teachers, the vice principal, the settlement worker at the school, with his mother and stepfather at their home and with other Chinese parents and grandparents at the Parent Centre. Zhi Gao crept into the mind of everyone with whom he was involved. Zhi Gao became the focus of my field work when I was seen as an important helper to Zhi Gao, especially during the time when he became defiant towards the school, the teacher and his parents. I became wrapped up in Zhi Gao's life when I helped the vice principal talk with him to find out why he swore at his teacher and when I helped Mr. Feng, a Chinese grandpa, who was a maths teacher and school principal in China and who volunteered at the school, to maintain order during his maths tutorial sessions. I translated at school meetings, such as parent–teacher interviews, for the teacher and Zhi Gao's mother and talked with the latter for hours about Zhi Gao when she phoned me at night because he smoked at home, came home too late, played video games all the time or got involved in a fight. I lived in the tensions in Zhi Gao's in-school and out-of-school lives and between my urge as well as others' expectations to help Zhi Gao and my need to get my work done according to the research agenda. I also existed with the tensions between my role as a volunteer at the school to make my work helpful and useful to those under my study and my role as a researcher who needed to finish my studies within a certain timeframe. These conflicting demands came to a climax when the students with whom I was working graduated from Bay Street Community School and attended different high schools. I used this period of time to reduce the frequency of my school visits and focus more of my time on my data analysis and writing. This plan was interrupted when I learned that Zhi Gao had dropped out of school before finishing his first high school term. My involvement with this family continued.

Following this new information, I called Zhi Gao's home several times, only to find more bad news. Zhi Gao was becoming increasingly bad-tempered. He slammed the door on the social worker and would not let him in when he came to talk with Zhi Gao at home. His mother also found cigarettes in his room. During one of my calls, Zhi Gao's mother asked if I could talk with the boy as she believed he might listen to me.

I went to their home, where Zhi Gao's mother gave me a pair of slippers and led me to the kitchen; I noticed that the house appeared to have been cleaned for my visit. After shaking hands with Mr. Chan, the boy's stepfather, we sat around the table exactly as we had on my first visit. Even the parents' worried facial expressions were the same. His mother showed me two sheets of paper listing Zhi Gao's attendance record. He had not been in school for almost two months. She said:

> [N]ow it is worse. He goes out around ten o'clock at night and comes back about five o'clock the next morning. I do not know where he goes and who he is with. He shouts at me and asks me not to follow him. He used to ask me for $2 or $3 for lunch money. Now he often asks for $20. He says he wants to fix the computer. First it was $20, then $30 and then $75. If we refused, he would become really nasty, swearing at us with 'f-words'. When he first asked for lunch money, I told him that I could bring him lunch to school. Zhi Gao said, 'If you dared to come to my school, I would call a group of people to beat you up!' He is very rude to me. He says I am stupid and fussy.

The mother looked confused, saddened and depressed. She said she did not know what to do. 'I know he is not going to school. I know he is playing video games, but I don't know what to do about it.'

Multiple roles taken by me which were other individuals' jobs

As I saw in Zhi Gao's case, his situation was so complicated that no one could solve his problems single-handedly.

Throughout my intensive fieldwork from my participatory observation at the school community in all aspects of school life of the newcomer children, I have noticed that in Canada, people's roles in the school system are clearly defined within the confines of specific boundaries. With clear-cut boundaries, responsibilities are defined. While home visits are common and part of the teaching practice in China, Canadian teachers are not supposed to go into students' homes, as this is a job that can be done only by social workers. During his two years at Bay Street School, Zhi Gao was close to his Cantonese teacher, who cared about him, encouraged him in class and spent hours talking with him after class. From my two-year observation of Zhi Gao during his Grades 7 and 8 in Bay Street Community School, as well as from my conversations with the Cantonese teacher and Zhi Gao, the Cantonese teacher played an essential role in preventing Zhi Gao from dropping out of school during his two struggling years as a newcomer. But the Cantonese teacher was not treated as a regular teacher in the school. Her job was counted by the hours of language classes. She was not appreciated as a valuable resource person. Her extra voluntary work was not appreciated. Instead, she was questioned a few times by the school administrator and other colleagues about why she would not leave school at 3:30pm but would instead stay to talk with students. Hence, well structured and well staffed as it appears, the system cannot function to its best advantage, as fragmentation is created in-between the boundaries. From my work with teachers at school, I learned that, according to the defined terms of the union, a classroom teacher cannot pay home visits to a student. A social worker is called upon if home visits are needed, but a social worker works according to his or her schedule, with a single worker covering several schools. The one who worked with Zhi Gao said he had to cover eight schools. Newcomer settlement workers help to make bridges between home and school, but one settlement worker usually covers two or three schools. More importantly, supporting staff such as social workers and settlement workers are bound to work with students in discontinuity, as they do not work with the students on a daily basis in their classroom and hence do not know the student's school life, and know even less of the student's home life. Zhi Gao would talk with me and tell me what had happened to him but bang the door in the face of the social worker. This shows the importance of dealing with children and youth educational issues with continuity and interaction of the actual in-school and out-of-school situations in which they live. For the same reason, Chinese mothers preferred me to translate for them at school council meetings and parent–teacher interviews rather than the professional interpreters because I knew their children's school life. I could also help parents convey their message in the meeting as I knew the family situation from my home visits and interaction with the family out of the school. The interpreters who are called upon by the school have little knowledge of the students' lived experience at school and at home.

While taking on roles beyond a researcher, I was aware of the ethical and professional boundaries in Canada. More importantly, I was aware of the urgent need for Zhi Gao and his parents to have professional help. I obtained contact information for local community centres and services for Zhi Gao's parents. Carmen, the staff member at the Parent Centre, recommended several organisations and schools. Freeman, the Chinese grandpa who frequently volunteered in the school and the community, drew a map for the mother to find a centre with a Cantonese speaking service. I accompanied her to another community centre to help her find the Cantonese service there. But Zhi Gao's mother continued to call me, sometimes late at night, telling me her worries and frustrations. She did not follow up on all the leads. Also, there were no follow-ups from the services I helped her to contact. With three to five messages being left on my home phone by the mother almost every week, I continued to search for professional help for the family. I also contacted the local school board trustee for help.

I was puzzled over the dilemma: With the abundant resources of professional help and government funded community services available, Zhi Gao's family seemed to be left in helpless situations and I seemed to be the only resource the family could and would turn to for help. His mother seemed to find no one who would take responsibilities or provide constant and consistent help and support for issues the family had to face. At the same time, I understood why she kept calling me for help, for I knew the narrative history of the child from his past in China to his two transitional years in Canada. I knew his situations both in school and out of school and hence understood the boy's and the family's situations in continuity. More important, because of the continuity and consistency of my presence and support in his life, I had established a trusting relationship with the boy who appeared to be defiant to others including his parents. The boy told me things that he would not tell his parents, his classroom teacher or the social worker. A narrative understanding of relationship and the lives involved helped me understand the situations and tensions in which Zhi Gao had to live in school and out of school.

Ethical considerations in cross-cultural narrative studies

In a study with ESL teachers in Canada, Ena Lee (2011) has a detailed discussion of ethical issues in cross-cultural research. Lee (2011) makes a good illustration of 'procedural ethics' vs. 'ethics in practice' by quoting from Guillemin and Gillam's (2004) work. Guillemin and Gillam (2004, p. 263; cited in Lee, 2011, p. 36), according to Lee (2011), make the distinction between 'procedural ethics' that involves institutional approval and 'ethics in practice' which entails 'everyday ethical issues that arise in the doing of research'. Just as what Lee (2011, p. 40) found out in her study, in my work with the Chinese newcomer families in Canada, 'my familiarity with and understanding of the institutional ethics policies did not fully prepare me for the complexities and situatedness of ethical issues that might and did arise'.

Procedural ethics

All researchers affiliated to a Canadian institution are aware of procedural ethics and have to obtain ethical approval from their institution's Ethics Review Board (REB) through an arduous process, which may take two to three months or longer, before they are allowed to do their research. Just as a researcher participant said in Koulouriotis' (2011, p. 11) study, 'Research is a western phenomenon', so is the institutional ethical review protocol. Many researchers in their cross-cultural studies have encountered such cases in which some participants were willing to give their oral consent to participate in the research, but backed out when the Letter of Information was presented with consent forms that required their signatures. Often a participant would have to sign more than one consent form.

These Western procedural documents appear to be too formal and institutional for them to make sense of the roles and implications although the documents are written in plain language and the researchers ensure the confidentiality and allow participants to have the right to withdraw etc. For example, following the institutional ethical review protocol, I used plain language and translated the documents into Chinese. I asked Freeman, the Chinese grandpa who could speak both Mandarin and several dialects of Cantonese, to review my documents to make the wording colloquial so that Chinese parents or grandparents could understand. In the Letter of Information, I explained the purpose and procedure of the study, how I would ensure the confidentiality and protect my participants, how I would make the study beneficial to my participants etc. I made it clear that a participant had his or her right to withdraw any time during the study without any negative consequences. Nevertheless, the institutional ethics package looked intimidating and paradoxical to participants who were not familiar with the Western research procedure. Some Chinese parents, for example, wondered why they had to sign the consent forms now that I had promised their anonymity in the research. They were very willing to share stories of their life, but refused to sign the consent forms. In the end I was not able to take them into account as my participants and could not use the interesting stories they had shared with me in the process of my negotiating entry into the research site or during my conversations with other participants.

On the other hand, many researchers affiliated to a Canadian institution – including postgraduate students – have to make an extra effort to explain in their ethical review application how to do their research according to the research ethics standards of the context in their cross-cultural and/or international studies. China and many other countries have no formal ethical review procedure for any research. In their ethical review application, researchers have to explain how they would be culturally sensitive in their process of obtaining consents from participants in these cross-cultural/international settings. In addition, they are often requested to prepare letters of information, consent forms and other research documents such as interview questions and survey questions, both in English and in a language that is the mother tongue of the participants.

Clandinin and Connelly (2000, p. 170) write about the tensions between the procedural ethics and relational ethics in narrative inquiry and the 'catch-22 position' that a narrative inquirer is often faced with:

> [I]n many ways, this process of obtaining ethical approval for our research proposals prior to beginning to negotiate our inquiries works against the relational negotiation that is part of narrative inquiry. However, as an institutional requirement, obtaining ethical approval is necessary. This places narrative inquirers in a catch-22 position. They should not approach participants until intuitional ethical approval is granted.

Clandinin and Connelly (2000, p. 170) point out the dilemmas faced by narrative inquirers: 'If they approach participants with ethical approval, then some aspects of the inquiry are no longer able to be negotiated. Furthermore, beginning participant negotiations with a set of already-approved forms and requests for signatures is a forbidding starting point.'

Situational ethics

Lee (2011), in her discussion of ethical issues in and through ESL research, points out the 'situatedness' of research ethics in cross-cultural studies. Resonating with Lee's (2011) consideration of ethical issues, I find understanding Dewey's (1938) notion of experience and education in terms of 'situation' and 'interaction' is helpful in understanding the situated experience of our participants in a narrative study at cross-cultural settings. Connelly and Clandinin (1988) illustrate why 'experience' and 'situation' are general terms in understanding curriculum as something experienced in situations. 'People have experiences. Situations are made up of people and their surrounding environment' (Connelly & Clandinin, 1988, p. 6). When I walked into the life space of Chinese newcomer families in in-school and out-of-school settings in Canada, I experienced 'a dynamic interaction among persons, things, and processes' (Connelly & Clandinin, 1988, p. 7) in my narrative inquiry into the situated experience lived by these newcomer children and families when I tried to make the curriculum meaning of new immigrant children's education. My inquiry path was shaped and reshaped by the newcomer children as I situated myself in all aspects of the school life and worked more intensively at the school with the newcomer children and their families, such as Zhi Gao and his family, teachers, other school staff members and the community people.

When illustrating the situatedness of research ethics, Lee (2011, p. 47) asserts that 'Ethical issues are identity issues'. This seems to have been true with my Chinese immigrant participants. As I mentioned earlier, I had obtained oral consent from a mother and a girl for my study with newcomer children at Bay Street School, but when I presented the Letter of Information and consent forms for my study, the mother said she would have to ask her husband first and later returned to tell me that her husband refused to sign the consent forms and would not allow her and the girl to participate in my study, either. I encountered several similar cases with families who were in Canada in a refugee status. I found that participants who immigrated to Canada under the category of professionals were more willing to participate in my study, although some of them would question the paradoxical nature of the procedural ethics. Someone like Freeman, who had been an active volunteer in the school community for over a dozen years and who could speak several Chinese dialects, wanted to have his real name used in my report as he said he felt proud to be part of the research and to be useful to the school and the Chinese community.

Hence, when it comes to research in cross-cultural settings, a researcher needs to be sensitive to the cultural differences and also to the situated experience that defines a participant's identity in such settings. I used Freeman as a pseudonym for the Chinese grandfather as he was so active and popular in the school community and the local Chinese community. If I had used his real name, I would have put some of my participants at risk of being identified, too, in my stories about Freeman and in his stories about the school.

Sensitivity to situated experience of the participants in cross-cultural narrative inquiry also involves our decision-making as to what to tell, what not to tell, who tell whose stories and how (Clandinin & Connelly, 2000; Connelly & Clandinin, 2006; Xu, 2006; Xu, 2012). Narrative inquirers, as pointed out by Clandinin and Connelly (2000) and also by Jill Bell (2011), are constantly balancing the ethics between causing no harm to the participants and the need to speak to a broader academic audience.

Relational ethics

According to Clandinin and Connelly (2000), narrative inquiry is a relational inquiry as we develop a participatory relationship with our participants in the process. Clandinin and Connelly (2000, p. 172) found themselves already in the midst of storied lives in Bay Street School prior to their arrival at the school back in the early 1980s. When I first joined their project as a research assistant and started my inquiry with the Chinese newcomer families, I was in the midst of research stories told and retold in Connelly and Clandinin's longitudinal research programme in the school. I had heard so many stories about Freeman before my first entry into the school. Just as Clandinin and Connelly (2000, p. 172) wrote, 'This web of stories led us to the school and set a context for the negotiation of our relationship'. Before I started negotiation of any relationship with my potential participants, I found myself walking into this web of stories that already existed in the school and in the school-based longitudinal project that had a long narrative history about this multicultural and multi-ethnic school. There were multiple layers of relationships: the relationship with a new principal when I first started my entry into the school as a research assistant for the ongoing project; with the main office staff members each time I had to sign in first before going to any other places in the school or when I helped the newcomer parents and/or children who could not speak English well; with Carmen at the Parent Centre and classroom teachers working with newcomer students; and with Freeman who was already in many of Connelly and Clandinin's research stories or stories about the school at our project meetings. With the dynamic social, cultural and demographic changes, Bay Street School has become much more linguistically, culturally and ethnically diverse. The children of Chinese origin have become the visible majority in the school (Xu, 2006; Xu, 2011; Xu and Connelly, 2010). To a great extent, it was the characteristics of narrative inquiry that had enabled me to 'follow the lead' in such a 'settling school' to make sense of the newcomer children's fluid life in their transitions between Canada and China, childhood and adolescence, school and home and Chinese language and culture and Canadian culture and English (Xu, 2006; Xu et al., 2007; Xu and Connelly, 2010). This in the end led to the multiple roles I took on in the school when the principal asked me to help with the translation at the monthly school council meetings and call the families to invite them to the school council meetings and other school events, and translate at the parent–teacher interviews. Freeman and I often worked together to translate the school flyers into Chinese, in which process I learned from the Chinese grandpa how to make my translation more accessible to those who understood little English and who also had limited education in China. Also through the multiple roles I took beyond a researcher to make myself and my study useful to the school and the newcomer families, as shown in Zhi Gao's case, I learned to understand why Clandinin and Connelly (2000) say that we need to think of ethics in terms of relational matters. I would not have got so involved in Zhi Gao's life if I had strictly followed the procedural ethics protocol, in which participants are seen as subjects under study. I might not have got Zhi Gao's and his parents' consent to participate in my study if I had only followed the procedural ethics protocol. Just as Clandinin and Connelly (2000, p. 173) point out, narrative inquirers need to negotiate the narrative unities of the ethics in narrative inquiry; that is, 'the ethics that emerge from our researchers' narratives of experience and those that emerge from the grand narratives via the institution upon the first negotiation of entry into the research field'. In my fluid narrative inquiry into the lives of newcomer children such as Zhi Gao, I became 'wakeful' to the 'shifting ground' (Clandinin & Connelly, 2000, p. 175) on which I had to renegotiate my role as a researcher throughout my inquiry journey when I took more additional roles beyond my research. Zhi Gao was hard to approach at the beginning, as he seemed to be the constant trouble-maker in his class. I was somewhat surprised when he was willing to bring my Letter of Information and consent forms to his parents. He appeared to be very excited. Later, when I met his parents, his mother told me that her son often talked about me to her, saying, 'She is a woman, but she is a doctoral student!' This narrative thread, in turn, helped me to understand Zhi Gao's struggles and seemingly hopeless misbehaviours. Deep in his heart, he wanted to become a good student and do well in his studies. He started to hate school when he could not follow due to language and cultural barriers and other personal and social factors in his transitional life from China to Canada, between home and school, between childhood and adolescence and, above all, between the Chinese language and culture and the Canadian culture and English. Hence in the process of negotiation of relationships with my participants, it was the relational ethics that had helped me to work with the newcomer families in need when I had to consider the ethical issues and boundaries in my study.

Both Li (2011) in her work with Chinese international students and Koulouriotis (2011) in her work with non-native speakers of English in Canada pointed out the ongoing nature of consent in cross-cultural studies. The relational ethics in narrative inquiry is ongoing by nature. Relational ethics is ethics in practice, which is an essential part of the inquiry process of narrative inquiry.

As Clandinin and Connelly (2000, p.170) point out:

> [E]thical matters need to be narrated over the entire narrative inquiry process. They are not dealt with once and for all, as might seem to happen, when ethical review forms are filled out and university approval is obtained . . . . Ethical matters shift and change as we move through an inquiry.

Ethical tensions in participants 'falling in love with' the researcher

As I mentioned in the earlier section, Clandinin and Connelly (2000, pp. 81–83) write about the need for, and the risks of, researchers 'falling in love' with their participants: researchers find themselves wrapped up in participants' lives and concerned about the particular outcomes. This was exactly what happened in my study, especially in my work with Zhi Gao and other newcomer boys. However, I also found myself on the other side to this phenomenon: participants 'falling in love' with the researcher. Freeman, Carmen and parents and grandparents in the Parent Centre, and Chinese students in the Grades 7/8 newcomer support class and Literacy Enrichment Academic Programme (LEAP), would ask, 'Where have you been?' 'How are you? Is everything OK?' when I started cutting back my school visits to wrap up my study. Zhi Gao's mother consistently called me for help after Zhi Gao had graduated from the elementary school and went to high school. She still turned to me for help after I had helped her to find various professional support services around the school community. I had worked with newcomer children in Zhi Gao's class for over two years and observed their transition from China to Canada and from their last two years of elementary school to high school. During those two years I often escorted Zhi Gao to the main office when he caused lots of trouble in class. I was the translator for him and his mother at the teacher–parent interviews and other school events. Therefore, he and his mother might have seen me as the one who could understand him and who knew both the school life and home life of the boy and was hence a resource person that they could rely on. Such a close and trusting relationship with my participants had made it hard for me to exit from the school. This phenomenon, 'the participants falling in love with the researcher', is another side of the ethical tensions that I encountered in my cross-cultural narrative inquiry. Just as Josselson (2007) pointed out, negotiating exit can be equally challenging as negotiating entry. In the end, I never did exit, as I have continued working with Dr Connelly, with the school and with the school board and more schools in new projects.

What I have learned from the ethical issues

The ethical issues and boundaries in my research brought me many more rewards than challenges and taught me much. In the end, ethical considerations merged with the interpersonal relational nature of the narrative inquiry, and what might have first appeared to be boundaries were essentially nuances in the learning process. I recognised that my 'insider' knowledge as a Chinese and a teacher who taught in China for ten years made it possible for me to establish relationships that would be difficult for others. I was in a privileged position by sharing a cultural background with my participants and helping them with my professional knowledge and, a newcomer myself, understanding their sorrows and joys through similar ups and downs in my own life course. Ethical issues, and their defined or imagined boundaries, ultimately merged with the inquiry, and I not only 'gained participants' but also learned as I did so. My 'wakefulness to questions arising from cross-cultural studies' (Clandinin & Connelly, 2000, p. 187) has led to my deeper understanding of newcomer children's cross-cultural schooling experience on landscapes in transition and to more new questions that have evolved into new collaborative projects with our research school and Toronto District School Board and other related partners to engage more people in an East–West bridge-making endeavour that aims to bring about broader social significance academically, professionally and publicly.

Note

1 As illustrated in Xu (2006), the preposition 'on' is used instead of 'in' to express a special notion of 'on landscapes in transition'. According to my lived experience with Chinese newcomer families, I notice that newcomer immigrants tend to stay 'on' the landscapes in transition, rather than getting immersed 'in'. On the one hand, they do not get fully accepted and immersed in the new landscape, and on the other hand, they find themselves no longer feel at home in their home country where dramatic changes have taken place both in the physical landscape and in social values and life style.

References

Bariana, A. K. (1997). *Broken covenant: Punjabi Sikh narratives*. Unpublished doctoral dissertation. Toronto: University of Toronto.

Bell, J. S. (2011). Reporting and publishing narrative inquiry in TESOL: Challenges and rewards. *TESOL Quarterly: A Journal for Teachers of English to Speakers of Other Languages and of Standard English as a Second Dialect, 45*(3), 575–584.

Clandinin, D. J. & Connelly, F. M. (2000). *Narrative inquiry: Experience and story in qualitative research*. San Francisco: Jossey-Bass Publishers.

Connelly, F. M. & Clandinin, D. J. (1988). *Teachers as curriculum planners: Narratives of experience*. New York: Teachers College Press, Columbia.

Connelly, F. M., & Clandinin, D. J. (2006). Narrative inquiry. In J. L. Green, G. C. Camilli & P. B. Elmore (Eds), *Handbook of complementary methods in education research*. Washington: AERA, pp. 477–488.

Dewey, J. (1938). *Experience & education*. New York: Kappa Delta Pi.

Gagne, A. (2004). Personal communication. Toronto: Ontario Institute for Studies in Education, University of Toronto.

Huber J. & Clandinin, D. (2002). Ethical dilemmas in relational narrative inquiry with children. *Qualitative Inquiry, 8*(6), 785–803.

Josselson, R. (2007). The ethical attitude in narrative research: Principles and practicalities. In D. J. Clandinin (Ed.), *Handbook of narrative inquiry: Mapping a methodology, vol. 21*. Thousand Oaks, CA: Sage Publications, p. 545.

Koulouriotis, J. (2011). Ethical considerations in conducting research with non-native speakers of English. *TESL Canada Journal, Special Issue 5*, 1–15.

Lee, E. (2011). Ethical issues addressing inequality in and through ESL research. *TESL Canada Journal, Special Issue 5*, 40–52.

Li, Y. (2011). Translating interviews, translating lives: Ethical considerations in cross-language narrative inquiry. *TESL Canada Journal, Special Issue 5*, 16–30.

Tse, V. K. (2002). Changing professional perspectives: Co-constructing stories about an elementary school principal and a teacher educator's personal experience across decades. Unpublished doctoral dissertation. Toronto: University of Toronto.

Xu, S. J. (2006). In search of home on landscapes in transition: Narratives of newcomer families'cross-cultural schooling experience. Unpublished doctoral dissertation. University of Toronto, Toronto, Canada.

Xu, S. J. (2011). Bridging the East and West dichotomy: Harmonizing Eastern learning with Western knowledge. In Janette. Ryan (Ed.). *Understanding China's education reform: Creating cross cultural knowledge, pedagogies and dialogue*. London, UK: Routledge, pp. 224–242.

Xu, S. J. (2012) Narrative inquiry, reflection, and researcher bias: Thinking about interactions of differing educational narratives. *Pratiche Riflessive in Educazione* (*Educational Reflective Practice Journal*), 2012(1), 69–87 (published in Italian).

Xu, S. J. & Connelly, F. M (2010). Narrative inquiry for school-based research. *Narrative Inquiry*, 20(2), 349–270.

Xu, S. J., Connelly, F. M., He, M. F. & Phillion, J. (2007). Immigrant students' experience of schooling: A narrative inquiry theoretical framework. *Journal of Curriculum Studies*, 39(4), 399–422.

11 What did I learn from studying one family?

A narrative inquiry into my family's cultural and educational experiences in Hong Kong and Toronto

Lau Chun Kwok

> [W]hen you're in the middle of a story it isn't a story at all, but only a confusion, a dark roaring, a blindness, a wreckage of shattered glass and splintered wood, like a house in a whirlwind or else a boat crushed by the icebergs or swept over the rapids and all aboard are powerless to stop it. It's only afterwards that it becomes anything like a story at all, when you're telling it to yourself or to someone else.
>
> Atwood, 1997, p. 298

Introduction

Due to the increasing trans-national and rural – urban migration and exchange in the world in the past few decades, experiences of people moving across different social, cultural and political boundaries have been a long-term focus of research in diverse disciplines including economic sociology (Portes, 1995; Thomas, 2011), psychiatry (Bhugra & Jones, 2001; Bhugra, 2004; Robert & Gilkinson, 2012), medical sociology (Noh & Avison, 1996) and psychology (Eyou *et al.*, 2000; Florsheim, 1997). These studies have revealed a general picture that migration is a stressful process and often brings detrimental effects to the immigrants' mental health. The settling process of immigrants usually includes a period of psychological, social and cultural dislocation and adjustment. The chance of successful integration and overcoming the difficulties depends on a wide range of factors including personality traits, language proficiency, social networks, economic resources and acceptance of others in their own ethnic group and from the host country.

This general picture describes in broad strokes the immigrants' experience from a distance. This situation could offer useful clues for governments and other agencies to provide more relevant services for people in the immigrant process to make a successful transition into a new society. Some of the studies that have just been reviewed were based on data collected through questionnaires and interviews from hundreds of research participants, while some analyses were generated from large scale census data from hundreds and thousands of respondents.

Following a narrative orientation, the stories in this chapter are based on one single case in a particular place and time in history. Thus, the chapter aims not to arrive at a timeless universal generalisation but to achieve a 'thick description' (Geertz, 1973) of the phenomena. It is an effort that is 'aimed at interpretation, at getting below the surface to that most enigmatic aspect of the human condition: the construction of meaning' (Eisner, 1991, p. 15).

In this chapter, I inquire into the cultural and educational experiences of my family as we moved in between Hong Kong and Toronto some 15 years ago. Throughout this inquiry, I explore the meanings of culture, learning, life and education. I position my inquiry in the curriculum field with the idea of curriculum as 'something experienced in situations' (Connelly & Clandinin, 1988, p. 6), an idea which is grounded in Dewey's (1938) theory of experience which proposes that there is an organic connection between education and personal life experience. While my family experience was idiosyncratic and located in a particular time and place, I am convinced that significant insights into broader issues – culture, life and education – can be gained through looking attentively into one instance of such experiences.

As the stories I am going to tell took place some 15 years ago, readers have to determine whether the phenomena I experienced and the questions I asked continue to have relevance today. I hope they do. I take Elliot Eisner's view that the logic in qualitative studies is more analogical. Through the stories, I might say something like this: 'This is what I did and this is what I think it means. Does it have any bearing on your situation?' (Eisner, 1991, p. 204). The focus is on the fluid meaning of the experiences that I ponder upon, not on the facts of a static picture.

The 'data' for the stories in this inquiry come from the daily journals I wrote during the year, plus some video recordings of our lives in Toronto and various artefacts like school work and report cards.

A synopsis of my inquiry phenomenon

My wife and I were both born and educated in Hong Kong and had been teaching in schools for many years. At the time the study began in 1999; our two children were of elementary school age. We had never been exposed to other educational systems or cultures except for short periods of travelling as tourists. When I began my doctoral study in Hong Kong in the summer of 1998, I was introduced to the idea of narrative inquiry as a way of looking into our life experience. In September 1999, I began my residency period in Toronto, my family came along with me and we stayed in Toronto for one year. We went back to Hong Kong in August 2000. During our stay, our two children attended a public school in Toronto. We experienced excitement and frustrations, puzzles and tensions in this different cultural and educational milieu. Exposure to a new culture led us to examine the values and practices we carried within ourselves as children, parents and teachers. As Dewey (1934, p. 15) stated, 'discord is the occasion that induces reflection'.

How it began – jet lag in April 1999

The idea of looking into my family's experience as a way of understanding life and education began with a jet lag experience. A few months before I started my residency year, I went to Toronto to attend a conference and at the same time had an initial exploration of Toronto's people and environment. During the week, I stayed alone in a hotel in downtown Toronto. Since I had travelled half way around the world, I often woke up in the middle of the night because of jet lag. I stayed awake and reflected upon the thoughts and experiences I had during the day.

During my stay in Toronto, I visited some preschools and elementary schools. I walked on the streets around the university campus and dropped into some bookstores and food courts. I also talked with friends who had emigrated to Canada some years previously and had their children studying in schools in Toronto. From these different snippets of observations and conversations, I sensed that the cultural milieu and educational philosophies and practices of Hong Kong and Toronto were very different. What I felt and observed during each day stirred up puzzles and called into question my relationships with my family members, the meanings and goals for my professional career and my doctoral journey. These bubbling puzzles and questions were the beginning of a narrative inquiry into the sojourn experience of my family in different educational and cultural landscapes.

My initial research ideas and obstacles

As I was gradually overcoming jet lag, these sleepless ideas evolved into doing a narrative inquiry into the cultural and educational experiences of my family in moving from Hong Kong to Toronto and back again.

When I went back to Hong Kong, I shared my Toronto experience and my research ideas with my family. Fanny, my daughter, immediately said that she did not want to be a guinea pig. Daphne, my wife, said this idea did not feel right to her. Andy, my son, said he did not know any English. My wife questioned the value of this kind of research, which was not representative of other people's experiences. She doubted that our particular experiences in one short year could be the substance of academic research. It was too subjective and at the same time, our family life could be complicated by the very act of doing research or being researched, which she felt would be intrusive and would make us uneasy.

My heart fell when I heard their reactions. The hesitation of my wife was my major concern. I knew that I could not proceed without the consent of my family members. It was impossible to find other participants for this particular study. If I could not persuade them, I had to find another research topic. I knew that if I wanted to do this inquiry, I had to be patient and handle the worries of my family with great care.

Their worries were understandable and not ungrounded. My wife and I were both educated in an all-embracing positivistic climate in Hong Kong, which honoured practical, scientific or social science knowledge and demoted stories and literature as soft and secondary. When Daphne thought of research, it was survey questionnaires and statistics that came to her mind. In our university education, we had never come across the idea of writing personal stories as a possible educational research genre. From then on, whenever I mentioned this research possibility, Daphne suggested I should think of other, more viable, research topics.

When I talked with some of my colleagues about my research intent, they often said that I already had my participants at hand and should have no problem to gain their consent and access to data. It turned out that it took me nine months to gain the understanding and consent of my wife and children to participate in the research.

Like the relationship in a marriage, the negotiation and nurture of the relationship between researcher and participant can be a never ending process, which might not be resolved even when the participant signs a consent form. I gradually came to realise that doing research on someone close to oneself was doomed to be a sensitive, delicate and risky business, especially when the key participant in my study was my wife and that we had very different temperaments and personalities. We loved each other but we sometimes quarrelled over petty little things. We had different experiences and expectations on many issues. Therefore I could imagine from the very beginning that my research journey would be anything but smooth. Unlike doing other studies in which I could schedule interviews or observations with my participants once or twice a week, I had to live with my participants every day and night, for the rest of my life. All the facets of our lives were intertwined together and confounded with my inquiry. This kind of relationship in research could either be a hurdle or, as I experienced it subsequently, a blessing if one enjoyed the challenges and had passion for it.

Our experiences as a family of new arrivals in Toronto

When we arrived in Toronto in late August 1999, we found that we had to work out hundreds of mundane details to settle our life there. We had to look for a place to live, find a school for our children, buy basic household furniture, organise utilities and dozens of other daily necessities. We also had to apply for bank accounts, credit cards, telephones, electricity, cable TV, health cards, student registration, house insurance and social insurance numbers (SIN). Some of these tasks were more important and some were of lower priority. The problem for us was that we could not always distinguish the two, since we sometimes received conflicting messages from different people. That made us confused and nervous. We often encountered more frustrations than satisfactions in these numerous applications and shopping experiences. To give one example, once we were told that we had to apply for SIN as a proof of our residence status immediately upon arrival in Canada. We went to a government office, filled in all our details on the application forms and handed them to the officer on duty, only to be told that we did not have to apply since we were not allowed to work in Canada. However, when we went to apply for other services as simple as a telephone line, we were declined because we did not have any one of the three proofs of identity (local credit card, SIN card and local driving licence) required. Later, we sought advice from the International Student Centre and were told that we were entitled to apply for SIN cards. We then went to another government office, filled in the forms again, handed them in and were accepted without further questions. The cards were mailed to us a few weeks later when we found that we did not really need them anymore.

In short, for the first two or three weeks, our initial excitement at arriving in a new country was soon overtaken by the overwhelmingly mundane details of our daily life. While all these similar tasks could be accomplished in one afternoon in Hong Kong, we had to visit different offices every day for two weeks and to keep our fingers crossed about getting things done.

Getting daily things done was an arduous challenge for us and made us feel clumsy. We had trouble sorting out the right coins in front of the checkout counters in the supermarkets. We had awkward feelings buying a sandwich or bagel when we did not know that there were so many varieties and we had to choose different toppings and sauces, the names of which we hardly knew. We were over-surprised to receive such individualised attention to our sandwich preferences when what we were used to were McDonald's-style choices. Getting off at the right bus stops and leaving the subway stations from the right exits were only achieved through learning by making many mistakes. One morning, I got off at the wrong bus stop and had to walk for miles to school with my children. Even the simple act of giving our address, telephone number and buzz code (what on earth was it – a bus code?) to pizza delivery people over the phone could become an embarrassing test of our English listening and speaking abilities. These difficulties, as I gradually realised, were not only due to our linguistic strangeness but also our cultural strangeness (He, 1999). There is always a significant part of a culture in a society that can never be learned by one who is outside it.

These were, of course, minor hiccups in adapting to a new environment. However, for new arrivals, confounded with other difficulties, these can cause frustration, anxiety and tears to a family in their early settlement period.

Unpacking our educational experiences in two cultures

As the subsequent stories illustrate, when we moved from Hong Kong to Toronto, we often '[fell] out of step with the march of surrounding things' (Dewey, 1934, p. 14); we had to learn to adapt to a new life. We experienced 'the rhythm of loss of integration with environment and recovery of union' (Dewey, 1934, p. 15). Things were not like what we were used to. On a more conceptual level, our daily exposure to a new culture often forced us to examine our values and the practices we carried within ourselves (He, 1999). Things we had taken for granted, values that we had upheld as universal and practices that had become our unthinking habits were all called into question. In a sense, this one-year period in our lives could be regarded as 'moments of escape from cultural walls' which might bring with it 'awakening to new ways of seeing' (Connelly & Clandinin, 1995, p. 81). For us, this experience of moving in between different cultures was a rare and invaluable experience that we treasured in our lives. We had to stop and think more about our life and education when things were not working 'as usual'. As we puzzled and reflected on our experiences, we gradually came to develop understanding on the themes, or recurring messages, both in different places and in our lives. These themes were embedded in the particular situations but extended beyond the situations themselves (Eisner, 1991, pp. 103–105). In the following sections, I unpack the educational experience of my children in schools and the cultural experience of my family as we explored the larger social landscape.

What's happening in school: report cards

As we move from one place to another, we leave behind things and places that are familiar and venture into unfamiliar situations. We change our daily routines. We speak a different language. We no longer take things for granted. We think and learn things anew (He, 1999; Hoffman, 1963; Phillion, 2002).

We were accustomed to a school system that placed high value on discipline, conformity and individual competition; in other words, learning in a lockstep way (Cheng, 1997). From a very young age, our children were well trained to conform to the school in every aspect of their behaviour, both in and out of the classroom, every day. They had to complete at least one to two hours of written assignments at home every night. Their daily homework (mostly copying and drilling), weekly Chinese and English dictations and monthly tests on different subjects were aimed at securing a high ranking in examinations held three or four times a year. While I would not deny that part of their hard work might have educational value, all their efforts were summarised in a report card with their marks or grades in every subject and an overall eye-catching number indicating their positions compared to other children in the same grade level.

When we went to Toronto, my son did not have to wear a school uniform. He could bring his own toys to school. He could usually finish his written homework in half an hour. (He was in Grade 3 in the North American school system, or Primary 3 in the British or Hong Kong systems.) The other daily homework item was reading – reading a storybook of his choice. While his English competence was obviously far behind that of his locally born classmates and he had difficulties in many aspects of his school tasks, he was evaluated on his own level and for his own accomplishments. He was given encouragement and affirmation for his diverse talents by his teacher.

The Ontario provincial report card recorded letter grades in each subject to indicate the student's achievement of the provincial curriculum expectations. There was no comparison or competition among students in a class. Instead of a numeric ranking of his position in class, my son got the following summary comments from his teacher in the first report card in December 1999:

> Andy has worked hard this term to make friends and establish himself in the Lillian [the name of the school] culture and has been very successful.

He can communicate basic concerns in English and follows simple instructions. He expresses himself creatively and very effectively through drawings. His diagrams are very well drawn and include a high level of sophistication. Andy persists and perseveres when confronted with daily tasks but is encouraged to ask for support when concepts and instructions are unclear. He is quickly learning basic reading strategies and reads simple texts during group readings. Andy you're amazing. Keep up the good work.

This type of evaluation is more personally centred as compared with the norm-referenced evaluation used in Hong Kong schools. As a father who had known his child reasonably well, I was not much surprised by these positive comments on my son's artistic talents, creativity and perseverance. However, I was amazed that the teacher could notice the individual potential and strengths in a child and make such detailed and accurate observations of him after just three months, despite his surface weakness in the classroom.

What was happening in the classroom? What were the underlying educational values and practices in the two educational milieus? How did the educational values reveal themselves in the differences in classroom physical settings, in teacher focus and attention on the children, in different styles and emphases in reporting students' progress? I began to wonder.

What's happening in school: a lesson in Black history for the father

My daughter was in Grade 5. Her school work was more demanding and required intensive study of language, mathematics, science and social studies. However, the teachers taught differently and my daughter learned differently in the two places. In terms of the number of subjects and topics, elementary students in Hong Kong had a great deal to learn in their class. There were many different subjects in their formal curriculum. Each subject was divided into teaching units that become chapters in textbooks to be taught by different subject teachers in 35-minute lesson slots. In Chinese language lessons, for example, the students were expected to complete one or two chapters in a week. They were expected to memorise the lesson or book content in order to pass tests and examinations. There was a set of supplementary exercise books accompanying the textbooks. However, the subject matter in different subjects was seldom integrated and tended to be learned in isolation. As Dewey (1938, p. 48) points out, when subject matter is acquired in a segregated manner, it becomes 'so disconnected from the rest of experience that it is not available under the actual conditions of life'.

In comparison to the Hong Kong situation, the subject topics my daughter learned in school in Toronto seemed to be comparatively fewer. For one single topic in science, clouds, she spent a whole month observing the cloud patterns every day after school. She had to make notes, fill in worksheets and draw conclusions from her own data. In Black History Month (February every year in Canada), she learned about African heritage. There were activity booths for the students to learn about African arts and music during the school day. The students had to research and write about prominent Black people and make presentations in their English language class. In social studies class, they watched a documentary on Martin Luther King Jr and the history of the struggle of the African Americans in North America. She watched performances and learned about African dance and music in music and drama lessons. She also made a paper sculpture of Martin Luther King as an art project and kept a journal on what she had done every day for several months.

One Sunday afternoon at home, when I was reading Maxine Greene's *The Dialectic of Freedom* (1988, p. 88) I came across a sentence: 'And we may recall the blacks, escaping in the slave years through the Underground Railroad, shipped northward in trucks . . . .'. As I had never studied history in school before, I had no clue what this 'Underground Railroad' was about. However, I remembered that my daughter had mentioned this to me a week before, so I sought help from her and I was immediately given a private lesson on the lives of slaves in the southern states of the USA in the mid-nineteenth century and how they had escaped from their masters and became free when they crossed the border to Canada. She also told me in detail the story of Rosa Parks and how the bus company was boycotted after King made a speech to the people, and was arrested because of this – a story I had heard about but not known in detail.

I was amazed that my daughter could make use of what she learned in school to answer my query. She was a diligent student in Hong Kong but I seldom saw her relate her book learning to real life problems. As I knew more about how she learned in school, I began to appreciate the wisdom of learning more with fewer topics. Since Black History Month, different subject matter in English, social studies, music, art, and drama in the school were geared towards a central theme. At the same time, the work she did under the central theme developed her learning in different subject areas. The history of human life was represented and learned through different modes and media – words, music, drama, images and artefacts. As different modes of teaching enable different ways of knowing (Heshusius & Ballard, 1996) and different forms of understanding (Eisner, 1991), her learning in different subject matter became part of her personal knowledge. This knowledge also enabled her to become her father's first teacher on Black history in America.

Exploring the social landscape: three images

My experience told me that when we come to a different country, we learn not only in schools or universities. Our daily life experience in society also revealed significant cultural lessons if we were attentive enough to the mundane and daily routines in our lives. I have several vivid images of my life in Toronto, three of which I will now share. These images are captured in little stories that prompted me to rethink some of the most simple and fundamental concerns in education – what, and how, does our society teach our children?

Image 1: a little coin box beside a printer in the children's section of a public library

My family often went to the North York Toronto public library during weekends. In the children's section on the ground floor there were computer facilities for the children to surf the internet. Printers were attached to the computers so that we could print the materials we needed. There was a little metal box beside the printer. On the box was a note which read 'Help yourself and put your money here – 20 cents per page'.

I had two related experiences of paying for my printing. I once used the printer in a hotel when I was in Toronto in April 1999. After I finished printing, I handed my pile of paper to the concierge for him to check the number of pages. He just asked me for the number of pages I had printed and told me the money I should pay.

Another time, I used the printer in the library in my workplace in Hong Kong. When I finished, I brought the printed sheets to the counter and told the library staff member there that I had printed 20 pages. She grabbed my pile of paper and counted them one by one.

Image 2: a middle-aged man with a ponytail sitting beside a fare box in a subway station

I often took the Toronto subway to go to classes from Finch Station, a few minutes' walk from where I lived. During morning rush hour, the station opened an extra entrance for passengers. The station master used a fare box to collect the coins or tokens from the passengers. I remembered seeing a middle-aged man with a grey ponytail sitting beside the fare box. He was not staring at the fare box to check whether the passengers tendered the exact fare. Instead, he looked into the eyes of each passenger and greeted them with a friendly smile, saying 'Hi!' or 'Good morning'. What a nice way to start a working day, I thought.

Image 3: a little boy holding a door open for his classmates

The school my children attended in Toronto was an old three storey building, outside of which was a large park where the children had recess. Once I went to the school during recess time and watched the children play. Some children were skipping, some were throwing and catching tennis balls high in the air, some were playing foot hockey, some were just strolling around talking with their friends and some were running wild in the open space. When the bell rang, I saw my son running swiftly towards the door of the school building. He pulled the door and proudly held it open so that all his classmates could walk through the door and return to the school building.

Epilogue: seeing the world through a grain of sand

When I first conceived my research proposal in May 1999, my thinking was filled with grand terms like 'culture' and 'education systems'. I looked for changes in our 'educational experiences', 'attitudes towards education, life and cultures', 'global perspective' and 'cross cultural awareness and understanding'. These are highly conceptual and high-sounding terms. Pondering our experiences in different landscapes in these years, I realise that we are not living in the abstract and conceptual world. The big word 'culture' is captured in the little stories in our lives. We can see the world in a grain of sand. When a society plants the seeds of trust, self-respect and respect for others in small children in the children's library, we can trust the adult passengers to tender the exact fare without being watched. A few dimes and nickels would be lost every day in this system. But this is the price we are willing to pay if we are to build a society of trust and cultivate a person with self-respect. We have to teach these lessons and provide chances for people, especially young children, to practise these virtues every day.

People landing in a new place usually tend to compare lives in the host and home countries. We might see that something in the host country is better than that in our home country, or vice versa. However, this is often an out of context, simplistic and hasty judgment. Things are never so simply dichotomised. Every practice in a society is interwoven with the social, historical, political and geographical fabric. There is no 'best practice' that can be taken out of its particular social and political institutions. Hong Kong is a small place with few natural resources except for the 7.2 million inhabitants. We might have a reason to stress efficiency, competition and cost effectiveness in our schools and society. We have few choices but to fully utilise our human resources. Hong Kong's economic success and vitality is undeniable. However, as I reflect on our experiences in moving between different cultures, I begin to wonder: What is education? What is life? What are schools doing to our children? What do we gain and what do we lose in the way we choose to live? How do our children learn? How is a person cultivated?

The value of a narrative inquiry, as I see it, does not rest upon how many questions it answers but on how successfully it can initiate and engage in a dialogue with readers on these significant questions in life. This concept of dialogue, following the legacy of Mikhail Bakhtin, the Russian philosopher and literary critic, is not simply a semantic device for explaining, convincing or manipulating others, but a way of life. For Bakhtin, dialogue is ontological – 'a way of living life in openness to others who are different from oneself, of relating to people and ideas that remain separate and distinct from our own' (Shields, 2007, p. 65). The narrative inquiry that I have undertaken and the journey that I travelled have not provided me with any definite answers to those questions I posed at their beginning. As I indicated in the introduction to this chapter, my family experience was idiosyncratic and located in a particular time and place, but insights into broader issues – culture, life and education – have been gained through looking closely at our experiences as a Hong Kong family living in an unfamiliar context. Through the narrative inquiry process, I learnt to live with inconclusiveness, uncertainty, paradox and ambiguity in a more humble manner. This methodological approach, therefore, has immense potential for research in Hong Kong as it encourages critical reflection on our cultural, social and political boundaries, which is imperative in our current, turbulent times.

References

Atwood, M. (1997). *Alias Grace*. New York: Anchor Books.

Bhugra, D. (2004). Migration, distress and cultural identity. *British Medical Bulletin*, 69(1), 129–141.

Bhugra, D. & Jones, P. (2001). Migration and mental illness. *Advances in Psychiatric Treatment, 7*, 216–223.

Cheng, K. M. (1997). The education system. In G. A. Postiglione & W. O. Lee. (Eds), *Schooling in Hong Kong: Organization, teaching and social context*. Hong Kong: Hong Kong University Press.

Connelly, F. M. & Clandinin, D. J. (1988). *Teachers as curriculum planners: Narratives of experience*. New York: Teachers College Press.

Connelly, F. M. & Clandinin, D. J. (1995). Narrative and education. *Teachers and Teaching: Theory and Practice, 1*(1), 73–85.

Dewey, J. (1934). *Art as experience*. New York: Perigee.

Dewey, J. (1938). *Experience and education*. New York: Simon & Schuster.

Eisner, E. W. (1991). *The enlightened eye: Qualitative inquiry and the enhancement of educational practice*. New York: Macmillan.

Eyou, M. L., Adair, V. & Dixon, R. (2000). Cultural identity and psychological adjustment of adolescent Chinese immigrants in New Zealand. *Journal of Adolescence, 23*(5), 531–543.

Florsheim, P. (1997). Chinese adolescent immigrants: Factors related to psychosocial adjustment. *Journal of Youth and Adolescence, 26*(2), 143–163.

Geertz, C. (1973). *The interpretation of cultures*. New York: Basic Books.

Greene, M. (1988). *The dialectic of freedom*. New York: Teachers College Press.

He, M. F. (1999). A life-long inquiry forever flowing between China and Canada: Crafting a composite auto/biographical narrative method to represent three Chinese women teachers' cultural experiences. *Journal of Critical Inquiry into Curriculum and Instruction. 1*(2), 5–29.

Heshusius, L. & Ballard, K. (1996). *From positivism to interpretivism and beyond: Tales of transformation in educational and social research (the mind-body connection)*. New York: Teachers College Press.

Hoffman, E. (1963). *Lost in Translation: A life in a new language*. New York: Penguin.

Noh, S. & Avison, W. R. (1996). Asian immigrants and the stress process: A study of Koreans in Canada. *Journal of Health and Social Behavior, 37*(2), 192–206.

Phillion, J. (2002) *Narrative inquiry in a multicultural landscape: Multicultural teaching and learning*. Westport, CN: Ablex Publishing.

Portes, A. (Ed.). (1995). *The economic sociology of immigration: Essays on networks, ethnicity, and entrepreneurship*. New York: Russell Sage Foundation.

Robert, A-M. & Gilkinson, T. (2012). *Mental health and well-being of recent immigrants in Canada: Evidence from the longitudinal survey of immigrants to Canada*. Ottawa, Canada: Department of Citizenship and Immigration Canada, Government of Canada.

Shields, C. M. (2007). *Bakhtin primer*. New York: Peter Lang.

Thomas, D. (2011). *Personal networks and the economic adjustment of immigrants*. Canadian Social Trends, Component of Statistics Canada, Catalogue no. 11–008–X. Canada: Statistics Canada, Government of Canada.

12 In the minority yet finding a voice

The value of using narrative inquiry in exploring multiple identities in Hong Kong

Eunice Pui-yu Yim

Introduction

Narrative inquirers are in the minority in Hong Kong, where traditional empirical research is more highly valued by academics and by funding bodies. In particular, the use of the first-person pronoun 'I' and the active voice in research are often considered to be unprofessional and 'non-academic' writing. As a narrative inquirer, I was questioned by colleagues about the 'scientific' and 'objective' values of using myself in the research process. In this chapter, I will present how I came to adopt narrative inquiry for a study on multiple identities in Hong Kong via a parent education programme, a vehicle for sharing between parents of diverse backgrounds. My study was constantly criticised and devalued for its emphasis on self-awareness and reflection on my life experiences and different identities; however, I show throughout the chapter how the latter elements were crucial in understanding multiple identities in group settings in Hong Kong.

Who am I?

I am a Hong Kong local and emigrated to Canada when I was 15 years old. This was the first time that I had been an immigrant in a foreign country. I received training on early childhood education after I completed my first degree in psychology. A few years later, I returned to Hong Kong and started participating in research related to early childhood education, new arrival families and special education. I am now a mother of two children. Having trained in a Western culture and now raising my own children in an Eastern culture, I experience conflicts in terms of values and beliefs in parenting and child development. I never thought that these experiences, together with the multiple identities that I had, could become a valuable research tool, until I encountered the methodology of narrative inquiry when I started my doctoral dissertation – a study on multiple identities in a group setting in Hong Kong.

Reflecting on prior experiences when participating in various projects funded by the government, I recalled that many of these projects adopted traditional empirical methods such as structured interviews and questionnaires to collect and analyse data. The Q sort test[1] was used as the major research method for one of the projects. I still remember a middle-aged man on welfare who was invited to participate in the Q sort test. Throughout the process, he tried to explain more about the rationale behind his responses to every Q item. However, since the data analysis for Q sort mainly took account of categorising the responses to the statements, I now consider the research process to have been quite inhumane as it overlooked the motives behind his choice or even ignored the role(s) and perspective(s) that the participant adopted throughout the research process. He may have sorted the given statements differently if he had responded to the study from the perspective of different life experiences at different times with different social roles or identities. Although the project also employed qualitative methods such as face to face interviews, the analysis concerned what the interviewee said in response to a set of pre-set interview questions. More importantly, the interpretation focussed on the literal meanings of the responses while, again, ignoring the values and beliefs associated with the particular perspective(s) and social role(s) that participants adopted throughout the research process.

Believing that de-contextualised meaning making is incomplete and inhumane, narrative inquiry became my choice for a study that investigated interpersonal interaction. With my assets of having multiple identities as mother, immigrant to a Western country and Hong Kong local, my flexibility in re-orienting myself and relating to similar experiences and identities put me in an advantageous position for exploring people, who experience culture clash, in transparent and authentic ways.

My approach to the study has been criticised vigorously by academic colleagues. From the presentation level of using the first-person pronoun 'I' and the active voice in the writing to using my own experiences as a core part of the process of data analysis, I have been criticised as being unscientific and too personal. I was even advised to replace 'I' with the passive voice and to follow the headings of most research papers to favour the taste of the majority of journal editors. It was suggested that the findings should be supported by a list of statements extracted from an hour long conversation. The meanings would then be interpreted at a literal level which de-contextualised data and de-humanised human experiences from which 'truth' would emerge in relation to contextual components. Not only were the interviewee's motives and uniqueness ignored, but my feelings, thoughts, and therefore interpretation, as an interviewer during the research process were also not valued and were described as too subjective and unprofessional.

I was surprised and puzzled by the resistance shown by my colleagues. Narrative inquiry was chosen as the methodological approach for my research project on group dynamics in parent education programmes in Hong Kong, because of the cultural nature of parenting studies and the methodological emphasis on contextualisation of meaning. I observed conversations among parents with different sociocultural backgrounds. When I analysed the 'data', I drew on my own perspectives and experiences of having been an outsider. This chapter presents a discussion of those processes.

Contextualising narrative inquiry

Narrative Inquiry in cultural studies

Group interaction and parenting are said to be social practices that reflect an individual's sociocultural values and beliefs (Alasuutari, 1995). People's actions are regulated by the cultural values and beliefs associated with their identities, which are context specific. In this regard, cultural studies reject the notion of universal phenomena, while emphasising cultural sensitivity and the holistic interpretation of data (Scupin, 1995: 411). A cultural study is therefore defined as a study that is focussed upon the dynamics of a culture within its historical context (Alasuutari, 1995). More importantly, cultural studies value all meanings as equally valid and important (ibid). In other words, no cultural value of a belief is superior or more important than any other and all behaviours can be explained through factors that require investigation and understanding within a context (ibid: 41). Based on my conviction that people's behaviours are guided by their values and beliefs, which result from their experiences and expectations associated with their particular social world, it is therefore important to understand the 'truth (s)' behind the perceived meanings conveyed by stories or narratives. Narrative inquiry explores the 'reality' within a context, with an emphasis on holistic and interpretive approaches in which 'reality' is not limited to an interpretation derived from one world but an infinite number of worlds relating to the subject's many attitudes and interpretations (Husen, 1988: 17; Pearse, 1983). People may differ in their responses to the same or similar situations, due to a person's interpretation within his/her own reference to his or her situated social context in a particular time and place (Gage, 1991; Crotty, 1998: 67). More importantly, meanings that are 'culturally derived' and 'historically situated' do not imply that a researcher's interpretations are bounded by the limits of the past. Instead, the past provides a frame of reference for the derived meanings of a person's current worldviews. The agglomeration of past and present worldviews on knowledge formation can be conceptualised as a spiral in which newly derived meanings become the foundation on which future knowledge develops (Crotty, 1998). Hence, the 'fusion' of the past and the present constitutes the 'reality' and 'truth' and 'knowledge' in that person's social world and the holistic interpretation of the participant can be achieved (Craig, 2007, Lindh *et al.*, 2009).

With this interpretation of 'truth', stories or narratives that are shared by research participants may yield multiple meanings and interpretations, since the participants adopt different frames of reference with different selves or identities across time periods and contexts. Relating this understanding to my study, although Hong Kong locals and Mainland Chinese people share similar cultural roots, their different social expectations from social roles, perhaps attributable to different sociopolitical factors, result in different behaviours and consequently different experiences within the shared context. In other words, these two groups of people experience different 'realities' within the same social context. With this, meaning contextualisation becomes critically important in exploring truths in relation to context across time and place.

Grounding narrative inquiry in the local context

The study was conducted within the context of postcolonial Hong Kong. Although Hong Kong was a British colony for over 100 years, it continued to be influenced by Confucian culture, which places strong emphasis on social hierarchy, power relations, group harmony and benevolence. With the reform of the population policy after unification with the People's Republic of China (PRC) in 1997, the number of new arrivals from Mainland China has been increasing dramatically and the cultural clashas between people of both areas have become more intense at all levels of society (Ip, 2014). I, as a narrative inquirer, re-oriented myself into multiple roles so that I experienced and interpreted the data from my understanding as a Hong Kong local and as a new arrival or immigrant in a different cultural context. Particularly, with the assets of having multiple identities with associated experiences, I can understand the cultural expectations and needs of a traditional Confucian Chinese person, a colonial Hong Kong local and a new immigrant from within my own frames of reference. When studying the narratives, I am aware of the implicit messages or feelings that might be associated with similar experiences and roles. Such awareness helps uncover and verify these unconscious hidden contextual issues and ensure that data are interpreted consciously and carefully.

Based on this, I, as the narrative inquirer, am never a neutral observer and analyst. Rather, I am the participants' partner in the process of interpretation 'from the historical and cultural context that defines one's interpretive framework' in which my interpretations of the stories are affected by my own frame of reference (Usher, 1996: 22). In this regard, my position on truth is that the interpretive process is a recursive activity generating new understandings or truths on a continuous basis, which could result in multiple or even an infinite number of truths and meanings (Pearse, 1983). The analysis and interpretation of participants' stories or narratives are not considered the products of either the participants or the researcher. Rather, they are the products of the researcher's and participants' accounts of a particular phenomenon – representing communal ownership with intersubjectivity (Craig, 2007).

Grounded in the contextualised meaning making approaches and my critical role in data interpretation in contributing to data transparency and authenticity, contextualising this study became particularly important in understanding the meaning of the narratives from the relevant cultural perspective and social roles that are adopted by individuals (Craig, 2007). A platform for self-representation through self-reflection was therefore needed to uncover the participants' conscious and unconscious identities and values, which help explain why they do what they do in a particular way at a particular time and place (Dillon, 2011). In this study, group discussion on parenting provided a platform for the participants to represent themselves from different perspectives on different parenting issues. Through sharing, all participants narrate and reflect on what they have said and done in the past, but also on the underlying motives, adopted identities and values behind the narratives which led to exploration of the 'truth' at that particular time as well as multiple truths across different life spans (Bamberg, 2009).

This study approached the investigation by using narrative inquiry wherein data, namely stories shared, are contextualised in relation to the cultural and social dimension of the participants. Throughout the storytelling process, the teller organises experiences into stories of important or critical events (Webster & Mertova, 2007). These critical events are considered to be important aspects of life in which meaningful information about who we are and why we behave in particular ways can be provided. The narratives that recount these events provide a specific structure for understanding meanings that convey participants' past and present values, beliefs and frames of reference to make the data interpretation more holistic and contextualised (ibid: 4). Hence, narratives allow researchers to present experiences holistically in all their complexity and richness in relation to time and place; aspects not usually revealed by more traditional research approaches such as questionnaires and individual interviews.

Narrative inquiry never aims at exploring causal relationships; it seeks to display how occurrences represent 'meanings' or 'truths' that show necessary connections between 'narratives' (Webster & Mertova, 2007: 19). Accordingly, using narrative inquiry enables me to gain a holistic understanding of the participants' experiences in two important ways. First, narrative inquiry helps me to become more aware of the multiple identities of people from diverse backgrounds in relation to the historical dimension and sociocultural values of the Mainland Chinese and Hong Kong locals. Second, narrative inquiry's emphasis on human-context relationships encourages me to reflect critically on my own relevant experiences, while the stories that are told help me understand how I can interpret and use their truths more responsibly (ibid, 2007: 7). In other words, through dialogue and reflection, both the narrative inquirer and the participants can not only construct (interpret within an adopted frame of reference) but also reconstruct or agglomerate the perceived truths (knowledge of the past and present) (ibid: 16).

As a narrative inquirer, I, myself, become the 'tool' to collect, process, analyse, interpret and present the data within the frame of my own experiences and those of the participants. The identity and contextual re-orientation in meaning making is considered as more humane in the sense that meaning emerges in relation to both researcher and researched, whereas the data were interpreted within context. The participants' and researcher's identities and cultural context therefore become the foreground of this study.

In this study, the dialogues between the participants and my reflections on their stories or narratives incorporate both participants' and researcher's stories or narratives that form the interpretations emerging from researcher and participants' frames of reference (Clandinin & Connelly, 2000: 4). Based on this assumption, after understanding what kind of story could be told, how, why, for whom and located within what context, I reached a position where I could make sense of the participants' experiences. In understanding meaning within context, the knowledge that emerges from the meaning making process becomes more meaningful and adoptable by people who share similar experiences. Investigating the stories with multiple lenses, my adopted frame of reference becomes critical in interpreting the stories and uncovering the contextual truth in order to obtain an empathetic understanding and completeness of data transparently and authentically (Mangan & Banks, 1999). In the following paragraphs, I will adopt the metaphor of a time machine to help readers to understand how, why, for whom and from what context I draw on my own perspectives and experiences of having been an outsider.

What, when, why and how do I study multiple identities in group settings?

In 2008, I was a research assistant for a family resilience project, which targeted families who experienced difficulties in their lives. Through this project, I met many families who were new arrivals from Mainland China and local Hong Kong families who were experiencing financial difficulties. While the structured interview was the major research tool used by the project, sharing sessions for the project participants were also organised to establish rapport with these families. My role in this project was as an observer who observed the sharing process and conducted structured interviews with the participants.

When I met the first group of participants, who were new arrivals and Hong Kong locals, I felt both familiar and yet not familiar with these labels. Although I am a Hong Kong local, I was once a new arrival in a foreign country. The new arrivals considered me to be a Hong Kong local, but I told them that I was once a new arrival in a foreign country in our informal conversation. I was not asked to compare myself to them by highlighting one of our shared identities, but the label of 'new arrival' that could be attached to me and to them drew seemingly different people together.

I will now show (1) how the participants were understood within the context, (2) how I used myself in data interpretation and analysis from different perspectives and identities to enhance the data authenticity and transparency and (3) how the inclusion of 'I' contributed to the discovery of multiple identities among parents with diverse sociocultural backgrounds via group sharing in Hong Kong.

The narratives of researcher and researched

Who are 'we'? Who are 'they'?

One autumn day in September 2008, I, as the research assistant of a government funded project, visited one of the research sites at Tin Shui Wai, a new town in northern Hong Kong, which is located close to the Hong Kong–China border. This research site is a community centre in Tin Shui Wai supporting the adaptation of new arrivals and was committed to a government funded project on family resilience. Negative media reports always describe Tin Shui Wai as a new town with a large population of new arrivals who have suffered family tragedies and financial difficulties. The centre supervisor helped to recruit participants from the community and informed them about the purpose of the project before they met together.

The participants arrived at the centre at around ten o'clock. They were all women. Without knowing anyone else in the room, they settled themselves in a pre-arranged semi-circle. To start the sharing session, the Principal Investigator (PI) introduced the project and me as a research assistant and as a student who was investigating multiple identities in a group setting. The PI started the sharing and invited the parents to introduce themselves to the group. There were six participants,all full time mothers of young children. There were three new arrivals from Mainland China who had resided in Hong Kong for less than five years and lived on welfare. The other three mothers were Hong Kong locals who lived in government subsidised public housing. I noticed that many of them spoke quite fast and softly, as if they wanted to finish their turn as quickly as possible. They seemed uncomfortable speaking in front of the group and being the centre of attention for even one minute or less. After the introductions, the PI briefed the participants about the family resilience project and started by asking them about their perception of 'new arrivals'. At first, I expected that the women would show some signs of discomfort, as the label of 'new arrivals' tends to carry a universally negative message. Surprisingly, the participants were very open and honest in discussing their views regarding the new arrivals. Mother A (new arrival) started the discussion in a frustrated tone. 'People always say that the new arrivals are lazy, don't work and rely on welfare. Many of us are very hard working and employed. I do admit there are some lazy ones, but many are not.'

Her assertive tone seemed to refute the public misrepresentation about new arrivals being a social burden.

Immediately after Mother A's claim, Mother B (new arrival), a medium-built female wearing fancy make up, continued, 'Yes, if jobs were available, nobody would want to rely on welfare. People always think we are lazy because the media only reports the bad parts.'

Mother C (Hong Kong local) nodded in agreement and joined the discussion. 'Just like Tin Shui Wai. The media's negative reporting causes the public to believe that Tin Shui Wai is a very poor district.'

The group lapsed briefly into silence. Mother F (new arrival) broke the silence by saying in a helpless tone, 'There are so few jobs in Tin Shui Wai. Many more jobs are available in Kowloon, but cross-district transportation is so expensive. The commuting time is also an issue. Nobody takes good care of our children.'

Suddenly, the women began to whisper to those sitting next to them. I could hear some expressing agreement regarding the difficulties they faced in this situation. The PI caught the group's attention and asked, 'Does anyone here have to work?'

The whispers faded, and the room became silent. None of the mothers raised her hand or said a word. They all looked at one another to check if any of them were employed.

The PI continued, 'So you all take care of your own children?'

They looked at each other and nodded. Then the PI asked, 'What difficulties do you face while raising children in Hong Kong?'

Mother B quickly replied,'Children in Hong Kong must be closely monitored.'

'Not those in China?' asked the PI.

'They need to be monitored to a lesser extent in China. We had very good relationships with our neighbours there. When we were young, we would never go hungry, as we would be fed by any one of our neighbours. But in Hong Kong, our neighbours do not even know one another,' Mother B complained.

All the new arrivals nodded in agreement. At this, a few Hong Kong locals in the group gave bitter smiles. Perhaps this claim was so familiar that they did not know how to respond. I could see embarrassment in their faces; however, this feeling did not last long.

A few seconds after Mother B's claim, Mother K (Hong Kong local) spoke up in defence.'The traffic in Hong Kong is chaotic; parents must hold their children's hand when on the road. But I see that some new arrivals let their very young children go out by themselves. These children play in playgrounds without any adult supervision.'

Immediately, Mother B, who had previously complained about the misrepresentation of the new arrivals, retorted,'There are two types of parents – those who closely monitor their children and those who let them run around without supervision.'

'Why would that be?' asked the PI.

'Some parents have no problems in letting their children go out on their own. We were brought up in China without supervision. Even now, the children in our home town grow up in the sun. However, the children in Hong Kong grow up indoors with toys. We are different,' Mother B further explained.

Both the new arrivals and the Hong Kong locals appeared to agree with Mother B's explanation, which was perhaps so familiar to them that nobody wanted to discuss it further.

Since there was no further response to Mother B's claims, the PI asked if the new arrivals and their children had ever experienced any discrimination. Rather than looking at each other, as they had done earlier, the parents simply stared at the PI, giving no further response. There was silence for a few seconds. Their faces showed some signs of hesitation, but I do not think they were surprised by this question. They just did not know how to answer – where to start. Suddenly, Mother B broke the ice again and said, 'The locals simply cannot accept the fact that we are smarter than them.'

'Can you explain what you mean? Smarter than them?' asked the PI.

'Yes. Previously, I worked in sales in Kowloon. Whenever I performed better than my Hong Kong local co-workers, they would do something to hurt me. For example, speak to the boss behind my back,' answered Mother B.

'Why, and what did they say about you?' asked the PI.

'They simply couldn't accept the fact that we could be better than them. They would spread rumours that the mainlanders must have done something underhand in order to get a better sales performance,' she elaborated.

At this moment, Mother F (new arrival) joined the conversation by declaring in a loud and angry voice, 'Once a lady called me a "mainlander ghost" when my arm accidently touched hers in a crowded bus. She pushed me. I kicked her in return.'

The participants' eyes, and even some mouths, opened wide on hearing that Mother F had actually fought with somebody on the bus. I assumed that both the new arrivals and the Hong Kong locals believe that fighting is not the right solution. Both groups were surprised that an accidental body touch could lead to a fight. Although Mother F recognised the astonished look on the participants' faces, she did not feel embarrassed or disgraced. She continued, 'She (the passenger) then got off the bus. I guess she was scared. We (both Mother F and the passenger) had the same skin colour. If she (the passenger) was not Chinese, then who was she? Was she a foreigner?'

The PI did not directly respond to this story. Instead, he turned to the group and asked, 'How do people know that you are not Hong Kong locals?'

'Accent,' Mother F replied with a pout.

The other mothers nodded.

Mother E (Hong Kong local), who had been settled in Hong Kong for over 20 years, said, 'Appearance . . . clothes.'

'What do they wear?' asked the PI.

'Mainlanders are not very fashionable,' Mother E answered.

'Mainlanders should be more fashionable; then they'll look much more beautiful than the Hong Kong locals!' Mother F responded with a laugh.

Immediately, laughter erupted in the room as the other mothers strongly agreed. Some said, 'That's so true', while all the participants laughed and nodded in agreement. Although nobody explained why they laughed and nodded agreement, the extraordinary laughter of the entire group conveyed an implicit message that was shared by all of them – young female mainlanders in Hong Kong are perceived and reported by the media as intruders who can break up the marriages of Hong Kong couples. I wondered if the mother who commented on the fashion sense of the newly arrived women was making a sarcastic joke. The discussion ended in laughter.

The narratives in relation to researcher and local context

The narratives illustrate the power of adopted identity in the group, which resulted in identity interpretation and group affiliation (Stets & Burke, 2000). The group participants were not only conscious of their identities as Mainland Chinese and new arrivals but also defended their identities vigorously and explicitly throughout the conversation. In this group, the new arrivals significantly outnumbered the Hong Kong locals. At the outset of the activity, the PI asked the participants to introduce themselves, including their years of settlement in Hong Kong. The self-introduction activity, therefore, already conveyed the clear message that there were two groups of participants in the sharing group. Following this, the PI's question about the participants' perception of 'new arrivals' further set the context for identity formation in this activity – new arrivals versus Hong Kong locals. Given that the new arrivals constituted the majority in this sharing session, it was understandable that they were not as quiet and timid as they were within the mainstream community (of Hong Kong locals). In the beginning, the new arrivals could not wait to describe the unfair treatment they received. They did not try to hide their status as new arrivals. Rather, they expressed their anger at being misunderstood and labelled as lazy and reliant on social welfare. Moreover, Mother B's attempt to speak up for the new arrivals elicited a chain reaction wherein others joined the protest. The new arrivals took this opportunity to explain why they were misrepresented by both the Hong Kong locals and the media. At this point, a local Hong Kong mother (Mother C) joined in the conversation and blamed the media for misrepresenting Tin Shui Wai as a very poor district. Hence, the common concern of both the groups was that the media's negative reports misrepresented their identities or images to the public. The new arrivals were concerned about their distorted images, while the Hong Kong residents focused on the economic status of Tin Shui Wai residents. Hence, although they focussed on different aspects, they were able to break through the silence between them, taking the first step to engage in discussion as one group with common concerns. However, this discussion was characterised by individual presentations of their own views or concerns, without much collaborative interaction and discussion about their shared identities and experiences: residents of Tin Shui Wai.

The very end of this activity was when a new arrival (Mother F) made the statement about the fashionable appearance[2] of the new arrivals, which united the two groups again, to a certain extent. Her comment conveyed that, unlike the stereotyped communist citizens of the past, the mainlanders kept pace with modern trends. Mother F's comment indicated that, in her view, the appearance of the new arrivals was comparable to that of the Hong Kong locals. At another level, she referred to the social issue of the 'second wife' that was prevalent in some Hong Kong families with low socioeconomic status. The hidden meaning of this reference was well understood by all the participants, who burst into sarcastic laughter at the comment. More interestingly, the new arrivals laughed extraordinarily loudly and nodded in response, possibly to indicate to the group that they were not second wives, as the public believed. Such a social response from both the groups reflects that they all shared the same social and moral values wherein having a second wife was unacceptable. Such shared values minimise intergroup differences and maximise intergroup similarities.

Throughout the sharing, the new arrivals interpreted themselves as a 'good and responsible group of new arrivals' comparable to the Hong Kong locals, as opposed to those new arrivals who were stereotyped as lazy and irresponsible with regard to their children. They explicitly differentiated the 'misrepresented new arrivals' from the 'irresponsible new arrivals', and their core message was, 'Many of the new arrivals are as good as the Hong Kong locals. It is only you (the Hong Kong locals and the media) who misrepresent us as intruders exploiting the welfare system in Hong Kong society'.

None of the new arrivals denied their identity as new arrivals. However, in their conversation, they emphasised that they were civilised new arrivals with citizenship qualities comparable to those of the Hong Kong locals. By doing this, they defended and sought respect for their identity as new arrivals while supporting the identity of the Hong Kong residents. The narrative data indicate that the process of identity interpretation and group affiliation, namely being in-group members, was decided by whether the participants' performed behaviour and held values were similar to those of the Hong Kong locals. These narratives thus explicate the dual identities of the new arrivals and the Hong Kong locals.

Researcher as an immigrant

I was an immigrant in Canada, where I experienced being treated unfairly. Nobody wants to be isolated, myself included. The easiest way to be 'perceived' as part of the mainstream is to change one's image, including one's outfits and accent. I still remember that when I was in school, I performed as a mainstreamer, raising my hand with the index finger pointing up, greeting teachers with a 'Hi!' and answering their questions while remaining seated. All these behaviours are considered disrespectful in a Chinese classroom. At that time, I was perfectly aware that I would be considered an 'alien' if I stood up to answer the teacher's questions or greeted the teacher with a bow. Under pressure to adapt, I felt an urgent need to be treated as an 'in-group' member, as my sole motivation was to be closer to the host culture. As an immigrant, I was always conscious that my performed identity required me to resemble the host culture in certain aspects, at least at the level of observation. Hence, a performed identity results from an individual's need to meet the requirements of a particular context in order to be considered in-group. A new immigrant will make every effort to assimilate, to be more similar to the host culture. This assimilation, however, does not imply a devaluation of the immigrant's own culture, beliefs and values (Brubaker, 2001). Instead, in my case, the attempt to seek common ground not only reflects my Chinese cultural values of group harmony and member inclusion and exclusion for interpersonal communication, but also the process of appropriating a particular group of people and context so that we can be understood by the majority and the environment to which we attach ourselves (ibid).

Understanding with shared experiences and identity

The narratives and my experience as an immigrant illustrate the issue of identity formation and fluidity to satisfy the desire to belong. Cultural minorities can easily adopt physical traits such as accents and outfits in order to resemble the host culture, while shared interests create a platform for different groups to identify their similarities and thereby minimise intergroup differences. However, certain perceived similarities emerge based on the information conveyed within a particular context at a particular time. As seen in the narratives of the first group sharing, the perceived similarities of particular aspects changed according to the shifts in the discussion topic. The narratives further showed that there are different values and beliefs associated with shared identity due to people being brought up with different sociopolitical backgrounds and different social expectations towards the same social role. Merely uniting people with different backgrounds by using shared identity is very fragile. Rather, exploring the shared context, such as the values and beliefs associated with the shared identity, can facilitate communication with respect and understanding. In this study, I related my own perspectives and experiences with the participants to show my understanding of their values and motivation within the context of having been an immigrant (a non mainstreamer) and a Hong Kong local familiar with the social issues (e.g. second wife) in Hong Kong. With shared context, identities and experiences, I became more sensitive, not over sensitive, to the feeling and motivation of 'wanting to belong', to the subtle interactions such as eye contact and gestures that communicate much deeper feelings than the face meaning of words.

Insights into revealing multiple identities in group settings in the local context

The narrative inquiry journey allowed me to re-orient myself into different perspectives and to reflect on similar experiences that helped me to understand the narratives from having shared or experienced similar social roles, perceptions and emotions. Taking account of Chinese cultural values, namely Confucian values, of avoiding conflict and maintaining group harmony, behaviour that positions people as in-group and out-group is very subtle and cannot be understood without contextualising the narratives within the cultural context. Building upon the groundwork of shared identities and data contextualisation of the narratives in relation to my local context, I found that the perceived similarities and differences significantly contribute to group affiliation and sense of belonging. While Confucianism emphasises group harmony and social hierarchy, the extent to which group members perceive themselves as similar or different affects the extent to which they interact with one another. The establishment of a shared identity enhances the perceived similarities and therefore positive group dynamics among group members. Self-perceived identity could range from an easily recognised one based on appearances to a deeper, unobservable level comprising shared social roles and expectations from the adopted role, which requires deeper understanding through intergroup communication.

The value of narrative inquiry in this study

This chapter has discussed the importance of contextualising research within the Hong Kong social and cultural context wherein it took place and the importance of developing methodological approaches that are grounded in these contexts. As a narrative inquirer, my experiences, as well as my multiple identities, strengthened the transparency and authenticity in interpreting participants' voices from multiple perspectives, not only the literal meaning but also their motivations in wanting to belong and their beliefs and feelings when they adopted different social roles in response to immediate contextual needs such as discussion topics and group norms. The methodological approach was grounded within the local context and lies on a continuum of self-centred perspective (perceived self) as well as a culturally and socially situated self and similarities with others.

Developing identity awareness and engagement require self-awareness and self-understanding in reviewing myself as well as similar others. One of the key conditions to develop self-awareness of multiple identities in participants is to engage them in a dialogic context where they acquire a sense of belonging and are supported with respect and understanding. The conversation among the participants was viewed as a dynamic process of positioning and re-positioning their self-identity and values in response to contextual needs across the life span, where the possible 'truth' is explored rather than an investigation leading to any understanding of an absolute or ultimate 'truth' (Hermans, 2003; Hermans *et al.*, 1992). The interactive conversation provided participants with the opportunity to conceive of themselves in many different ways.

Drawing on meaning contextualisation and discussing the appropriateness of using narrative inquiry in this study, there is no doubt that 'I' cannot be left out in the process of data interpretation and presentation. Although I have been criticised by local academics for being unprofessional and subjective in using 'I' in data analysis and presentation, I would argue that the inclusion of 'I' helps readers to experience and understand the contextual information.

Conclusion

In this chapter I have acknowledged the relevance of the cultural and social dimension of narrative in exploring multiple identities across time and context via the platform of sharing among parents in Hong Kong. Rather than understanding the narratives based on a single episode, they are interpreted and understood on a continuum where the researcher and researched move between different thoughts and feelings across time and place, and reflect their lived realities by making connections with these 'realities' (Clandinin & Connelly, 2000) The issue of contextualising narratives and looking at multiple identities and realities has strong ethical implications, as it calls for the development of a new understanding of the individual as well as the collective experience of researcher and researched. The exploration of multiple identities and realties and their connections alerts us to a bigger picture of understanding truth and our world.

Notes

1 In the Q sort method, the evaluator/assessor is given a set of statements or previously developed items. The assessor orders the Q-items into a designated number of categories, with an assigned number of items placed in each category. At one end of the continuum are placed the items most characteristic of the person being described, or most 'salient' in describing the person. At the other end of the continuum are placed the items most 'salient' in a negative sense. For each item, the number of the category in which it was placed is recorded (Block, 2008: 12).

2 The stereotype is that communists are perceived to be detached from the rest of the world, including social life. However, the modern Mainland Chinese women are very fashionable in appearance and often marry Hong Kong locals and later settle in Hong Kong.

References

Alasuutari, P. (1995). *Researching Culture: Qualitative Method and Cultural Studies.* London; Thousand Oaks, California: Sage Publications.

Bamberg, M. (2009). Identity and Narration. In Hühn, P., Pier, J. & Schmid, W. (Eds). *Handbook of Narratology.* Germany: Deutsche Nationalbibliothek, pp. 132–143.

Block, J. (2008). *The Q-Sort in Character Appraisal: Encoding Subjective Impressions Of Persons Quantitatively. American Psychological Association.*

Brubaker, R. (2001). The Return of Assimilation? Changing Perspectives on Immigration and its Sequels in France, Germany, and the United States. *Ethnic and Racial Studies,* 24(4), 531–548.

Clandinin, D. J. & Connellly, F. M. (2000). *Narrative Inquiry: Experience and Story in Qualitative Research.* San Francisco: Jossey-Bass Publishers.

Craig, E. (2007). Hermeneutic Inquiry in Depth Psychology: A Practical and Philosophical Reflection. *The Humanistic Psychologist,* 35(4), 307–321.

Crotty, M. (1998). *The Foundations of Social Research: Meaning and Perspective in the Research Process.* Thousand Oaks, California: Sage Publications.

Dillon, L. (2011). Writing the self: The emergence of a dialogic space. *Narrative Inquiry,* 21(2), 213–237. John Benjamins Publishing Company.

Gage, N. L. (1991). The Obviousness of Social and Educational Research Results. *Educational Researcher,* 20(1), 10–16.

Hermans, H. J. M. (2003). The Construction and Re-Construction of a Dialogical Self. *Journal of Constructivist Psychology,* 16(2), 89–130.

Hermans, H. J. M., Kempen, H. J. G. & van Loon, R. J. P. (1992). The Dialogical Self: Beyond Individualism and Rationalism. *American Psychologists,* 47(1), 23–33.

Husen, T. (1988). Educational Research and Policy Making. In J.P. Keeves (Ed.). *Educational Research, Methodology, and Measurement: An International Handbook.* Oxford: Pergamon Press.

Ip, P. K. (2014). Harmony as Happiness? Social Harmony in Two Chinese Societies. *Social Indicators Research,* 117(3), 719–741.

Lindh, I., Severinsson, E. & Berg, A. (2009). Nurses' Moral Strength: A Hermeneutic Inquiry in Nursing Practice. *Journal of Advanced Nursing,* 65(9), 1882–1890.

Mangan, J. M. & Banks, C. K. (1999). *The Company of Neighbours: Revitalizing Community through Action-Research.* Toronto: University of Toronto Press.

Pearse, H. (1983). Brother Can You Spare a Paradigm? The Theory Beneath the Practice. *Studies in Art Education,* 24, 158–163.

Scupin, R. (1995). Cultural Anthropology. A Global Perspective (2nd ed.). New Jersey: Prentice Hall.

Stets, J. & Burke, P. (2000). Identity Theory and Social Identity Theory. *Social Psychology Quarterly,* 63(3), 224–237.

Usher, R. (1996). A Critique of the Neglected Epistemological Assumptions of Educational Research. In Scott, D. & Usher, R. (Eds). *Understanding Educational Research.* London: Routledge.

Webster, L. & Mertova, P. (2007). Using Narrative Inquiry as a Research Method: An Introduction to Using Critical Event Narrative Analysis in Research on Learning and Teaching. London and New York: Routledge.

13 Identity and identity education of Hong Kong Chinese people

A narrative self-study of an educator

Chan Nai Kwok Francis

Introduction

In this chapter, I explore my personal experience in two historical events relating to the world-shocking June 4 Incident[1] that took place in the People's Republic of China (PRC) in the summer of 1989. The first is a story of how Hong Kong Chinese reacted towards the Incident when it was unfolding. As a secondary school history teacher at that time, I was among those actively taking to the streets in Hong Kong to support the protesters in Beijing when they were in action. The second is one of the aftermaths of the June 4 Incident in Hong Kong. It was a controversial debate in 1994 on whether the June 4 Incident should be mentioned in history textbooks. As a curriculum officer of history and civic education working in the Department of Education at that time, I was caught in the midst of the controversy.

The issue of identity among Hong Kong Chinese has stood out prominently in the June 4 Incident per se and its aftermath. Through this narrative self-study, I inquire into the puzzles of Hong Kong Chinese over their identity in the face of the political handover of their city from Britain to China in 1997. In the first part of this chapter, I reconstruct my experience of the collective activism of Hong Kong people during the June 4 Incident in 1989, followed by a reflection of its relationship to our identity issue. The second part is a narrative of the History textbook controversy in 1994 and discussion on the concerns of people in Hong Kong over the identity education to be promoted in schools for the political handover.

Background of Hong Kong Chinese and the 1997 issue

Hong Kong was ceded and leased to Britain by Qing China according to three treaties signed in the nineteenth century. In the Treaty of Nanjing (1842) signed after her defeat in the First Opium War (1839–1841), China gave away the Hong Kong Island. In 1860, the Kowloon Peninsula was further conceded to Britain after the Second Opium War (1856–1860). Finally, in 1898 the New Territories were leased to Britain for 99 years, a lease that was to expire on June 30, 1997. Probably unforeseen at the time of signing these treaties and lease, 1997 was to become a magic number for Hong Kong people many years later.

Under these treaties, Hong Kong people had been living under British colonial rule for nearly one and a half century. The great majority of Hong Kong people (over 95 per cent) were ethnic Chinese but politically they were British subjects. For a long period of time, people in Hong Kong lived their daily life peacefully with a mix of traditional Chinese and Western cultures and institutions. Being sheltered from the political upheavals in the mainland, Hong Kong had acted as a temporary safe haven for many Mainland Chinese, with large numbers of people moving across the boundary in times of social and political turbulences, especially during the Second World War (1941–1945), the Great Leap Forward (1958–1960) and the Cultural Revolution (1966–1976) in China.

For a long time during the colonial period, most people in Hong Kong identified themselves as Chinese in a historical or cultural sense. National identity in a political sense had been vague. Discussion of national identity was mostly avoided in schools and in the society in general. However, as Hong Kong approached the end of the 99-year lease, the Chinese and British governments began negotiation on the future of Hong Kong in the early 1980s and finally settled on a Sino-British Joint Declaration in 1984. It was then that the issue of national identity arose for people in Hong Kong.

The issue of identity of the Hong Kong Chinese in the face of 1997 was one of the key concerns among scholars during the transitional period (Cheng & Wong, 2002; Lau, 1997; Lee, 1995, 1998; Lui, 1997; Wong, 1995, 1998, 1999). Various groups of Hong Kong Chinese reacted to the 1997 issue differently, depending upon their personal backgrounds. While some were excited or frightened by the prospect of a Chinese takeover in 1997, a large proportion of Hong Kong Chinese felt puzzled, ambivalent or confused by the key question of their identity: "Who am I and where am I going?" For many of the Hong Kong Chinese, the emergence of the 1997 issue was the occasion on which they questioned their identity seriously for the very first time.

One evening in May 1986, I went to watch a slide show on the destiny of Hong Kong with one of my best friends, Fok (a pseudonym). The show was produced by a local Christian organisation in the mid 1980s when the 1997 issue became the talk of the city. In one entry from my 1986 diary, I wrote the following:

[A]fter watching the slide show, we walked on the street without saying a word for quite a long while. It was Fok who broke the silence.
"Which identity should come first," Fok asked me with a puzzling look, "as a Hongkongese, a Chinese or simply a human being?"

Diary entry, May 18, 1986

Fok emigrated to Toronto some years later in 1991.

Hong Kong's return to China in 1997 turned out to be a significant moment for Hong Kong people to ask themselves who they were and what it meant to be Hong Kong Chinese. According to the Basic Law (The People's Republic of China, 1990), Hong Kong Chinese were going to be a special type of Chinese, living in their motherland, yet under a different political system. They would become citizens of a communist country but allowed to continue their 'capitalist' way of life in Hong Kong. However, the concept of *Hong Kong Chinese* could be interpreted differently, as it involves various identities of the people of Hong Kong. According to Lau (1997), the Hong Kong identity and the Chinese identity are the two most prominent identities of Hong Kong Chinese. In the past, most of them identified themselves with the culture of China, but not with the political regime in Beijing. With the handover in 1997, however, their Chinese citizenship implies a civic identity, which they cannot decline if they choose to become Hong Kong Chinese living in the Special Administrative Region (SAR) after 1997.

The June 4 Incident

Suddenly, the June 4 Incident in 1989 complicated the whole issue of identity of Hong Kong people. They became bewildered by the fact that the Beijing government, which had crushed the peaceful pro-democracy movement of the patriotic students, was going to rule them in less than ten years. In the following section, my autobiographical narrative of the reactions of Hong Kong people during the June 4 Incident aims to help illuminate part of the complexity of the issue of identity of Hong Kong Chinese. My own diary records, apart from other references, are the key source materials of the reconstruction of my personal experience in the episode.

The death of Hu Yaobang

The pro-democracy movement in Beijing was triggered by the death of Hu Yaobang, the ex-party general secretary, on April 15, 1989. He was mourned by university students in Beijing as a liberal reform leader who was forced to step down in December 1986 for tolerating 'bourgeois liberation' among young people in China (Baum, 1994). Immediately, the mourners took the opportunity of the funeral of Hu to call for an end to corruption, nepotism and abuse of power among officials of all levels, particularly the senior cadres. They saw greater democracy of the people as the solution to all these vices (Tsang, 1997).

They put up wall posters in their own university campuses, organised sit-ins near the Great Hall of the People in Tiananmen Square and in front of the most senior party leaders' residences. Not only were their pleas ignored, the demonstrators were stunned by an editorial in the *People's Daily* on April 26, 1989 commenting on their movement as a planned conspiracy. The students became outraged and responded with massive rallies which were joined by academics, workers, professionals and even government employees.

Students began a hunger strike in Tiananmen Square on May 13 when the government stood firm and refused to retrieve the editorial of the *People's Daily*. This act proved to be catalytic in enlisting the support of more people who had so far been concerned by-standers. The students' firm dedication to their cause, even at the expense of rapidly deteriorating health, powerfully moved a large local population from all walks of life. More and more people went to the Square to give support to the students suffering from the hunger strike (Zhang, 2001).

Hong Kong people: from onlookers to demonstrators

Though the people of Hong Kong had been keeping a relatively low profile towards what was happening in Beijing, they were greatly concerned and well informed by the daily and hourly news updates from the newspapers, radios and televisions in Hong Kong. During those days, I read at least three newspapers every morning to follow stories of the movement. In my school, the radio in the staff room was turned on during recess and lunchtime to catch the most recent news stories. The atmosphere was tense and heavy.

The development in Beijing took a drastic turn on the night of May 19 when Premier Li Peng imposed martial law in Beijing with immediate military rein- forcements. It was clear that actions would be taken against the students still occupying Tiananmen Square. On hearing that, I immediately decided to join a hastily organised protest rally on the following day at Victoria Park, one of the major parks on Hong Kong Island.

I can still remember clearly that Hong Kong was struck by a strong typhoon and heavy rains the next day. Three colleagues and I, all wet to the skin, were run- ning feverishly along the streets to distribute leaflets to all the passers-by we met, inviting them to join a rally in the afternoon to protest against the imposition of martial law in Beijing.

The following day, I wrote in my diary: 'The rally held in the midst of a typhoon at Victoria Park was really unforgettable. We made history in stormy weather'(May 21, 1989). I felt outraged by the high-handed measures adopted by the Chinese Government to suppress the peaceful movement of the dem- onstrators and wrote: 'Deng Xiao-ping and Li Peng were really too much and should be condemned'(May 21, 1989).

A one million people rally

On Sunday, May 21, we joined the first territory-wide mass rally to protest against the Beijing government. It was roughly estimated that over one million people joined the rally (Wong, 2000), an unprecedented event in the history of Hong Kong. Having lived under colonial rule for a long time, most Hong Kong people were politically aloof but on that day, things changed.

Though I had studied and taught history for years, I had never felt the close relationship between Hong Kong and Mainland China to such a great inten- sity. The fate of these two places had never been so strongly connected to one another, both being hinged upon the outcome of this same historic event.

During the two following weeks, I joined nearly all the major mass rallies. I felt puzzled about the outcome of the incident. On the one hand, I hoped that 'I might have the chance of witnessing the collapse of the Chinese Communist

Party' (June 1, 1989). On the other, I had a feeling that the prospects did not look so optimistic. I wrote:

> [I] hate the brutality of the totalitarian regime of China. It seems that China is going to miss a good chance of transforming herself. Though the student movement, if abortive, might still contribute to the building of a new China in the long run, much time will be wasted. Indeed, China cannot afford such a waste. She is going to lose a historic opportunity.
>
> June 2, 1989

This entry was written two days before the military crackdown on June 4. The erection of the Statue of the Goddess of Democracy in Tiananmen Square on May 30 by the students and the mobilisation of troops into the capital by the government on June 1 further intensified the situation. I sensed that the final showdown between the government and the protesters was not far away.

The military crackdown

The military crackdown on June 4 came as a great shock for many people, even though they had sensed that the government would definitely clear Tiananmen Square occupied by student demonstrators for more than two weeks. Given the uncompromising attitude upheld by both sides, it was expected that some sort of force, like tear gas or hydraulic jets might be employed to accomplish the task.

What had actually taken place in Tiananmen Square in the early morning of June 4 in 1989 has yet to be fully revealed (Zhang, 2001). The core of contention over the last 25 years has been the question whether soldiers killed any students in the process of 'clearing' the Square. The Government denied any casualties in the Square, while a number of people claimed that they were eyewitnesses of a massacre there.

In Tsang's (1997, p. 162) description, 'the whole world was stunned and dismayed by the massacre they saw on their television sets. The people of Hong Kong were utterly devastated'. Most people in Hong Kong believed that there was a massacre in Beijing and reacted with feelings of shock, horror, disbelief and outrage. I noted in my diary that I felt extremely tired physically and spiritually for several days following June 4. Above all, I was extremely worried about the situation of China after the crackdown.

In the afternoon of June 4, Black Sunday, over half a million mourners attended a massive rally at the Happy Valley Race Course. My friends and I volunteered to help keep order and discipline along the way. Two or three days later, I helped organise a mourning assembly for all our students in the school chapel. Teachers and students shared their feelings about the massacre, showing great sorrow and anger. On June 11, I gave a talk on the historical account of the Incident in a mourning ceremony organised by a Catholic body. In my diary, I wrote: 'I was responsible for retelling the story of the student movement and felt deeply moved in my own narration' (June 11, 1989).

The June 4 Incident and the identity issue

According to some scholars, the Tiananmen Incident in 1989 brought the Hong Kong people's identity issue to a head, and even to the extent of a crisis (Lau, 1996; Lee, 1995; So, 1999; Tsang, 1997). For the very first time, Hong Kong people became strongly aware of and worried about their Chinese identity. They identified with the student protesters in Beijing as fellow Chinese and showed great concern about the future of China as their own country. However, they condemned the Chinese Government as repressive and illegitimate in the way it reacted to the peaceful pro-democracy movement. The Chinese identity of people in Hong Kong was no longer a merely distant and abstract idea. It had immense practical implications for how we were going to live our lives in the transition to 1997 and thereafter.

We are Chinese but with mixed feelings.

For many Hong Kong people, their ambivalence towards their Chinese identity was suddenly swept aside, at least temporarily during this period with passionate sentiments of patriotism and nationalism. The June 4 Incident consolidated a new Hong Kong ethnic identity vis-à-vis a Chinese national identity (So, 1999).

In Wong's (2000, p. 73) view,

> [T]he emergence of the mass pro-democracy movement in China unleashed the suppressed sense of Chinese national identity and the patriotic sentiments of many Hong Kong Chinese. This 'reactive' nationalism was an important driving force in mass mobilization, galvanizing Hong Kong people to stand shoulder to shoulder with the Chinese people and to oppose the repressive communist regime by peaceful means.

The intensity of the emotional commitment shown by the people of Hong Kong in May and June of 1989 suggested that we recognised China as our mother country and wished her success in her modernisation. As we valued democracy, human rights and freedom, we were also eager to see China acknowledge these values to become a modernised society as soon as possible. Since I took a positive view of the pro-democracy movement in Beijing, its suppression was seen as a setback of the nation on her road to modernisation. I wrote in my diary: 'As the government had chosen to push over the Statue of Goddess of Democracy and gun down her people in Tiananmen Square, where was China heading to?' (June 6, 1989). I was extremely worried and puzzled and even depressed during those days.

Identity crisis of the Hong Kong Chinese

Two weeks after the crackdown, I wrote: 'The tragedy has outraged all people. It will be hopeless for the future of Hong Kong if the existing regime does not collapse' (June 19, 1989). I felt that the fate of the PRC regime was linked to the future of Hong Kong. The June 4 Incident touched upon the core of the China complex and the identity crisis experienced by Hong Kong Chinese.

Indeed, the mentality and activism of the Hong Kong people in the pro-democracy movement could only be properly understood in the context of their own fate. In 1989, Hong Kong was nearly halfway in her transition from a British colony to a Chinese SAR in 1997. The Beijing government promised Hong Kong the 'maintenance of the status quo for another 50 years' with a 'high degree of autonomy' and 'rule by Hong Kong people'. However, ever since these promises were promulgated in the Joint Declaration in 1984, the Hong Kong Chinese had cast serious doubts on both the sincerity and competence of the Chinese government in honouring them (Chan, 1997). Before the June 4 Incident, there had already been the first round of exodus of emigrants, a sign of mistrust of the promises (Wong, 1995). Given the track records of the PRC regime on human rights, people in Hong Kong preferred to secure some sort of political insurance in foreign countries against any possible woes after 1997.

For many people in Hong Kong, the Tiananmen Square crackdown was a double shock. Apart from experiencing an outburst of their high hope of building a democratic China, they suddenly realised that the sovereign power greeting them in 1997 might likely be this same tyrannical and repressive PRC regime. 'Whither Hong Kong?' The intensity of a sense of crisis over their identity had never been experienced before, as vividly captured by a comment made immediately after the Tiananmen Square crackdown:

> [N]ow, the most urgent and important question concerning the future of Hong Kong is: whether the United Kingdom should implement the Joint Declaration to hand over the six million of Hong Kong people to a communist rule as brutal as the Pol Pot regime of Cambodia.
>
> Li, 1989, p. 51

In the first few years after the June 4 Incident, Hong Kong experienced a sudden upsurge of the number of emigrants (Wong, 1995). At the same time, many people joined the annual June 4 candlelight vigil year after year. I am one of those who attended it every year, even during the three years (from 1993 to 1995) when I worked in the Education Department as a senior curriculum officer of history and civic education. In fact, the June 4 Incident continued to loom large in the identity politics of Hong Kong as 1997 was drawing closer and closer.

An aftermath: the textbook controversy in 1994

A few years after 1989, I left teaching in the frontline and joined the Curriculum Development Institute of the Hong Kong Government. I was responsible for the development of the secondary school history curriculum.

On June 27, 1994, when I was busily editing the draft of a new history curriculum guideline, a newspaper reporter came to my office to seek my view on a comment made by the Director of Education on an issue of history education. There was a feature article in a local newspaper that morning reporting that the June 4 Incident of 1989 appeared for the first time in one of the local Chinese history textbooks in Hong Kong. It was only a brief account of the Incident in 81 Chinese characters. Two university teachers and one publisher commented that it was inappropriate to teach about the Incident in school history because it was too recent and the account was too brief to understand the whole picture.

Dominic Wong, the then Director of Education of Hong Kong, in response to an inquiry from a newspaper reporter that morning about whether the contro-versial June 4 Incident could be mentioned in local history textbooks, answered in the negative. He considered that what happened within 20 years should be regarded as current affairs instead of history because it took a much longer time to discern historical trends ('Events within 20 years', 1994).

His view was immediately challenged by the chairman of the Hong Kong Professional Teachers' Union, who insisted that the Incident was part of history and there had not been any official ban on teaching it so far ('Events within 20 years',' 1994). On the following day, Wong issued an official statement on his stance on the issue.

Coverage of history textbooks

Following a discussion between the Education Department and representa-tive of the publisher concerned, the latter has agreed with the Education Department that, as far as history textbooks are concerned, events which took place within the last 20 years and which have not yet been established by objective analyses, verification and assessment should not be covered. Twenty years is considered to be a reasonable minimum period.

The Education Department will strengthen its textbook reviewing pro-cedures and will reiterate its advice to publishers that events within the last 20 years, of which the full facts have not yet been established, should not be covered in history textbooks.

The publisher's decision to remove the section concerned from the text-book is unrelated to any political considerations.

It is noted that history textbooks should always be handled with care.

Press release No. 12 by the Education Department,
June 29, 1989

This official statement sparked off heated debates in the following few days. On the one hand, there erupted a roar of condemnations. Academics, educators and teachers criticised it as a political rather than educational or professional decision.

On the other hand, those who were more pro-China supported Wong's deci-sion. They argued that the Incident was too controversial and it was difficult to have any consensus as a historical fact and that even in the USA or some European countries there existed a ban on releasing confidential information within a certain period of time. Therefore, in their view, it was more appropriate to discuss it as current affairs in civic education. The controversy quickly went beyond purely aca-demic or educational confines and was turned into a political issue. The Governor, Chris Patten, also asked the Director to review his decision ('Chris Patten', 1994).

A few days later, the Director issued another statement, denying

> any administrative directive regarding the time-frame within which history should not be taught. In other words, historical events in recent years can still be printed in history textbooks. . . .
>
> The Government and the Education Department have no (repeat no) power to censor school textbooks, or delete any part of it . . . publishers can publish whatever they want . . . .
>
> The Education Department has only offered comments on some of the wording, which may carry implications of value judgment of events. The June 4 Incident can still be included in textbooks.
>
> The Director of Education's Explanation and
> Clarification dated 4 July, 1994

Though his critics welcomed the Director's ambiguous retreat from his former stance as a back down, the controversy over the episode lasted until early September, with more speculations on the Director's motives and interpretations of the significance of this incident in the fields of politics and education, particularly in the context of the transition to 1997.

As a senior curriculum officer of world history at that time, I was only indirectly involved in this episode, which originated from a textbook of Chinese history.[2] My counterpart of Chinese history was asked to help the Director to handle the case. He provided the Director with information about the curriculum and met the publisher of the textbook to see what could be done about the disputed paragraph on the June 4 Incident. I was requested to conduct a literature search to see whether any eminent professional historians had ever written something that could be quoted to support the Director on the 20-year rule on history education.

I remember that I found the stance of the Director on the 20-year rule absurd. As a history educator, I viewed that history, after all, was an interpretative business and any interpretation was tentative. The understanding of the nature of history as 'events, which have been established by objective analyses, verification and assessment' was regarded by me to be at least outdated if not misconceived. Furthermore, this view of history education as a transmission of a body of factual information was not in line with the skills-based and inquiry-oriented approach in the teaching and learning of history we were promoting at that time.

Though debate on the textbook controversy was officially closed on July 4 with the Director's back-down, its repercussions could still be felt in the following months. In retrospect, the major criticisms against the Director's decision, apart from his misconception of the nature of history and history education, included attempts of bureaucratic control of the curriculum and textbooks (Morris, 1997), administrative interference into professional and academic autonomy (Siu, 1996) and implications of self-censorship on the part of publishers and teachers (Lee & Bray, 1995). These accusations have to be understood in the political context of Hong Kong at that time and, in my view now, the identity of the people of Hong Kong was mingled with this textbook controversy.

Why is it so sensitive?

First, the main concern here was not only the importance of the learning of the history of contemporary China. It was rather the content of the story of communist China to be told. Should we teach our students the negative aspects along with the bright side of the PRC regime? What kind of story of the PRC do we construct for our next generation and what sorts of identities as Chinese do we expect our youngsters to compose from the story of China we tell them? Do we expect our children to forget all about the trauma of the June 4 Incident or to learn from its bitter experience the real situation of China, their sovereign country, after 1997? These queries, as I come to understand now, were related directly to the issue of identity formation in history education.

Second, it was an issue of attitude towards the PRC government. The pro-China people in Hong Kong argued that those who insisted including the June 4 Incident in history education bore a sinister purpose of making use of the Incident to stimulate sentiments of anti-China and anti-Chinese leaders among students in Hong Kong (Hang Man, 1994). They assumed that teaching the June 4 Incident in schools might bring up disloyal or alienated Chinese citizens among the younger generation of Hong Kong and was thus unfavourable to a smooth transition to 1997. Thus, logically, there was a need to facilitate the cultivation of a sense of belonging with emphasis on a positive attitude towards the PRC regime. This was easily understood from the pro-China stance on identity education for 1997, which focused on converting youngsters in Hong Kong into supporters of the PRC regime (Lee & Sweeting, 2001). Accordingly, the crackdown on the student movement in 1989, as one of the stigmas of the future sovereign power of Hong Kong, should be avoided as far as possible.

Third, in my view at that time, this episode could arouse an immediate concern because it touched upon the nerve of the people of Hong Kong in relation to the transition to 1997. I wrote in my diary that 'The Director's attempt to ban history within 20 years has opened the Pandora Box of 1997 again. It is going to add another controversial issue to destabilise the transitional period' (June 29, 1994).

The core of concern was clearly summarised in the editorial of a local newspaper on the day following the Director's backdown on his decision.

> [T]he June 4 Incident is regarded a totem of democracy. Whether the Incident is allowed to be reported in the media, discussed in academic circles or touched by politicians after 1997 has become the litmus test of the "one country, two systems" . . . . The most significant feature of the "two systems" lies in the maintenance of the pluralistic character of Hong Kong. Different opinions and ideologies are permitted to co-exist and people of Hong Kong are given the freedom of speech. In case the right of discussing the June 4 Incident is scraped, the spirit of the "one country, two systems" will vanish.
>
> 'Ban irritates the public', 1994, translated from the Chinese text

As one newspaper commented, 'the people of Hong Kong reject the system of China. They want to defend their freedom of speech and press and academic autonomy' (Siu, 1994, B5). The author of the disputed textbook was also, interestingly enough, the Chief Executive designate of the Curriculum Development Institute within the Department of Education at that time. He also encouraged the territory's teachers 'to stand up and say that learning history in Hong Kong is different from that in the mainland', because 'the way that history is taught in the mainland is mainly through indoctrination to promote patriotism' (Moyes, 1994, C4).

It seemed in the end that academic autonomy triumphed and the identity of Hong Kong was asserted. However, I took it with reservation. I remember that I shared with my colleagues my great disdain for a primacy of political over academic or professional considerations in curriculum development. There were genuine and widespread worries among academics and educators in Hong Kong, who spoke out aloud during this episode, about whether political considerations would dictate the school curriculum in post-1997 Hong Kong, as they thought it was practised in the mainland. This incident had brought to the surface the uncertain fate of academic autonomy after 1997, though its safeguard was solemnly promised in the Basic Law of Hong Kong. I became more aware of the difficult situation history education might have to face after 1997. History teachers might need sound personal integrity or great moral courage to honour academic and professional autonomy in face of political pressure. Were our history educators well prepared for all the challenges ahead? I did not have great confidence at that time.

Retrospection and implications

This is a narrative self-study into my personal experience of the issue of identity of Hong Kong Chinese people in the context of Hong Kong's return to China in 1997. My own personal stories of taking part in the June 4th Incident in 1989 and of being involved in a textbook episode relating to the Incident five years later have been reconstructed for the purpose of illustrating the dynamics, complexity and challenges over the issue of identity confronting the Hong Kong Chinese during one of the most significant periods in our history.

In inquiring into these two pieces of personal experiences relating to the June 4 Incident, I have tried to explore my personal Chinese identity as well as a case study of the collective experience of Hong Kong people at large in face of the political handover in 1997, depicting how we felt, thought and acted in response to the Incident unfolding in Mainland China at that time. In fact, after 25 years, the story of this Incident can still be illuminative for Hong Kong people to examine and understand our own identities.

It is worth inquiring into the June 4 Incident even after 25 years because some of the most disputable issues in Hong Kong society today are rooted in this collective memory and its interpretations. Only with a proper resolution of this painful tragic memory could there be hope for a more humane and just society to come about and resolve the problems we are facing. One of them is the lack of identification with their motherland among the younger generation of Hong Kong. They are resentful of the SAR government in Hong Kong and the sovereign power in Beijing behind it. The refusal of the Beijing government to admit its tragic error of suppressing the June 4 Incident 25 years ago has proved to be a major cause and excuse for the alienation of the younger generation from the regime of China today.

It seems that I tried hard to uphold my story as a Hongkongese by emphasising values such as democracy, liberty, open-mindedness, pluralism, fair play and rule of law on the one hand and that I showed great reservation of cultivating an uncritical Chinese identity, especially through education, on the other. My outrage towards the Beijing regime in 1989 and the move of the Director of Education in the textbook controversy in 1994 can be understood in terms of my belief that the Chinese identity of Hong Kong Chinese should not be developed at the expense of their Hong Kong identity.

As illuminated in this narrative self-study, in the wider context of the political transition towards 1997 in Hong Kong, the contention aroused from the issue of identity lay in the relative importance assigned to the Hong Kong and Chinese identities. During the June 4 Incident, Hong Kong Chinese turned patriots, supporting the Beijing students' demand for democracy, liberty and rule of law, which, as argued previously, have long been cherished as core components of the Hong Kong identity. In the textbook controversy, while the contention revolved around issues of academic freedom and professional autonomy in education, its significance lay in a defence of the Hong Kong identity amidst calls for promoting a cleansed image of the PRC regime. A major concern in the debate was focused on the approach to be adopted in inculcating the national identity among youngsters in Hong Kong. Should we prepare a generation of Hong Kong people who were critical and independent minded or who were loyal but submissive and subservient? The testing case was the proper attitude towards the PRC regime. Should history education prepare informed critics of the PRC regime? Such a focus of the controversy has clearly shown that the Hong Kong Chinese were still living with the memory of the June 4 Incident at that time. Both episodes had much to do with the issue of identity of Hong Kong Chinese.

Narrative inquirers are informed by a range of philosophical perspectives – critical theory, post-structuralism, social constructionism – in addition to postmodernism. The nature of historical narratives has been discussed by postmodernist scholars such as Michel Foucault (1972), Hayden White (1978) and Keith Jenkins (1995, 1997, 2000). Jenkins (1995) argues that all history is interpretive and never literally true. In history discourse, historians transform into ultimately imagined narratives a list of past events that would otherwise be only a collection of singular statements and/or a chronicle.

Jenkins makes it clear, however, that it is not part of any postmodernist argument to deny the material existence of the past or the present. It is argued, instead, that the once actual past is only accessible to us through texts and thus as a 'reading'. History just is, and always has been, textual. The historian does not narrate past facts but retells past stories from a current perspective. Viewed from such a stance, I have reconstructed my past experience of the episode from a present perspective. Although I have tried hard to reconstruct, with the help of various sources, my experiences as they were in the past to the largest possible extent, I understand that it is unavoidable that it is always more a reconstruction than a direct re-presentation of them.

By employing narrative as a research tool to explore my personal experience, I find it useful and possible to capture in greater depth and detail not only what happened at that time, but more importantly how the people of Hong Kong saw and felt about their identity as Hong Kong Chinese.

The unique strength of narrative inquiry in exploring an important historical event lies in the possibility of reconstructing vividly the complexities, contradictions as well as consensus of the issue of identity experienced by the Hong Kong Chinese in an important historical period. This mode of representation can depict powerfully and adequately the personal passions and actions of such a dramatic experience.

The story is still unfolding

This year (2014) is the twenty-fifth anniversary of the Incident. Every June 4 evening since 1989, there has been a large scale candle-light vigil at the Victoria Park with tens of thousands of people to commemorate it. As a regular attendee every year, I have noticed that in recent years, more and more young people who were not even born in 1989 have flocked to attend it. Their attitude towards the Beijing government is, surprisingly, even more critical than the generation of mine and their parents who had actually taken part in the protests in person. In the June 4 Incident 25 years ago, while we condemned the Beijing regime for the massacre, we did so from the perspective of a Chinese. Now, many of the young protesters go to the extent of not only refusing to acknowledge the legitimacy of the current Beijing regime but flatly denying their own Chinese identity.

It is obvious that the identity crisis germinated by the takeover of Hong Kong by China in 1997 has been deteriorating among the people of Hong Kong in the last 17 years. Such a phenomenon has annoyed and alerted both the Beijing and the Hong Kong SAR governments. As a result, the SAR government has attempted to put forth a series of remedial measures to strengthen the identification of youngsters with their mother country. In the summer of 2013, it proposed to make national education a compulsory subject in all primary and secondary schools. While the Director of Education tried to avoid mentioning the 'dark side' of the communist regime in the textbook controversy in the 1990s, the SAR government now prefers to propagate the 'bright side' of the sovereign power in the curriculum of a new school subject called national education. However, the proposal was met with immediate and strong opposition from parents, students and political activists. The concerns and worries of Hong Kong people over the issue of political indoctrination, so powerfully expressed in the textbook controversy twenty years ago, resurged suddenly to the great surprise of the government. Eventually, the government had to back down and shelve the proposal. It seems the issue of identity will continue to haunt the Hong Kong Chinese with the identity education in school still facing a crossroads in the years to come. Narrative inquiry and its value in reconstructing personal and collective meanings of past events and their relevance to the current day, will, undoubtedly, have a place in the continuing story of Hong Kong.

Notes

1 The June 4 Incident here refers to the whole student-led movement starting from the mourning over the death of Hu Yaobang in mid-April, 1989 to the final military crackdown on Tiananmen Square on June 4, 1989 and its immediate aftermaths. 'June 4' is used in this chapter instead of '4 June' as this is the Chinese style of date notation and more importantly, this has become a proper noun in the Chinese history.
2 In Hong Kong school curriculum, there are two history subjects, namely, world history and Chinese history.

References

Ban irritates the public (in Chinese) (1994, July 4). *Wah Chiao Daily.*
Baum, R. (1994). *Burying Mao.* New Jersey: Princeton University.
Chan, M. K. (Ed.) (1997). *The challenges of Hong Kong's reintegration with China.* Hong Kong: Hong Kong University Press.
Cheng, W. T. & Wong, S. L. (2002). Identity of Hong Kong Chinese: Changes before and after 1997 (in Chinese). *Twenty First Century* (73), 71–84.
Chris Patten demands a review of the decision on the limit of 20 years (in Chinese). (1994, July 2). *Ming Pao.*
Events within 20 years should not be regarded as history (in Chinese). (1994, June 28). *Ming Pao.*
First mention of the June 4 Incident in a Chinese History textbook published in Hong Kong (in Chinese). (1994, June 27). *Ming Pao.*
Foucault, M. (1972). *The archaeology of knowledge.* New York: Pantheon.
Governor considers it inappropriate to set time limit (in Chinese). (1994, July 8). *Ming Pao.*
Hang Man. (1994, July 21). Anti-China in name of history education. *Ta Kung Pao.*
Jenkins, K. (1995). *On "What is history?" – From Carr and Elton to Rorty and White.* London: Routledge.
Jenkins, K. (1997). *The postmodern history reader.* London: Routledge.
Jenkins, K. (2000). A postmodern reply to Perez Zagorin. *History and Theory.* 39(2), 181–200.
Lau, S. K. (1996). National education under the one country two systems (in Chinese). *Mingpao Monthly* (9), 19–20.
Lau, S. K. (1997). *Hongkongese or Chinese: The problem of identity on the eve of resumption of Chinese sovereignty over Hong Kong* (in Chinese). Hong Kong: Hong Kong Institute of Asia-Pacific Studies.
Lee, M. K. (1995). Community and identity in transition in Hong Kong. In R. Kwok & A. So (Eds), *The Hong Kong-Guangdong link: Partnership in flux.* Armonk and London: M. E. Sharpe, pp. 119–134.

Lee, M. K. (1998). Hong Kong identity – past and present. In S. L. Wong & T. Maruya (Eds), *Hong Kong economy and society: Challenges in the new era*. Hong Kong: Centre of Asian Studies, The University of Hong Kong, pp. 152–175.

Lee, W. O. & Bray, M. (1995). Education: evolving patterns and challenges. In J. Y. S. Cheng & S. S. H. Lo (Eds), *From colony to SAR: Hong Kong's challenges ahead*. Hong Kong: The Chinese University Press, pp. 357–378.

Lee, W. O. & Sweeting, A. (2001). Controversies in Hong Kong's political transition: Nationalism versus liberalism. In M. Bray & W. O. Lee (Eds), *Education and political transition: Themes and experiences in East Asia*. Hong Kong: Comparative Education Research Centre, The University of Hong Kong, pp. 101–121.

Li, Y. (1989). The impact of the massacre on the Sino-British Joint Declaration. *The Nineties, June 15, 1989* (special issue), 51–53.

Lui, T. L. (1997). The Hong Kong new middle class on the eve of 1997. In J. Y. S. Cheng (Ed.), *The other Hong Kong report 1997*. Hong Kong: The Chinese University Press, pp. 207–225.

Morris, P. (1997). Civics and citizenship education in Hong Kong. In K. Kennedy (Ed.), *Citizenship education and the modern state*. London: Falmer Press, pp. 107–125.

Moyes, J. (1994, August 15). Keeping history books straight. *South China Morning Post*, C4.

Siu, C. H. (1996). *Political transition and curriculum reconstruction: The inclusion of local history in the history curriculum of Hong Kong*. Unpublished M.Phil. thesis. Hong Kong: The Chinese University of Hong Kong.

Siu, M. (1994, July 29). Row over the syllabus of Chinese History (in Chinese). *Ming Pao*, B5.

So, A. Y. (1999). *Hong Kong's embattled democracy: A societal analysis*. Baltimore: The Johns Hopkins University Press.

The Director of Education's Explanation and Clarification dated 4 July 1994 (1994, July 5). *Ming Pao*, A1.

The People's Republic of China (1990). *The Basic Law of the Hong Kong Special Administrative Region of the People's Republic of China*. Hong Kong: The Consultative Committee for the Basic Law of the Hong Kong Special Administrative Region of the People's Republic of China.

Tsang, S. (1997). *Hong Kong, an appointment with China*. London: I. B. Tauris.

White, H. (1978). *Tropics of discourse*. Baltimore: Johns Hopkins University Press.

Wong, P. W. (2000). The pro-Chinese democracy movement in Hong Kong. In S. W. K. Chiu & T. L. Lui (Eds), *The dynamics of social movement in Hong Kong*. Hong Kong: Hong Kong University Press, pp. 55–90.

Wong, S. L. (1995). Political attitudes and identity. In R. Skeldon (Ed.), *Emigration from Hong Kong: Tendencies and trends*. Hong Kong: The Chinese University Press.

Wong, S. L. (1998). Hong Kong society: Problems of transition and future challenges. In S. L. Wong & T. Maruya (Eds), *Hong Kong economy and society: Challenges in the new era*. Hong Kong: Centre of Asian Studies, The University of Hong Kong.

Wong, S. L. (1999). Changing Hong Kong identities. In G. W. Wang & J. Wong (Eds), *Hong Kong in China: The challenges of transition*. Singapore: Times Academic Press, pp. 181–202.

Zhang, L. (2001). *June fourth: The true story* (in Chinese). Hong Kong: Mirror Books.

Index